Wasafiri

Volume 21, Number 1, March 2006 Issue 47

Articles

Reviews

The Lifting and the Lifted

Prefaces to Colonial Modernist Texts

Amardeep Singh

> This is no longer the sanctity of the cell and of the scourge; being but a lifting up, as it were, into a greater intensity of the mood of the painter, painting the dust and the sunlight. (Yeats xix)

Modernism: Totalised Space, Absolutist Textuality

The word 'modernism' suggests an aesthetic strongly associated with an idea of time. But it can also be described spatially, as a 'lifting up' (or *Aufhebung*), where the writer's goal is to conceive of the world as a totality. It is a powerful gesture, and an essential part of the modernist aesthetic, but it is nevertheless linked to a colonial power play. In fact, the 'worlding' gesture in high modernism – where writers deliberately embraced a global self-image and rejected geographical binds – was also very much a performative gesture and bound by the performative's many contextual limitations. So, however enabling the perception of authorial globality may be, the story of totalisation continues to be a troubling one. Many modernist writers (especially the canonical ones) articulate a vision for the role their work might play on a world stage. They want their work to have a face, but this face would be pointedly affixed to the universal idea of the literary text, and not the particular image of the author associated with it.

Formally, a textual preface can be such a 'face' (other faces might include: packaging, publishing house, reviews, and cover-blurbs). For the most part, modernist writers follow the Hegelian line and pose their texts as absolutes, and refuse elaborate packaging or prefaces written by more established writers. Consequently, prefaces in modernism are generally much rarer than they were in earlier literary periods.[1] And when prefaces do appear – such as the prefaces to Oscar Wilde's *Picture of Dorian Gray* (1891) or Joseph Conrad's *The Nigger of the 'Narcissus'* (1897) – they are written by the authors themselves, and foreground the absolute qualities (timelessness, spatial universality) of the work of art that follows, eschewing any reference to the biography or positioning of the author in favour of aesthetic principles. Perhaps the aesthetic absolutism expressed in these rare modernist prefaces is belied by the supplementary quality of the prefaces themselves (one might ask why an autonomous literary text should *need* a preface). In short, and despite the occasional prefaces that do appear before major texts, the tendencies in modernism that entail the rejection of the authorising power of literary tradition also unmake the precedence of the preface.

The spatial and temporal axes of the preface become important in the debates over whether, and how, modernism may have been an international movement. Represented in a wide range of postcolonial scholarship is a growing critical awareness of the modernist movements in Africa, the Caribbean, India, and East/Southeast Asia, and questions about exactly how, or whether, to include these texts in dominant stories about 'modernism' as a whole. Many accounts of non-European modernism emphasise the derivative nature of these modernisms, and read them as a complement to the European representation of various forms of non-European alterity in primitivism. If Aimé Césaire or Mulk Raj Anand are important, they are so as the lower half of Picasso's African primitives or E M Forster's colonial crisis. They are local modernists, low modernists, or 'also modernists', rather than modernists *tout court*: discussion of writers like Mulk Raj Anand, for instance, are generally limited to South Asian studies circles.[2] It remains unthinkable for critics to think of a modernism that encompasses a day in the life of Clarissa Dalloway in Virginia Woolf's *Mrs Dalloway* (1925), alongside a radically dissimilar (but technically contemporaneous) day in the life of Bakha, the untouchable

Wasafiri Vol. 21, No. 1 March 2006, pp. 1–9
ISSN 0269-0055 print/ISSN 1747-1508 online
http://www.tandf.co.uk/journals DOI: 10.1080/02690050500475328
Routledge Taylor & Francis Group

protagonist of Mulk Raj Anand's *Untouchable* (1935). As Johannes Fabian delineates it in his influential book *Time and the Other* (1983), the concept of time in Eurocentric modernism produces a 'denial of coevalness'. If modernism, as I have suggested, entails a gesture of lifting up, it also seems to rely on a tacit concomitant gesture of *putting down* and *pushing away*.

Under the force of this structure of thought, it may seem difficult for writers and critics from colonial locales to claim the discourse of modernism without also replicating its exclusionism. Nevertheless, new possibilities are emerging in postcolonial criticism. Even if non-European modernism is still somewhat marginal, post-orientalist and anti-racist critics, in recent years, have successfully mainstreamed their challenge to the slanted representations of Africa and India in key European texts such as Conrad's *Heart of Darkness* (1902) and Kipling's *Kim* (1901). Ironically, these critiques have so prevailed that many seminal texts of modernism now need prefaces to explain historical context for contemporary readers. It is thus fitting that the recent Norton edition of *Heart of Darkness* has a preface by the Afro-Caribbean writer Caryl Phillips, while the recent Penguin edition of *Kim* has a preface by Edward Said.

Though they generally refused prefaces to their own works, most European modernist writers did write prefaces for *other* writers' works, including poems and prose by non-European writers. There is a small body of prefaces written by white European writers to poetry, prose, and criticism in the modernist idiom by non-European writers from colonial locales. This genre of the preface is especially important, as it challenges European modernism's temporal and spatial universalism through a visible textual proximity: the modernists' preface-texts appear in *books* alongside the literary efforts of non-European writers. Such prefaces benefit the colonial writers considerably by legitimating them as serious literary authors, though the actual phrasing of the praise in the prefaces often re-delimits their range and vision. Despite the complexities associated with such forms of address which often display profound orientalism, these prefaces perform an important kind of work upon European modernism. Namely, by foregrounding a scene of exchange between Europe and non-European writing, they help to *push modernism outside of itself*. In place of an Olympian universality outside of the historical time and space of the colonial world, these prefaces model a concept of a dis-placed literary production in European literature and also outside of it. The prefaces, in short, facilitate the rethinking of modernism, from colonial internationalism to a kind of postcolonial globalism.

Though all of the prefaces I am working with here challenge modernism in this way, each of the prefaces also has qualities – problematic qualities – that set it off from the others, and each deserves to be read closely. Yeats's 1912 preface to Tagore's *Gitanjali*, E M Forster's 1935 preface to Anand's *Untouchable*, and André Breton's 1943 preface to Aimé Césaire's *Notebook of a Return to My Native Land* seem to form a group, as they are all prefaces to literary works by famous European literary modernists.[3] Each of the three participates in the dis-placing of modernism into colonial space, though each also reinscribes the political order of colonialism and leaves the coevalness of the colonial writers' texts in question. The philosopher Jean-Paul Sartre also wrote prefaces of this type, including the famous 1938 essay 'Orphée Noir', which prefaced Léopold Senghor's collection of 'Negritude' poetry.[4] He wrote a preface to Fanon's *The Wretched of the Earth* (1961) — which I will generally refer to as Sartre's 'Preface'. It seems helpful to draw a historical divide between Sartre and the others because Sartre's essays, published after the Second World War, are decisively marked as part of an anticolonial (or postcolonial) political mobilisation. They are, one could say, 'postcolonial', while the earlier Forster, Yeats, and Breton prefaces are late colonial. Finally, it is impossible to consider Sartre's prefaces without referring to Fanon's response to Sartre in *Black Skin, White Masks* (1952) — Fanon's account of what it is like to be the subject *to* a preface, to be constituted by the prefatory.

Who is Lifting Whom? Forster, Yeats, Breton

> Hegel's objection to prefaces reflects the following structure: preface/text = abstract generality/self-moving activity. His acceptance of prefaces reflects another structure: preface/text = signifier/signified. And the name of the '=' in this formula is the Hegelian *Aufhebung*. (Spivak xi)

Before entering into a discussion of the preface-texts themselves, it would be helpful to think through the idea of the preface as a modernist performance. Here Gayatri Spivak's comment in her translator's preface to *Of Grammatology* (1967) seems apposite. Among many other things, Spivak creates an analogy between preface and text, 'abstraction' and 'activity' to demonstrate a relationship between Hegelian abstraction and the signifier in Derrida. The preface is the face, or the name, which points to the text itself that is in the signified position. The historical and continuing pervasiveness of literary prefaces certainly bears out the implications of this analogy: just as the preface is nothing without a text, the text cannot act without a face. Of course, Spivak's proper aim is to deconstruct this analogy: if the stability of the text itself as a linear entity, with a front and rear, may be questioned, the preface's position comes into question in terms that are either *spatial* (the preface in front of the text), or *temporal* (the preface must be written after the text is read). Spivak sees her preface to Derrida, as well as Hegel and Derrida's own prefaces to themselves, as ultimately both inside and outside, both preceding and subsequent to, the greater scene of the text.

However, even as it seems imperative to deconstruct the line between preface and text, the split between the two is nevertheless extended and enhanced in the colonial context, where the distinction between preface and text can be the very site of enforcement of colonial authority. For the mere presence of the preface, in the context of dominance, can challenge the independence of the text that follows. If a word from a 'Breton' or a 'Forster' legitimises a young Caribbean or Indian writer, that legitimation can also be seen as instituting dependency or vassalage: Yeats, we could say, uses the name 'Tagore' to extend the domain of his own authorship, and subsumes Tagore into his own image of a worldly modernism. On a different register, this formal divide also operates on the level of the projected audience: the preface-writer assumes a European readership and poses the non-European writer's culture as remote and unrecognisable, either because of its idealism or because of its grotesque violence. And yet each of the prefaces I am interested in also deconstructs the gap between preface and text, colonial subject and colonial centre, through the preface-writer's own reading.

Proceeding out of chronological order, I will begin with Forster's preface to Mulk Raj Anand's 1935 novel *Untouchable*. Anand began the novel in Simla, worked on it on the passage to England, *S S Viceroy of India*, and completed it in Bloomsbury.[5] Whilst in England, Anand studied philosophy at Cambridge, and afterwards lived in Bloomsbury, working and writing there until the end of the Second World War. Forster's preface to *Untouchable* still appears with every American or British printing of the novel.

Forster's presentation of the text that follows his preface, Anand's novel, perfectly exemplifies the kind of modernist displacement I have been referring to, though it is not without its problems. First, Forster blurs the line between himself and Anand, but this blurring is absorptive rather than equalising. That is to say, the preface describes the subsequent literary text largely in terms of the preface-writer's own work. Forster begins the preface with a conservative European's response to *A Passage to India* (1924) — he mentions an 'indignant Colonel' who disliked a particular scatological reference in *A Passage to India*.

> Well, if the Colonel thought *A Passage to India* dirty, what will he think about *Untouchable*, which describes a day in the life of a sweeper in an Indian city with every realistic circumstance. Is it a clean book or a dirty one? Some readers, especially those who consider themselves all-white, will go purple in the face with rage before they have finished a dozen pages, and will exclaim that they cannot trust themselves to speak. I cannot trust myself either, though for a different reason: the book seems to me indescribably clean and I hesitate for words in which this can be conveyed. Avoiding rhetoric and circumlocution, it has gone straight to the heart of its subject and purified it. None of us are pure — we shouldn't be alive if we were. But to the straightforward all things can become pure, and it is to the directness of his attack that Mr. Anand's success is probably due. (v)

Forster's point of departure is the potential for scandal in Anand's book — its figuring of an untouchable toilet sweeper as its protagonist. In a way a dirty book in 1935 is an admirable accomplishment, since it is the great era of scandalous modernist fictions, including D H Lawrence's *Lady Chatterley's Lover* (1928), Radclyffe Hall's *The Well of Loneliness* (1928), and James Joyce's *Ulysses* (1922). But Forster quickly turns away from modernist scandal of dirty art to its antimodernist expiation — a cleansing that Forster's own *Passage to India* refuses. Forster suggests that Anand's passionate and direct treatment of his subject rejects corrosive irony and corrupting shock value in favour of the earnestness of religious ritual. This is damning praise if the goal is to pose Anand's text as having the potential to push European modernism outside itself. To put it narratively, by insisting upon Anand's self-purifying qualities, Forster provides a *finish* (ie a reading) to Anand's text before the reader holding the book *Untouchable* even starts to read it. But note Forster's reference to race: 'those who consider themselves all-white, will go purple in the face with rage before they have finished a dozen pages, and will exclaim that they cannot trust themselves to speak'. In this phrasing Forster stakes out a privileged position between the 'all-white' Colonel and that of the all-brown Anand — a kind of hybrid position. Forster uses Anand's novel to push forward his own worldly authority, but the terms of his preface seem to fix Anand's text in place at the periphery.

Complexion is also a major issue in Breton's preface to Césaire's *Notebook*. Breton's preface is unpromisingly entitled 'A Great Black Poet' ('Un Grand Poete Noir'). Here Breton describes his excitement at discovering a copy of the Césaire-edited literary journal *Tropiques* while in Fort-de-France in 1939.[6] Breton likes Césaire's references to French avant-gardists, and begins with an emphasis on Césaire's tone rather than his literary accomplishment or style:

> I shall not pretend that I did not at once take some pride in the fact that what he expressed was in no way unfamiliar; the names of the poets and authors he referred to would have been in themselves sufficient evidence; but even more the tone of those pages rang true. (x)

Breton's interpretation of Césaire's modernism is approving insofar as Césaire offers him what he perceives as a mirror of his own approach to modernism. The room may be different, but all of the furniture (meaning, the authors and their ideas) are in the identical locations. Breton, in short, interpellates Césaire as a satisfyingly accomplished mimic-man, but this fixing is nevertheless challenged at times in the course of Breton's own presentation.

Breton's pressing concern at the moment of his writing is of course the plight of France under Vichy, and he reads Césaire as resisting that 'darkness': [this is Breton quoting Césaire:] 'We belong . . . to those who say no to darkness' (xi).[7] But is it the darkness of Vichy France that Césaire resists and refuses, or is it France itself? An even cursory reading of Césaire's poem (which I do not attempt here) reveals that Césaire's worry is much less the government of France than the life of Martinique; it seems that Breton wants to see resemblance so strongly that he reshapes Césaire's political preoccupation to match his own. Breton writes: 'This land he was revealing and that his friends helped reconnoitre, it was my land too, yes, it was our land that I had wrongly feared obliterated by darkness.' In seeing Césaire as a comrade in the struggle against fascism, one braver than many of his own avant-gardist peers, Breton seems unable to actually read a key element of Césaire's poem, namely the latter's struggle with race and racism.

The heart of Breton's preface is a literal presenting of Césaire's face, that is to say, an account of his first meeting with Césaire in Fort-de-France in 1939. In his description of the meeting, Breton moves away from the rhetoric of 'darkness' as a metaphor for political occupation, and towards 'blackness', in the image of Césaire's face. Breton's attraction to Césaire's face is the site at which the barrier between them might be undone:

> I recall my first quite elementary reaction at finding him of a black so pure and even more unnoticeable at first because he was smiling. Through him (I already know it, I see it, and everything will confirm it later), human essence is heated to a point of maximum effervescence in which knowledge – here of the highest order – overlaps with magical gifts. . . . And it is a black who handles the French language in a manner that no white man is capable of today. And it is a black who guides us today into the unexplored, establishing along the way, as if by child's play, the contacts that make us advance on sparks. And it is a black who is not only a black but all of man, who conveys all of man's questionings, all of his anguish, all of his hopes and all of his ecstasies and who will remain more and more for me the prototype of dignity. (xii)

Césaire's blackness is pure, an immediate mark of difference that Breton addresses up-front. We can even say that for Breton, Césaire's difference *precedes himself* on the wings of stereotype. But it is a blackness that Breton finds appealing. He sees Césaire as the future, embodying a *blackness* that can possibly lighten the '*darkness*' of Vichy with his language. But note that Breton avoids using images of a sun-like 'light' in favour of other images: 'effervescence' (energy that may not be light), 'sparks' (ie light that is inconstant), 'ecstasies', and 'child's play'. In the sense that he marks Césaire as the future, Breton's preface seems to be genuinely prefatory — the text that follows is not just that signified of racial difference, it is the future of the human. But can it really be, that in Breton's attempt to posit a 'face of blackness' against the 'heart of darkness' that is the rise of Nazism, he remains unaware of the implicit semantic association between the black and the dark?

Unlike Césaire's face in Breton, Tagore's physical face is absent from Yeats's preface to his *Gitanjali*. Though this preface comes much earlier chronologically, Yeats's attraction to Tagore and his joy at discovering the Bengali poet is described by Yeats in terms that are equally salvific. Like Breton, Yeats saw Tagore as rising prophetically to the demands of the battle for truth and light that Yeats felt he, himself, had lost. As for Tagore's poems themselves, Tagore translated them from the original Bengali in roughly the same way that Anand wrote much of *Untouchable*, namely, in a brief period of activity on a ship from India to England.[8] Yeats's preface has no image of Tagore himself, but it recounts Yeats's conversation with a Bengali interlocutor present in London, who knew Tagore's work and reputation in Bengal. In contrast to Forster, Yeats generally avoids the ethnographic tone, though the Bengali interlocutor gives Yeats's claims about Bengali 'civilization' a certain stamp of legitimacy. The absence of Tagore's face enables Yeats to pose an image of the poems themselves at the front of his account:

> I have carried the manuscript of these translations about with me for days, reading it in railway trains, or on the top of omnibuses and in restaurants, and I have often had to close it lest some stranger would see how much it moved me. (xiii)

Note Yeats's emphasis on his context, the social and technological space of London. Despite the fact that he is reading Tagore not on the tops of mountains but on the tops of omnibuses, his rhetoric is intensely romantic and naturalistic. He recounts his personal experience of being moved by the poems, and uses his preface as a performance of that movement. Yet there is a paradox in his fear of exposure to the English strangers on London trains and buses — are these not the very strangers who are now holding the book *Gitanjali*, reading his preface to the same poems, witnessing Yeats being moved by Tagore? The split between manuscript and book, between the concrete William Yeats and the author-signifier named W B Yeats, is also the gap of signifier and signified, preface and text, all over again.

If Yeats has to wait until the moment of the book to allow the poetry of the colonial subject to move him in public, the final question to ask might be whether his account of being moved has the potential to move incipient modernism (ie in 1912) outside of itself. As with each of the other prefaces in play here, there are two answers, or rather a double answer, Yeats sees the signs of difference in Tagore's writing as both radically other, and radically assimilable, to the desires of his concept of modernism:

> A whole people, a whole civilization, immeasurably strange to us, seems to have been taken up into this imagination; and yet we are not moved because of its strangeness, but because we have met our own image, as though we had walked in Rossetti's willow wood, or heard, perhaps for the first time in literature, our voice as in a dream. (xvi–xvii)

Yeats poses the image of Tagore as his own mirror image, and Tagore's voice as Yeats's own echo. The mirror and the echo in Yeats's rhetoric foreclose the possibility of a link to a space outside of Europe, and sustain a modernist economy that is able to assimilate others but unable to cede priority to the other. In other words, when Yeats sees Tagore as his own mirror image, he rejects the idea that his own work might be a reflection or an echo, in an economy, where Tagore (or India) could be positioned as the source of light.

However, Yeats is ultimately less interested in mirrors and echoes than he is in Tagore's worldly aesthetic, which he describes in semi-Hegelian terms:

> This is no longer the sanctity of the cell and of the scourge; being but a lifting up, as it were, into a greater intensity of the mood of the painter, painting the dust and the sunlight. (xix)

Yeats reads Tagore's refusal of Hindu *askesis* as a self-lifting that rejects the 'sanctity of the cell', and he finds in Tagore a distinctly modernist aesthetic of worldly asceticism. If for Yeats the only gesture that describes the worlding of modern literature is 'lifting up', a question nevertheless remains that figures equally for Breton and for Forster: who is lifting whom? All three of these prefaces by European modernists may aim to rhetorically lift colonial modernists into their own space — the space of European universalism. But is it not also just as viable to reverse this dynamic, and argue that European modernism does not lift, but is itself lifted, by the access to the dramatic image of alterity presented by colonial modernism. To invoke Hegel (and Spivak) again, perhaps the prefaces are thus merely European 'abstractions' that ride the back of the 'self-moving' modernist texts that follow. These various prefaces present these alternate possible readings but do so in such an ideological cloud that the issue is never resolved. In Sartre, by contrast, the ideological and formal implications of these issues are made to intersect quite directly.

'Europeans, you must read this book': Sartre

Both the 'Preface' to *The Wretched of the Earth* and 'Orphée Noir', the preface to Senghor's 'Negritude' anthology, also provoke the question of who is lifting whom into universality. However, they differ substantially from the three prefaces discussed above, largely in the substance and tenor of Sartre's approach to race and colonialism. Intensely dialectical, Sartre uses his prefaces to make strong political arguments, rather than to familiarise (or exoticise) his subject to his readers. Moreover, Sartre at no point worries over the status of his own worldly reputation, or the importance of his more substantial philosophical and political work (published without preface elsewhere). Indeed, he allows that his prefaces may in fact be superfluous, as when he writes of Fanon's *The Wretched of the Earth*: 'This book had not the slightest need of a preface' (Sartre, Preface 21). Despite Sartre's evident anti-colonial and anti-racist commitments, his prefaces aim to overwrite the texts that follow. Sartre's analyses of both the Negritude writers and Fanon superinscribe the latter and bind them in the time and space of his own dialectic. Fanon, of course, identifies and resists Sartre's superinscription, and critiques Sartre's preface to *Black Skin, White Masks*; I will turn to Fanon's non-prefatory text after first looking at Sartre.

Both of Sartre's prefaces foreground the politics embedded in the prefatory genre with self-referential theatricality. Early on in the 'Preface' to *The Wretched of the Earth,* most strikingly, Sartre marks the rhetorical moment in a direct confrontation with the reader who is identified as European and male. But even as he clearly identifies his audience, Sartre suggests the same audience may be in some sense superfluous. It is a playful gesture choreographed to leave the troubled European reader in a state of invisible abjection:

> And if you murmur, jokingly embarrassed, 'He has it in for us!' the true nature of the scandal escapes you; for Fanon has nothing in for you at all; his work – red-hot for some – in what concerns you is as cold as ice; he speaks of you often, never to you. (10)

Sartre singles out the complicit European reader as the subject of his address in the preface, but then suggests that the very text following the preface is in fact directed not to 'you' at all. Sartre puts it even more bluntly elsewhere, when he asks, 'What does Fanon care whether you read his work or not?' (12). In passages like these, Sartre skilfully plays both sides of the fence: Sartre's preface is alternately directed *at* European readers who are about to be shocked/scandalised by Fanon's polemic, and, simultaneously, self-inclusive in that community. Sartre is perfectly comfortable slipping between 'you, the reader' (and the presumed 'I' who occupies a different position from 'you'), and 'we, Europeans'. Sartre positions himself both in and out of Europe, as well as in and out of the idea of black subjectivity that is the issue at the heart of both prefaces here.

Sartre begins 'Orphée Noir' with a similar shock to his readers that sharply identifies the scene of address. Instead of locating his readership (derived, one would assume, from the readership of the text that *follows* the preface) in an idealised, world-space of high modernism, Sartre begins his preface by sharply identifying the readers of the preface by their position and by their complicity in colonialism. The politics of reading is Sartre's subject here, much more than the timeless and universal qualities of the work of art:

> When you removed the gag that was keeping these black mouths shut, what were you hoping for? That they would sing your praises? Did you think that when they raised themselves up again, you would read adoration in the eyes of these heads that our fathers had forced to bend down to the very ground? Here are black men standing, looking at us, and I hope that you – like me – will feel the shock of being seen. For three thousand years, the white man has enjoyed the privilege of seeing without being seen; he was only a look — the light from his eyes drew each thing out of the shadow of its birth; the whiteness of his skin was another look, condensed light. The white man . . . lighted up the creation like a torch and unveiled the secret white essence of beings. Today, these black men are looking at us, and our gaze comes back to our own eyes; in their turn, black torches light up the world and our white heads are no more than Chinese lanterns swinging in the wind. (Sartre, 'Black Orpheus' 291)

The aggressive second-person address here, which is strongly reminiscent of the language of the 'Preface' to *The Wretched of the Earth,* aims to implicate the reader in the mythic scene of the colonial master–slave dialectic that is the subject of Sartre's essay. In Sartre, it is not simply Europeans who are culpable, but *you*, the reader, who ungagged black men and are now subject to their words as well as their gaze. Alongside this rhetorical manipulation is a theory of race and racialisation. Here, Sartre situates the present moment as one where 'blacks' (read: colonial others) are both ungagged and developing the power of the gaze. Sartre's radical perspectival reversal turns whiteness itself into a mask – a performance of itself – that is inherently illegitimate. This reversal points to one possible larger implication of the politicised reading of these and other prefaces. Namely, Sartre, Yeats, Breton, Forster, and others are experimenting with allowing the 'other', whose text follows the preface, to speak. The prefaces may aim to preserve the colonial writer as subject, but each in its own way also acknowledges the objective gaze/speech of the cultural other that Sartre is describing here.

Importantly, Sartre directs his Preface (as well as the 'Preface' to *The Wretched of the Earth*) at a reader who is a white man; he does not seem to be concerned with the probability that many readers of the negritude volume would themselves be black. In an echo of the Hegel/Spivak comment above, it is also possible that Sartre conceives the preface as the 'abstract generality' that the book's white readers will *have* to read, while the text itself will be the Hegelian self-moving activity, the organic presence, that black readers can access immediately.

The reference to dialectic is not incidental; it is in fact at the core of Sartre's idea of Negritude in 'Orphée Noir'. Sartre posits an important distinction between black self-consciousness and the class-consciousness of the European working class. The proletariat derives its argument from an 'objective' awareness of its 'position'. But racism, because it aims to attack the subjectivity of people of colour, can only be fought subjectively. It is based in the 'black soul, or, rather – since the term is often used in this anthology – on a certain quality common to the thoughts and conduct of Negroes which is called *negritude*' (Sartre's emphasis) (297). The turn to the subjective is fraught in Sartre, whose work until 1963[9] tends to reflect a strict rationalism that belies his occasional claims to subjective truth. This approach to Negritude has a number of problematic consequences, one of which is, of course, that it diminishes the value of the literary. If Sartre appreciates the urgency and sense of mission of the Negritude writers, he also suggests the subjects of negritude writing are much more limited than those found in European poetry. Sartre praises black poetry as 'evangelic', a 'revealed' literature more than a literature that is written by individuated writers (Sartre, 'Black Orpheus' 298). The subjective, however, is only one part of the process of black expression represented by negritude. There is also an objective moment, at which art is radically depersonalised. Art is ripped from the artist in an act of violent parturition that is also a conjoining of subjective and objective elements:

> And finally, *negritude-object* is snatched from Césaire like a cry of pain, of love, and of hate. Here again he follows the Surrealist tradition of *objective* poetry. Césaire's words do not describe negritude, they do not designate it, they do not copy it from the outside like a painter with a model: they *create* it; they compose it under our very eyes. Henceforth it is a thing which can be observed and learned; the subjective method which he has chosen joins the objective method we spoke about earlier: ejects the black soul from himself at the very moment when others are trying to interiorize it; the final result is the same in both cases. (Sartre, 'Black Orpheus' 313)

In becoming objective, negritude loses its personal associations with Césaire. It becomes universal, everyone has access to it, and everyone can learn it. Sartre clearly enjoys the violence in the aggressive depersonalisation that occurs in writing (it is not so clear that a black poet in the 'Negritude' anthology would see it in the same way).

Fanon responds to Sartre's 'Orphée Noir' in *Black Skins, White Masks* with seething frustration. It is not that there is anything fundamentally wrong with Sartre's conclusions; Fanon concedes that negritude is heavily dependent on ahistorical generalisations that reify race. But Sartre's critique of the absoluteness (or finitude) of negritude strikes Fanon as both insufficiently dialectical and rhetorically excessive. For

Fanon, Sartre uses his prefaces not to introduce the texts that follow so much as to *conclude* them and the movement of ideas they propose. Fanon is particularly irked at Sartre's attack on negritude as epistemology and as politics at the end of 'Orphée Noir', and he quotes Sartre at length in *Black Skin, White Masks*. Here is the passage from Sartre that Fanon cites:

> [L]ike all anthropological notions, negritude is a shimmer of being and of needing-to-be; it makes you and you make it: both oath and passion. But there is something even more important in it: the Negro himself, we have said, creates a kind of antiracist racism. He wishes in no way to dominate the world: he desires the abolition of *all* kinds of ethnic privileges; he asserts his solidarity with the oppressed of every color. . . . In fact, negritude appears like the upbeat of a dialectical progression: the theoretical and practical affirmation of white supremacy is the thesis; the position of negritude as an antithetical value is the moment of negativity. But this negative moment is not sufficient in itself, and these black men who use it know this perfectly well; they know that it aims at preparing the synthesis or realization of the human being in a raceless society. Thus, negritude is *for* destroying itself; it is a 'crossing to' and not an 'arrival at,' a means and not an end. (Sartre, 'Black Orpheus' 326–27)[10]

Sartre aims to think through the implications of the 'other' text that follows his preface as well as the meaning of his own newly marginal (ie merely prefatory) position. At the same time, Sartre insists on resolving the contradictions of the negritude position he outlines, thus denying the Negritude writers a reason for writing. Fanon reads this denial as troubling not because of its erasure, but because it is a misreading of the dialectic itself. Here is Fanon:

> When I read . . . [the passage quoted above], I felt that I had been robbed of my last chance. I said to my friends, 'The generation of the younger black poets has just suffered a blow that can never be forgiven.' Help had been sought from a friend of the colored peoples, and that friend had found no better response than to point out the relativity of what they were doing. For once, that born Hegelian had forgotten that consciousness has to lose itself in the night of the absolute, the only condition to attain to consciousness of self. In opposition to rationalism, he summoned up the negative side, but he forgot that this negativity draws its worth from an almost substantive absoluteness. (*Black Skin* 133)

Fanon sees the flaw in Sartre's reasoning as Sartre's failure to see the negative term in the dialectic as carrying a 'substantive absoluteness' of its own. Fanon's critique, softened somewhat by its anecdotal and personalised phrasing ('When I read that page'), considerably rehabilitates his own work, that of the Negritude writers, as well as that of other colonial modernists. The absolutism of the non-European, in Fanon's thinking, should not be confused with the same absolutism of one stream of European modernism. Rather, it is merely the absolutism that advocates the text as *substance*. In order for the text to perform its decolonising work, it must be read in its material particularity. Fanon does not complain that Sartre misreads negritude, but that Sartre fails to allow negritude to run its actual course. Sartre, in other words, uses his preface to *preempt* rather than *prefigure*.

Preface the prefaces

Whatever their limitations, the prefaces to colonial modernist texts succeed in pointing to European modernism outside of Europe. They show a surprising self-consciousness about race and colonialism operating within European modernism, and presented by its canonical 'core', from a very early moment. The prefaces add texture to the debates occurring within modernist studies about the discourses of universalism and globalism operating at the moment of high modernism. If European modernism frequently deployed a rhetoric of universalism that aimed to absorb (or subsume) the non-European world, these prefaces show a side of Euro-modernism that is potentially more worldly and inclusive.

Though I have been critical of the rhetoric of these prefaces, I do not aim to argue that these prefaces should be ignored in contemporary readings of writers like Anand or Fanon. For one thing, the prefaces are a crucial part of the historical moment of the emergence of postcolonial writing. They tell us about the conditions of publication of these texts, and help situate and explain the rhetorical strategies employed by modernists who were African, Caribbean, and Indian. The prefaces add to the texts without supplanting them; it is possible, in a poststructuralist vein, to read the prefaces as both inside and outside the primary texts with which they are associated. Furthermore, close reading shows that these preface-texts themselves play with, and at times reverse, the categories of value produced by the split between preface and text. A preface can be either 'below' (as in, subordinate to), or 'above' (as in, authorising), the text that follows it, and this dual possibility, I have argued, is especially intense when the preface-writer is white and European, and the text that follows the preface is written by a non-white colonial subject.

Notes

1 There is a long and complex history of preface-writing, which I do not have room to address here. Many prefaces from canonical British literature, for instance, can be found compiled in Alisdair Gray's anthology, *The Book of Prefaces*.

2 A good critical source on Anand, with mainly lesser-known critics, is R K Dhawan, ed. *The Novels of Mulk Raj Anand.* Dozens of books on Anand have also appeared in the Indian academic press since the 1960s. A useful volume is C D Narasimhaiah's *The Swan and the Eagle.*

3 The texts I've chosen are generally ones first published by a European publisher with the preface attached. The one exception to this rule is the Breton preface to Césaire, which appeared in 1943, in the first American bilingual edition of Césaire's *Notebook*; Césaire's poem was first published in the Parisian journal *Volontés* in 1939, without preface.

4 In addition to Sartre's preface in the original 'Negritude' anthology, there are prefaces to each author in the anthology written by Senghor himself, as well as an 'Avant-Propos' by André Julien. None of the other prefaces are especially important in themselves, though the preponderance of prefaces does rather overwhelm the actual poetry in the volume. The 'Negritude' anthology seems to be more about the work of editors explaining the political and anthropological implications of the volume than the actual poetry that follows the prefaces.

5 Anand briefly joined Gandhi's camp before returning to Europe, where he wrote several other novels, including one novel of Indian soldiers on the western front — actually written in Madrid and Valencia during the Spanish Civil War.

6 Breton, a member of the French Communist Party, was in exile from Vichy France, and on his way to the United States with Marcel Duchamp and Max Ernst. He stayed in the United States for most of the war years, except for occasional trips to Martinique with such people as Claude Levi-Strauss. See Mark Palizzotti's *Revolutions of the Mind.* For a simple biography of Breton, see <http://www.kirjasto.sci.fi/abreton.htm>.

7 This is Césaire's language, as quoted in Breton: 'Nous sommes . . . de ceux qui disent non a l'ombre.'

8 Unlike Anand, Tagore was coming to England in 1912 not to study (though he had studied there, earlier in his life), but to broaden an already formidable literary reputation. According to critics like Krishna Dutta, the translations do not do justice to the sound and spirit of the same poems, as Tagore wrote them, in Bengali. Tagore was only too aware of his limited skills with English verse, and allowed Yeats to select the poems he thought to be the best, as well as make some minor changes in phrasing. See Krishna Dutta and Andrew Robinson, *Rabindranath Tagore.*

9 In 'Sartre: the "African Philosopher"', Robert J C Young argues that Sartre's work begins to go in a different direction after the Algerian War, when he begins to advocate revolutionary violence as the only way to thoroughly achieve decolonisation. Young's essay is the Preface to Jean-Paul Sartre, *Colonialism and Neocolonialism.*

10 Alternate translation of the last sentence: 'Thus negritude is the root of its own destruction, it is a transition and not a conclusion, a means and not an ultimate end' (*Black Skin* 133).

Works Cited

Anand, Mulk Raj. *Untouchable.* 1935. New York: Penguin, 1990.

Breton, André. 'Un Grand Poete Noir' ['A Great Black Poet']. Preface. 1943. *Notebook of a Return to My Native Land.* By Aimé Césaire. Trans. Annette Smith and Clayton Eshleman. 1939. Middletown, CT: Wesleyan UP, 2001. ix–xix.

Césaire, Aimé. *Notebook of a Return to My Native Land.* Trans. Annette Smith and Clayton Eshleman. 1939. Middletown, CT: Wesleyan UP, 2001.

Conrad, Joseph. *Heart of Darkness And Selections From Congo Diaries.* 1902. New York: Modern Library, 1999.

Dhawan, R. K., ed. *The Novels of Mulk Raj Anand.* New York: Prestige, 1992.

Derrida, Jacques. *Of Grammatology.* Trans. Gayatri Chakravorty Spivak. 1967. Baltimore: Johns Hopkins UP, 1974.

Dutta, Krishna, and Andrew Robinson. *Rabindranath Tagore: The Myriad-Minded Man.* New York: Griffin, 1999.

Fabian, Johannes. *Time and the Other: How Anthropology Makes Its Object.* New York: Columbia, 1983.

Fanon, Frantz. *Black Skin, White Masks.* Trans. Charles Lam Markmann. 1952. New York: Grove Wiedenfield, 1967.

——. *The Wretched of the Earth.* 1961. Trans. Constance Farrington, 1963. London: MacGibbon & Kee, 1965.

Forster, E. M. Preface. 1935. *Untouchable.* By Mulk Raj Anand. New York: Penguin, 1990. v–viii.

Gray, Alisdair, comp. and ed. *The Book of Prefaces.* 2000. New York: Bloomsbury Publishing, 2002.

Kipling, Rudyard. *Kim.* 1901. New York: Penguin Classics, 1987.

Narasimhaiah, C. D. *The Swan and the Eagle.* Delhi: Motilal, 1987.

Palizzotti, Mark. *Revolutions of the Mind: The Life of Andre Breton.* New York: Farrar, Strauss & Giroux, 1995.

Phillips, Caryl. Preface. 1999. *Heart of Darkness And Selections From Congo Diaries.* By Joseph Conrad. 1902. New York: Modern Library, 1999. xi–xviii.

Said, Edward. Preface. 1987. *Kim.* By Rudyard Kipling. 1901. New York: Penguin, 1987. 7–46.

Sartre, Jean-Paul. 'Orphée Noir' [Black Orpheus]. Preface. 1948. *Anthologie de La Nouvelle Poesie Negre et Malgache.* By Léopold Sédar Senghor. 1948. Paris: Presses Universitaires de France, 1969.

——. 'Black Orpheus'. *What is Literature? And Other Essays.* Ed. Steven Ungar. Trans. John MacCombie. Cambridge: Harvard UP, 1988. 291–330.

——. Preface. *The Wretched of the Earth.* By Frantz Fanon. 1961. Trans. Constance Farrington, 1963. New York: Grove Wiedenfield, 1965.

Senghor, Léopold Sédar, ed. *Anthologie de La Nouvelle Poesie Negre et Malgache*. 1948. Paris: Presses Universitaires de France, 1969.
Spivak, Gayatri Chakravorty. 'Translator's Preface'. 1974. *Of Grammatology*. By Jacques Derrida. 1967. Baltimore: Johns Hopkins UP, 1974. ix–lxxxix.
Tagore, Rabindranath. *Gitanjali*. London: Macmillan, 1912.
Woolf, Virginia. *Mrs. Dalloway*. 1925. New York: Harvest Books, 1990.
Yeats, William Butler. Preface. 1912. *Gitanjali*. By Rabindranath Tagore. 1912. London: Macmillan, 1913. vii–xxii.
Young, Robert J. C. 'Sartre: the "African Philosopher". In Jean-Paul Sartre, *Colonialism and Neocolonialism*'. Ed. Robert J. C. Young. New York: Routledge, 2001. vii–xxiv.

Diana Bridge

the gopuram

You're for ever looking above your head.
This time it's a bone-white tower, a gateway,
one of six, struck like a pyramid off its base,
flung into contrast by a companion tower
still swathed in the shadow gauze of morning,
the shade where we linger, glued to its hold-
your-breath outline: the world mountain, lifted,
like your face, to the unerring blue of sky.

the god of hills

1
You want him, if it is him, not there,
or there in the sense of an arrow: three twigs
laid on earth's autumn-coloured surface;

or splash-painted onto a peg for
someone or other to pass,
the connection that chancy.

2
But walking these red tracks,
our country, you assume, as safe
as anywhere on earth,

the colours of the day so sharp,
your habit to take one thing at a time,
you ask yourself, why look?

Wellington

she adds god

she adds god to every stone
an idea new to me

who makes museums of
her temples

and takes god out of statues
to better worship stone

Hampi

the way you see him

You come upon him as you turn the corner
like the surprise of an idea, one that hits you fluid
as light welling from a niche, complete as sculpted form;
not there, of course, for safety, those dipped eyes
unable to be met, mouth caught between compassion
and the joke that presence, yours as well as his,
is an illusion, a theory capable of turning on its head
the weary human limit in your observation that
from here to the base of the statue is quite a long way.

seated buddha

What do you think as you stand there, your mind re-
arranged into perceptions, feelings, consciousness;
not that I'm saying the compartments are fixed,
or that you and your thoughts are the same, just
what do you think as you stand at the end of the hall
lined with statues by the great knees looped in a bow?

It's obvious, I'd say; you like your statue leavened
with a dash of theory. I am simply addicted to looking.

Museum, Sarnath

Wasafiri Vol. 21, No. 1 March 2006, p. 10
ISSN 0269-0055 print/ISSN 1747-1508 online
http://www.tandf.co.uk/journals DOI: 10.1080/02690050500475344
Routledge Taylor & Francis Group

She's a Little Bit Unsure About the Formation of Clouds

Erica Johnson Debeljak

For most of the day, the television screen in the living room is a dull, lifeless grey. At times, it almost seems to function as a cipher: obliterated by the winter sun that floods the room at midday, reflecting the bright stacks of cumulus clouds that float through the afternoon sky, capturing the outlines of a shadow as it glides through the room. At one minute before three, just such a shadow moves across the dead surface of the screen. It is the shadow of a woman about forty years old: slender, dressed in blue jeans, a black short-sleeved turtleneck, low-heeled shoes. She enters the room, leans in toward a low glass coffee table positioned in front of a red couch, picks up a slender, black, rectangular box and points it at the television. Dust motes explode outward, escaping the heat with a soft static blast. A bright orange three-lettered logo begins to take shape in the darkness. The woman, focusing intently on the letters that have replaced the impressionist blur of clouds, lowers herself to the couch. She wears no make-up and her features are so pale and expressionless as to be nearly monochromatic. She throws her head back against the sofa and lets her arms flop outward and open at her sides, exposing the tiny bluish veins running down the crooks. She is ready for her daily dose.

It usually comes in three discreet acts:
TSUNAMI IN THE INDIAN OCEAN
CAR BOMB IN IRAQ
DEADLY MUDSLIDES IN CALIFORNIA

or:
CAR BOMB IN IRAQ
TSUNAMI IN THE INDIAN OCEAN
MULTIPLE SHOOTINGS IN GAZA

or:
TSUNAMI IN THE INDIAN OCEAN
FATAL AVALANCHES IN UTAH
POLITICAL ASSASSINATION IN IRAQ

or:
TSUNAMI IN THE INDIAN OCEAN
STAMPEDES IN HINDI RELIGIOUS FESTIVAL
SUICIDE BOMBER IN IRAQ

The order doesn't much matter. The shifting trios of events seem to fit a random cyclical variation. There is the occasional spike, the occasional dull dip, but day after day, the number of dead rises and falls, rises and fall, creating what over time becomes a regular, even monotonous pattern.

Today the anchor begins the broadcast by reporting an upward revision in the death toll from around 225,000 to more than 250,000 from the tsunami that swept across the Indian Ocean on the day after Christmas. The anchor adds that the numbers will probably go up again: that now it is more a matter of numerical estimates – historical population figures, missing persons reported, statistical extrapolations of one kind or another – than an actual physical body count. The woman almost wishes that they would provide her with some sort of a ceiling, an upward figure, so that she could align her expectations, put a theoretical cap on this natural holocaust. The unsettling vision of a sideways figure eight hovers briefly in her mind. *Infinity*. No ceiling. The roof blown clear off.

From the first day the tsunami appeared on her television screen, the numbers had been too large for her to grasp in any meaningful, non-statistical way: too large in other words for them to represent anything but an abstract idea. It was like the mathematical term asymptote that defines the remote end of a curve, a point you can get infinitely close to, but never actually touch or measure or put on a graph. Five hundred thousand

Wasafiri Vol. 21, No. 1 March 2006, pp. 11–15
ISSN 0269-0055 print/ISSN 1747-1508 online
http://www.tandf.co.uk/journals DOI: 10.1080/02690050500475377
Routledge Taylor & Francis Group

people had attended the presidential inauguration in Washington DC the week before and she had watched the mass of affluent-looking Americans captured in the camera lens as they surged through the cold grey streets of the capital, flooding the intersections, pouring into the monumental squares. She squinted at the broad aerial shot that filled the screen, closing one eye then the other, trying to imagine that half of those people were no longer there. But she couldn't do it. It didn't work. There were simply too many of them.

The anchor segues smoothly into acts two and three where the numbers are more manageable: one hundred and one killed in a stampede at a religious festival in India, thirty-one killed in various incidents in Iraq. One hundred and one is a prime number, the atomic weight of mendelevium, exactly half of the number of students that were enrolled in the natural science and mathematics doctoral programme at Northwestern University in 2002, the year she finished her dissertation. Thirty-one: another prime number – she marvels briefly at the coincidence – equal to the square root of 961, the atomic weight of gallium, the number of children in her daughter's sixth-grade class minus one.

In general, she prefers anecdotal stories: stories about individuals that don't slip into mathematical abstraction. During the opening days of the tsunami story, she used to lean forward expectantly whenever the anchor turned to the experiences of Western tourists caught up in events. A couple of years back, she had complained to her husband about always going to his mother's for Christmas. She wanted to alter the routine and go to the Maldives one year for a change. A colleague in her programme had gone and said it was heaven on earth. So when she listened to the accounts of survivors, she could quite easily imagine herself and Martin and the children being swept up by the great waves. How they would have had only an instant to choose which of the three children to hold on to. She could take Sybil, the eldest, who was a decent swimmer and not prone to panic, and Martin could take care of the twins. But then he wouldn't be able to grab hold of anything else – a tree or a fence post – to stay afloat, and might have to let go of one of them. She could let Sybil swim on her own and then she and Martin could each hang on to a twin, and have one arm free. Still, level-headed or not, Sybil was only eleven, a pretty fragile eleven at that, and might not be strong enough to withstand the powerful currents. Chances were good that at least one of the children would be drowned. She pondered the various combinations: how breakfasts would be without Henry, the family comic whose infectious laughter allowed her to indulge in a secret smile when she heard it from the pantry. How would they manage without gentle Max, the conciliator, or – oh! – without her beloved Sybil. She allowed a shudder to pass through her body and a thrilling sort of horror to engulf her mind as she wondered at how she would react to such a loss. Would she blame Martin for letting one of the twins go? Would he blame her for suggesting the Maldives — just to get her out of her doldrums? Would she finally be cured of the malaise that had seized her since her babies were grown and her doctoral studies finished? Cured from what she sardonically termed her meaning-of-life crisis?

A mechanised song explodes in the room. She picks up the cell phone from the table and glances at the numerical display. At the same time, she points the remote control toward the television, muting the sound but leaving the images.

'Yes,' she says to her husband.

'Belle.' His voice is subdued, solemn even. He is not supposed to call her from work. His boss admonished him the week before when he stepped out of an interminable meeting in legal in order to check up on her. 'How are you doing?' he whispers into the phone.

'Okay.' She stares into the screen at a mangled wreck of a burnt car. 'Same.' Wisps of smoke hover above the black skeletal beast, while in front of it a puddle of dark liquid – gasoline or blood – widens on the pavement.

'What are you doing?' His voice barely registers.

'Watching the three o'clock news.' A man in dungarees runs across the street in front of the smoking hull. His mouth is open in a ragged oval shape. He holds his arms in front of him: blood runs in thick rivulets from his hands to his elbows. He is yelling frantically to someone beyond the camera's field of vision. She cannot hear his voice, only the sigh let out by Martin on the other side of town. 'What's the tally today?' he asks.

Belle closes her eyes and rapidly calculates. 'Twenty-five thousand one hundred and forty-two.'

'Jesus Christ.' The volume of his voice rises. 'What the hell happened?'

'Nothing,' she picks up the remote and flicks off the television. 'Nothing. Just an upward revision of the tsunami numbers.'

She stares at the tall, cottony clouds that fill the dead screen. She can sense her husband's presence on the end of the line. Even when not speaking, he seems to saturate the airwaves with impotent concern. 'What are you going to do now?' he asks, voice low and controlled again.

'Pick up the kids. What else would I do?' The words quiver with a bright sarcasm and a sort of put-on despair. She doesn't know why they come out of her mouth like that. She had wanted him to call.

'Hey, Belle. I talked to someone today about a job possibility for you. It's not great, but it's something. And it would get you out of the house a couple of days a week.'

'What is it?' Now she moulds her voice into a dull and unresponsive shape, disguising the nearly imperceptible quickening of blood in her veins, the sense of something dilating and expanding inside of her. Another voice is silently screaming: *Stop! Stop!*

Stop what? she wonders to herself. *Stop what?*

'Substitute teaching. Not university level. High school. Evanston High. Math, geometry, maybe a little calculus.'

Without saying goodbye, she presses another button on the little phone and places it quietly on the table in front of her.

Across the street from the house stands a low factory that was built in the 1940s and abandoned in the 1990s. It squats behind a red-and-white property sale sign in a thinning copse of oak trees. Two silos rise above the dull concrete mass. A faded black-and-white dairy cow is painted on the side of the first silo, an ear of pale yellow corn on the second. The images strike her as relics from another civilisation, from a distant time — like hieroglyphics or cave paintings that have yet to be catalogued in the archives of a natural history museum.

Belle steps out into the world and regards the quiet afternoon. A dusting of fresh snow lies on the ground, the temperature not having risen sufficiently during the day to melt it. White crystalline sleeves of frost cling to the branches of the oak trees, lending them a fairy-tale aspect. A flock of dark birds, startled perhaps by the slam of the house door or by the beep and flash emitted by the remote auto-lock device, take sudden flight, circling and swooping around the abandoned factory, and then ascending. Their black silhouettes traverse the fragile eggshell sky and disappear into the vault of clouds.

She stands entranced for a moment. How perfectly beautiful are these natural creations – frost, branch, bird – next to the brute ugliness of the factory. She is often struck by the contrast. And yet, as she opens the car and lowers herself into its metal frame, she asks herself: isn't this car also natural? And what of that terrible wave? What of that terrible war? All part of the natural order of things, she shrugs, though she seems to have lost the will to penetrate the meaning of this order. Belle had once prided herself on her ability to penetrate the meaning of things, and she had once been – or so she thought – something of an expert on natural cycles, or at least natural cycles at their most mathematically abstract. She wrote her dissertation on the classification of rational symmetry and periodic cycles of order in three-dimensional space. She knows – as intimately as she knows the contours of Martin's long telephone silences, or the slope of Sybil's downcast eyelids – that every point in space is attracted to periodic cycles of order, and that she herself is no exception to that rule. She too has tried to draw comfort from cycles. Not from the long, nearly linear cycle from birth to death – that one is too ruthless, too inexorable – but from the repetitive everyday cycles of rising and sleeping, nutrition and elimination, evaporation and precipitation. Martin often urges her: 'Don't always take the long view. Just forget about publishing your dissertation, or getting the perfect job — at least for now. Enjoy the small moments of each day. That's the key to happiness.'

The critically finite, she calls this compromise. Though Martin is certainly right: his words, banal but true. Words to live by, and she had tried. One advantage of being pregnant or writing a doctoral dissertation or having small babies is that, for a brief spell, the world is indeed critically finite and meaning-of-life issues all but disappear. During those years, she and her life possessed a clear purpose. She was a vessel: a container for something other than herself. But such clarity, such purpose rarely endures. Eventually the small periodic cycles of order breed tedium and despair: the endless piles of laundry to be washed and folded and worn and piled up again, the university job listings to be checked, cover letters written, stamps licked, envelopes posted, food bought at the grocery store, put into bags, taken out of bags, cooked and swallowed and turned into shit, asses to be wiped, diapers changed, only to be filled with more shit. The sheer physical relentlessness of it all makes her think of the fingernails and hair on corpses that continue to grow even as the living calcium in the bones is slowly transformed to dust.

She often yearns for the abstraction of numbers, or perhaps for an even deeper abstraction. When Sybil was still an infant, Martin had taught Belle – who had somehow never bothered to learn – how to drive a car. They practised on the same Evanston streets that she now traverses to get to the elementary school. They practised on the highway from the university into Chicago. Once she mastered the basics of highway driving, she used to project her gaze out over the orderly rows of traffic in front of her and imagine her car careening off the side of the road and into the dividing wall. She visualised the accordion crunch of metal, the baby's car seat lurching violently in the backseat, the path of her own head as it soared forward into the steering column and bounced back again: the parting of skin, the snap of vertebrae.

'What's the matter?' Martin had once asked her from the passenger seat. 'You just shuddered.'

'Sorry.' She shook the vision out of her mind. 'I was imagining the car crashing on the divider — what would happen to me, the baby, the car. Don't you ever do that?' she asked. 'Not just with cars, but at all? Sometimes I stand at the top of a flight of stairs and imagine my toe catching the step, and me tumbling down, falling into a heap at the bottom. Or I imagine an explosion blasting out the front windowpanes of our house — the heat of it, the destructive force.'

He turned and gave her a long look with his dark hazel eyes. 'No, Belle,' he annunciated the two syllables slowly as if he were addressing a beloved lunatic. 'I don't do that.'

'Oh, come on,' she insisted. 'You never project your life forward toward some tragic, violent incident – plane crash, earthquake – whatever? Everybody does that, don't they?'

'I don't think I do that,' Martin reflected. A few minutes passed in silence and then he suddenly remembered. 'When I used to take the L-train to work, I would imagine stepping forward and nonchalantly shoving someone off the platform in front of an oncoming train. I'd imagine the mayhem that would follow: the body being taken off the tracks, the arrest, a trial maybe, the victim's family sitting in the front row all righteous, teary-eyed, bewildered. With one impulsive gesture, my life would change into something totally different from what it was supposed to be.'

Today recalling this conversation as she turns the car down Lake Street where her three children stand on the curb waiting for her to pull up, she has to admit that Martin's homicidal vision possesses a certain perverse logic. When he dreams of a single violent, transformative instant that would catapult his life out of its ordinary cyclical routine, he imagines a stranger's death, not his own. Or hers. Or the children's. Which make more sense in a way than her endless fantasies about precisely what she fears the most, more sense than her strange brooding on impossible choices — which child to be carried away in a tidal wave, which crushed in a car accident, which blown to bits by a bomb. And sometimes she has to wonder: what does she truly fear most? Years ago, when she was still nursing the twins, she sat on the edge of the bed massaging her breasts and looking at the two baby boys in a rare moment of simultaneous sleep. All of a sudden her fingers stumbled upon an unmistakable lump in her right breast, and vast quantities of survival-driven adrenaline pumped into her system. In the end, it turned out to be nothing more than a clogged milk duct, but in that second of discovery, a thought – a prayer really – had sprung fully-formed into her mind: 'Don't take me. Take one of them instead of me. Take one of the children.'

At times, she can't escape the feeling that she has become a walking anachronism: a mathematician spooked by infinity; a melancholic clinging to a life barely lived; a suicide terrified of her own extinction.

She pulls up beside her row of offspring, their three small heads poised on delicate necks, their growing bodies hidden beneath the armour of down parkas, their backs bent slightly beneath the burden of school bags. 'Get in.' Belle unlocks the back door. The children tumble noisily into the back seat, pulling off hats, making adjustments, storing their backpacks between their knees. 'How was your day?' Belle asks the routine question as she pulls out from the curb.

'I have a test tomorrow,' Sybil responds.

'In what?'

'Environmental studies.'

'What's going to be on it?'

'You know, the usual: the hydrosphere, clouds, rain, pollution, the ozone layer, global warming, stuff like that.'

'Can I see your notebook?' Sybil passes the notebook forward and, while waiting at a red light, Belle flips through the pages, her gaze travelling down the neatly written section headings:

PRECIPITATION
CONVERGENCE
FRONTAL LIFTING

'What about you boys?' she asks the seven-year-olds. 'Anything going on in your class?' They don't answer. The light turns green. Reluctantly she pulls her eyes away from the bold capital letters and presses her foot down on the accelerator, the lovely words still floating though her mind:

NIMBUS
CIRRUS
STRATUS
CUMULUS

'We're not supposed to talk about it,' Max answers at last.

'What do you mean you're not supposed to talk about it?'

'They're really not supposed to,' Sybil rushes to their defence. 'The teacher said . . .'

'What happened?' Belle glances around quickly, looking at the children in the back seat, wondering at the suddenly sombre mood in the car. 'You can trust me. I won't tell anyone. Who would I tell?'

'Somebody's mother died,' Henry blurts out the terrible words and then, with the power of a breaking dam, the interior of the closed car fills with palpable excitement and release. The children's voices overlap and interrupt, rising in agitation as they search for the right expressions, the expressions adults might use in such an extraordinary situation.

'I was so upset when I heard . . .'

'The teachers couldn't stop talking about it all day long . . .'

'. . . something in her brain.'

'. . . out of the blue . . .'

'. . . a stroke or something . . .'

'She was so nice, so pretty . . .'

'Stop!' cried Belle. She despises their excitement, recognising her own. 'Whose mother?'

'Tommy's,' answers Max, who is crying now, rubbing his eyes with the back of his mittened hands, contemplating, perhaps for the first time in his short life, the potential of the world to strike such a personal blow.

'Did I know her?' Belle asks, trying to visualise the woman, to create a person out of the abstract number one — another prime number, the first prime number. When Henry describes her short red wavy hair, the rectangular black-framed glasses, the plaid car coat, she realises that she and Tommy's mother had spoken briefly outside the school last Friday afternoon, only three days ago, the day before she died. About trivial everyday things: the weather, winter break, husbands.

'What happened to her?'

'She was driving home from the grocery store on Saturday afternoon, and she pulled her car over to the side of the road – she must have felt funny – and then she just closed her eyes and died. They're not sure why. That's how they found her,' Sybil explains in a serious voice. 'Alone in the car. Dead.'

Belle spots a gap in the line of parked cars on the right side of the street, and pulls into it, turning off the engine as she coasts in. It's a quiet residential street not far from her own. She looks to the left where two leggy teenage girls stand conferring in front of a bright red clump of dogwood that glimmers flame-like above the dull grey sidewalk. The two girls, heads together, peek into a small plastic bag. One pulls out a silky something, and the other touches it gently, and makes a whistling sound. They move down the street laughing. Belle looks to the right where an old man wearing bedroom slippers emerges from an apartment building and turns over a garbage pail into a dumpster. Then she leans in close to the windshield, places both palms of her hands on the glass, and looks up into the wan winter sky, the towering clouds turning a pale shade of purple as afternoon heads toward night. *Cumulus, nimbus, cirrus*: she mouths the silent incantation.

'What are you doing, mommy?' Max's voice sounds small and unsure.

I'm trying to see what she saw in the last instant of her life.

'Mommy?'

I'm trying to sort it out.

'Are you okay?'

Belle rests her back against the seat and closes her eyes.

'Did they tell you how to treat Tommy when he comes back to school?'

'Yeah,' Henry says. 'The nurse came and said we should treat him normally, *not* avoid him, but *not* ask about her — about his mother. We're supposed to talk about the usual stuff: like homework, cafeteria food, football, whatever.'

Aha, thinks Belle, trapped in our small periodic cycles of order, we thirst for the occasional statistical spike, and when it comes, we turn away. We retreat into the routine, into the splendid ordinary.

She starts the engine again, flicking on the left-hand blinker as she pulls out.

'Oh yeah, and we're supposed to bring five dollars for a wreath tomorrow.'

Martin comes home at six-fifteen on the dot. He's a good man that way. Reliable. The television screen records his shadow crossing the room to the liquor cabinet where he pours himself his single bourbon of the day. 'Anything new?' he calls out to the kitchen where Belle and the children sit around the table drawing and doing homework.

'The daily tally went up by one.'

'One, huh?' Martin says, staring into the liquid as it swirls around his glass. 'They don't usually report one death. Must have been someone important.'

It was.

'But then again,' Martin waxes philosophical as he enters the kitchen, drink in hand, and leans against the frame of the door, 'everyone's important.'

Infinity equals one. It makes no sense at all.

'What are you all doing?' he looks down fondly at the four bent heads.

'Getting ready for Sybil's test. Environmental studies.' Belle turns her face up toward Martin and examines him as if she is seeing him for the first time after a long separation — his slouching comma-shaped frame in the rumpled tan jacket, the shadow of a black beard coming in grey in patches, the lines of concern that have recently become a permanent feature of his complexion, the dark hazel irises surrounded by even darker black rings. When they were first falling in love she used to spend what seemed like hours gazing at those dense planetary rings, searching for – and finding more often than not – the meaning of life right there in his eyes.

'Is she ready for it?'

'Well,' Belle pauses, and a terrible and inexplicable surge of emotion rises in her throat, the kind of overwhelming feeling she used to get when standing in a church full of singing people, their collective voice rising up toward the rafters.

'She's a little bit unsure about the formation of clouds.'

'Hey,' Martin puts down his drink on the counter, strides over to the table and places a rough hand on Belle's wet cheek. 'What is it?' he laughs softly. His eyes are working overtime now, trying to reach into hers and catch hold of her foundering soul. 'We're all a little bit unsure about the formation of clouds,' he says reassuringly. 'Aren't we, Sybil? Isn't that right, Henry? Max, back me up here.'

'Yeah, yeah,' the children begin uncertainly, catching hold of their father's stray wisp of gaiety. 'We're all a little bit unsure . . .' they echo. Martin leans over and kisses Belle, passing his bourbon-wet tongue over her front teeth.

'Stop,' Belle says. 'Stop it.'

Stop what? she wonders to herself, but she's smiling now and for once not trying to hide it. 'You know, Martin, I was wondering . . .'. She looks beyond Martin out of the kitchen window into the night sky. 'I was wondering: do you think they teach the theory of quantum entanglement at Evanston High?'

'I have no idea. I don't even know what quantum entanglement is.'

'It's the theory that two particles – photons or electrons – that have once interacted in some way will always retain a connection, always, even if they are spatially separated by incredible distances, even if one ceases to exist.'

'I don't know, Belle, I kind of doubt it. But there's one way to find out.'

Her gaze returns to the night sky. A light snow is falling through the darkness outside. The street light in front of the house illuminates a broad halo of individual silver flakes, catching just a small part of their long descent to earth.

Over the Barricades of Indian Nationalism in Raja Rao's Short Stories

Stefano Mercanti

In the welter of historiographical perspectives conveyed by the West in its intellectual – essentially unilateral – traffic with the Orient, India's struggle for independence has often been viewed through various stereotypes ranging from those theorised by the imperialist school of historians – known as the Cambridge School – to those emerging from the Marxist school.[1] Their viewpoint of the Indian national movement vehemently converged in seeing the freedom struggle against British imperialism as a mock battle ('mimic warfare'), a structured bourgeois movement or 'as a cloak for the struggle for power between various sections of the Indian elite, and between them and the foreign elite' (Chandra et al. 19). This denied its existence as a genuine anti-colonial movement of the Indian masses aimed at overthrowing British imperialism and established an approach to historical events relevant to Western hegemonic needs. However, when this 'imaginary' freedom movement is closely examined against the Indian socio-historical and literary backdrop, it turns out to have been for the colonised a very profound experience in embodying a radical vision of anti-colonial nationalism in which Gandhi built the need for a national ideology as a means of cultural survival. Moreover, he recognised that India, 'would either have to make a break with the post-medieval western concept of nationalism or give the concept a new content' in order to avoid an imaginary nation-state shaped by a response to western imperialism (Nandy 154). This critique of nationalism arose almost spontaneously among the colonised as the British rule imposed, as A R Desai noted, 'basic handicaps on the free development of the subject nation' (308).

At a literary level, India's movement for independence not only provided many novelists with rich material for their fiction but also shaped the essential human conditions of Indian consciousness during the emergence of a national identity. Many were the 'Gandhian' novels written both in English and Indian languages around the social and political upheavals spanning the 1930s and 1940s with varying degrees of success and commitment.[2] Whether this great national upsurge was treated as a central theme or as the background to a personal narrative, it ultimately triggered off a vigorous resistance to the 'benevolent Raj' at all levels of Indian society and pushed many writers to re-define their country and identity with intense emotional and artistic vibrancy. As Meenakshi Mukherjee rightly noted:

> this was an experience that was national in nature. It traversed boundaries of language and community and, since Indo-Anglian novels aim at a pan-Indian readership, this unifying experience has served to establish Indo-Anglian writing as an integral part of Indian literature. (34)

This essay explores, mainly through an analysis of the three explicitly nationalistic short stories written by Rao in the collection *The Cow of the Barricades*, the political and philosophical preoccupations which inspired the author to depict Gandhi's national movement as a significant expression of the complex Indian consciousness. In examining his artistic vision of Indian nationalism, this study will also show Rao on his intellectual and spiritual journey from the rustic portrayal of Indian village life found 'In Kandesh' to the more spiritual and mythical depiction of Gandhi's national 'liberation' of

Wasafiri Vol. 21, No. 1 March 2006, pp. 16–21
ISSN 0269-0055 print/ISSN 1747-1508 online © 2006 Wasafiri
http://www.tandf.co.uk/journals DOI: 10.1080/02690050500475435
Routledge Taylor & Francis Group

India in 'Narsiga' and 'The Cow of the Barricades'. It is a journey between myth and historical fact made by one who, with his first novel *Kanthapura* (1938), became one of the most distinguished writers of Indian English literature and perhaps the most authentic novelist in describing the complex combination of many forces grouped under the wide multi-class Gandhian movement.[3] Surprisingly, Rao's short stories, have not been given the distinction they deserve, a critical negligence that we also generally observe in the case of the Indian English short story as a genre. Yet, if we consider that the short story developed in India during those turbulent years of the freedom struggle and has 'since ... remained a mode for expressing the suppressed/repressed', it undoubtedly deserves a much more serious scrutiny (T Mukherjee 95). For, by the time of the social and political upheavals of the 'Gandhian whirlwind', the short story – along with the novel and poetry – already displayed a remarkable degree of indigenisation of both the English language and the narrative structure which most Indian English writers achieved by a deliberate use of a living orality, the native techniques of fiction as well as the fabular orientation of an old Indian narrative tradition.[4]

All the three stories discussed here first appeared together in *The Cow of the Barricades* in the same year as the Indian publication of *Kanthapura* — and were also both published rather emblematically in the year of India's Independence. By avoiding a direct portrayal of Gandhi, Rao's stories bring to focus his early social and political concerns in which the timeless and the temporal, the metaphysical and the social, the local and the national merge in his highly poetic imagination. 'In Kandesh' is the story of a small South Indian village which appears animated by the excitement of its inhabitants in welcoming the visit of their Maharaja, escorted by some British officials. Except Dattopant who is awoken by the hammering sound of the drums – 'Tom-tom ... tom-tom ... Tira-tira ... Tira-tira' – after a long sleepless night full of nightmares which portend his death:

> A terrible pain in the stomach had kept him awake late into the night. And then, what with the heavy monsters that rolled over his belly, the horse that galloped without neck or tail, the noise of the grand-child near him, the breathless flight in the air, funeral processions, death-drums, temples and rupees, and mimicking monkeys ... Deep in the night he heard an owl hoot somewhere ... Death, said the elders ... Sleep indeed came but the owl changed into a sheep, the sheep grew long, twisted horns and became a buffalo. A black rider sat on it, a looped serpent in one hand. The buffalo put its muzzle on Dattopant, licked his flesh, sniffed — then with a dart flung into the depths of the raging clouds, and was lost. Dattopant too was lost. A noose was around his neck. The black rider was dragging him against the amassed clouds ... Where? (Rao, *The Cow* 142–43)

The same nightmarish tension marks the unfolding of Dattopant's troubled mind in a kind of Kafkian re-awakening which assumes a more sinister tone through the dark description of the village:[5]

> In Kandesh, the earth is black. Black and grey as the buffalo, and twisted like an endless line of loamy pythons, wriggling and stretching beneath the awful heat of the sun ... Then, suddenly, there is a yawning ravine in the endless immensity of the python-world, the chief python of pythons, with his venom flowing in red and blue and white. The red venom shines in the sands. The blue one lies in the shadow. And the white is the bubbling, steaming water that crawls over the bed, as though the pus of heaven had turned liquid. The blood of the earth mingles with the pus of the skies — to bear cotton. Rows and rows of cotton. Thin, unmoving, bone-like plants, with little skulls in their hands that split and crackle with the heat of the sun. (146–47)

Here the eerie atmosphere, previously evoked during the night, becomes so confused and creeping that it permeates not only the village, but also the earth and the sky, now saturated with venom. Trapped within a fantastic territory, Dattopant is searching for his own self, lost in the physical and cultural spaces between his Indian native roots and the contamination of the British colonisers, the 'red man' — *the chief python of pythons*. Dattopant's inner conflict is enhanced by Rao through the use of an idiosyncratic style – like the sound of the beating drums – which sustains the unreal atmosphere of the village and blurs the boundaries amongst animals, nature and human beings. Thus the colours of the British flag – *his venom flowing in red and blue and white* – insidiously merge in the colonised India's natural elements. In this light, Dattopant's experience appears even more rending as his confused consciousness inevitably derails from the British loyalist fold of his colonised community in order to preserve his spiritual and cultural alterity. While the unceasing drumbeat frames, on the one hand, the exceptionality of the royal visit and confines the whole village to the enthusiasm of the happy event, on the other, it forebodes the ominous death stored in Dattopant's fate. Accordingly, the pressing sound of the drums and the arrival of the train merge in his confused and labyrinthine imagination which inescapably isolates the agitated protagonist from the welcoming crowd, thus leading him to death:

> Clutter-clutter – clutter-clutter – 'The train! The train!' ... Curtains follow curtains. It is like the prison-house – the storm. Walls of curtain that tear with a violent breath. Curtain again. Then suddenly the trees, like policemen, hard, gory, smeared with black running blood. Clutter-clutter – clutter-clutter – like a leopard the rain scratches on the back, brusque, snarling, satisfied ... Clutter. Rama, Rama, there – the train! Dattopant jumped forward and the train

> squashed him with a thud. It was a ballast train. The Viceroy's special followed it. Special trains like kings need heralds. Life is not bought at the market. (162–63)

Interestingly, if the Indian railways had an important role in the unification of India as an instrument designed by the British Empire to maintain their military hold on the subcontinent, they also became, as Pramila Garg has pointed out, a useful means for organising political movements to overthrow the Empire (24). Yet, 'In Kandesh', Dattopant's individual resistance remains unnoticed and Rao's bitter comment at the end of the story is followed by Dattopant's cremation. Kandesh, however, is a microcosm in which everything takes place at the same time as it has already happened at some other point, and 'the fire burns as elsewhere' (163).

Whereas 'In Kandesh' we have a story of human alienation in which freedom is only a glimmer of a possibility, 'Narsiga' shows the triumphant exuberance of a poor five-year old orphan over his difficult childhood: 'his father had died of cholera, his mother of famine, and one sultry afternoon, a thin tall woman, angry and effusive, turned up and calling herself his aunt carted him away into a distant village' (97). To his aunt's affection is added that of a spiritual master who offers Narsiga the chance of making a small profit by leading his sheep to pasture. The world of Narsiga is animated by a fervid imagination which finds expression in spending a pleasant time with animals and nature. Escaping from the sunny and dusty everyday monotony, Narsiga plays with dogs and pulls the tails of tethered cows, and by projecting his dreams even further, he rides his sheep, suddenly becoming

> one of those powerful gods that have animals for their vehicles. Now he would be Shiva, the Serpent-garlanded, and the knotted grass became the serpent and the long-horned goat the bull. And now he would ride on Rama's chariot of flowers, a bael flower at the sheep's tail, and two others behind his ears. And, my, such a rain of flowers welcomed him back to Ayodhya! (100)

The metaphors holding his strong imagination are those belonging to Indian mythology and popular folklore which aim at preserving the natural equilibrium of his innocence. Even when Narsiga sings *Vandé Mataram* he cannot avoid asking himself to whom those verses are really dedicated.[6] He knows that it is a song addressed to the Mother Goddess, but his being an orphan makes him incapable of clearly understanding who this Mother is, a concept that is further complicated by the red man's colonial conquest which makes her appear brutally imprisoned. It is worth noticing that the religious symbolism of motherland in the Indian anthem carried the primordial appeal of Indian idolatry which strongly appealed to the Indian mind in the nation-building process. Accordingly, the personification of the nation as an abstract idea became a natural means of investing old archetypes of Indian culture in a sort of 'intuitive leap towards an imagined future through remembrances of the past' (Bhattacharya 94). But Narsiga's world is a small one and the overarching concept of a motherland is too complex for him as is also the figure of Gandhi as a Mahatma (Great Soul) who is likewise imprisoned. It is his aunt who tells him about Gandhi:

> An old man — bewitching man, a Saint, you know! He had come from village to village, and I have beheld him too . . . He looks beautiful as the morning sun . . . He is an incarnation of God, that is why everybody touches his feet, even Brahmins, my son. (Rao, *The Cow* 105)

While Narsiga senses there is a bigger world outside his own, his limited experience confines him to the narrow confines of his own imagination: it is an inner landscape from which he is finally rescued, and all events eventually merge into the world of mythology, providing explanations to his troubled mind. He comes to terms with the mysterious figure of the Mother by closing his eyes and seeing the Master's wife or his aunt juxtaposed to the image of the Goddess:

> Mother who was good, Mother who was kind. Mother who grew rice. Mother, Mother, Mother . . . a huge big goddess, sitting on a swan, like the one in the picture by the sanctum door, a huge light behind her head, a conch in one hand, a wheel in another, and a tamed lion at her feet. She held rice in one hand and a lotus in the other . . . and when it came to the end, 'Mataram, Mataram, Vandé Mataram,' Narsa's eyes suddenly grew full of tears, and the whole earth seemed to grow soft and radiant, and he felt his head resting on the lap of a great big mother. (111)

It is this strong imagination, coupled with a natural simplicity, that enables Narsiga to find solutions to those troubling thoughts of the Goddess and the Mahatma Gandhi. How to explain that Gandhi, being a saint, had no temple? Or was able to show love to everyone even when you are brutally enslaved and imprisoned by the 'red man'.[7] Narsiga wonders 'if my sheep were to stray away, I have to beat them. Now, if I have not to be cruel should I beat them, or should I not? . . . And the snake, it is a wicked thing. It comes rushing towards you when it sees you' (114). We also see him involved in an innocent act of rebellion against the colonisers by throwing stones at a passing train, an episode that gives him a shivering fever as a result of his guilt at breaking the Gandhian admonishment 'Love the red man'. It is only through seeking forgiveness that Narsiga finds a solution to his mischief:

> 'Saint Gandhi', he said, beating his cheeks to ask forgiveness, 'pardon me, O Saint. You are great. You are next only to God. You are by the Mother. Saint, I shall never hate the red man again. Take away the

devil from me, Saint. Saint, I fall at thy feet and kiss them. O Saint!'. (115–16)

Thus, his experience results again in a fancy amalgam in which reality takes flight and facts are juxtaposed to a mythical symbology as also with Gandhi's release from prison, news which overwhelms him with so much joy that he imagines the Mahatma as a mythical hero 'going in the air — like Rama and Sita going back to Ayodhya. Master says, the Mahatma will fly like that, with four white steeds, such as even the District Collector never had' (117). The story of Narsiga undoubtedly shows Rao's ability to give voice to a world seen through the eyes of a child. It is indeed an adolescent dimension insightfully rendered through a distinctive Indian peasant sensibility and folk imagination, a truly authentic response to the Independence movement as experienced in Indian villages.

Rao's complete involvement in the national movement succeeds in creating a more complex symbolic vision of independent India in the title story 'The Cow of the Barricades'. If the critical appraisal given by several scholars of this story is questionable, Rao's poetic imagination is undoubtedly remarkable here as it finds expression during a period of growing discontent with Gandhi's political strategies, a sentiment that is also echoed at the end of the story:[8] 'the Mahatma may be all wrong about politics, but he is right about the fullness of love in all creatures — the speechful and the mute' (182). During the 1930s, Rao felt certain that the Gandhian ideology would have led the country towards its independence, a passionate patriotic conviction which is depicted in the story by the use of the fantastic to serve a metaphysical end, thus exerting noble resonances with man's human depths. Like in 'Narsiga', 'The Cow of the Barricades' is a story of how the Gandhian struggle for Independence comes to a small village in South India, yet this time the central figure is not a human being but a cow, the many-faceted symbol of India *par excellence* which here primarily conveys the idea of the country in the bondage of foreign rulers. Gauri is the symbol of the holy cow which stands against the British rule by representing the Gandhian values of non-violence (*ahimsa*) and truth (*satya*). Its religious significance is directly related to the ancient myth of *Kamadhenu* (also known as *Surabi*, *Savala* or *Nandini*), the first mother of cattle who gives prosperity whenever needed to gods and sages. According to several *Puranas* (a body of Vedic Hindu texts), she belonged to the sage Vasishtha and was produced as the ocean was churning. Amongst the many examples of her supernatural powers, she gave birth to a host of warriors who aided the sage Vasishtha to defeat the arrogant king Vishvamitra, thus turning him into a royal saint (*Rajarsi*). Added to this puranic myth is that of the Hindu Goddess (*Devi*) in which Gauri is known as *Parvathi* (wife of *Shiva* and mother of *Ganesha*). *Devi* emerges as the ultimate feminine principle, the Universal Life Energy itself, the original *Shakti* (psychic and spiritual power) inherent within creation which embodies the ability of her divine male consort to create the manifest world. In analysing Rao's 'The Cow of the Barricades' it is necessary to consider this philosophical and religious lore in order to fully understand the symbolic meanings and the inherent messages conveyed by the author. The story itself is woven together by Rao in a sort of puranic style which unfolds stirring, mesmerising and rhythmic cadences. Here the reader almost participates in the vigorous resistance of this small southern Indian village and is directly taken behind the barricades of India's freedom movement in which Gauri heroically stands up the British troops. Rao evokes the mythological stature of the cow-goddess by depicting her paying regular visits to a spiritual master every Tuesday at which she only takes a handful of grain from him and then disappears into the bushes and is not seen for the rest of the week:

> And the Master's disciples gathered grain and grass and rice-water to give her every Tuesday, but she refused it all and took only the handful of grain the Master gave. She munched it slowly and carefully as one articulates a string of holy words, and when she had finished eating, she knelt again, shook her head and disappeared. And the Master's disciples said, 'This is a strange creature' . . . And they went to the Master and said: 'Master can you tell us who this cow may be?' And . . . he said: 'She may be my baton-armed mother-in-law. Though she may be the mother of one of you. Perhaps she is the great Mother's vehicle.' And like to a mother, they put kumkum on her forehead, and till Tuesday next they waited for Gauri. (174–75)

The symbolic meanings conveyed by the cow and the chance that she represents of achieving India's independence through a peaceful resistance become more clear in the subsequent description of Gandhi's freedom movement. It is indeed in this period in which the country was forging its national and self-governed (*swaraj*) identity that Rao synthetically restates the key principles of Gandhi's non-violent resistance (*satyagraha*):

> 'Don't buy their cloth.' And people did not buy their cloth. The Mahatma said: 'Don't serve under them.' And people did not serve under them. And the Mahatma said: 'Don't pay their taxes.' And people gathered, and bonfires were lit and processions were formed, and there were many men wounded and killed and many taken to prisons, but people would not pay taxes nor would they wear foreign clothes. (176)

With the oppressive imposition of taxes by the foreign rulers, peasant life becomes increasingly unbearable and eventually the village is transformed into a battlefield in which barricades are erected to stop the advance of the British troops. Yet, the spiritual Master of the village spurs the peasants on following the peaceful message spread by Gandhi: 'No barricades in the name of the Mahatma, for much blood will be spilt,' but the workmen said, 'It is not with "I love you, I love you," you can change the grinding heart of the Government' (178). The happiness that reigned at the beginning of the story – represented by the snake and the rat playing under the Master's bed – is now contrasted by the tremendous sufferings created by the 'grinding heart' of the colonial government. The symbol of the cow as Mother India (*Bharat Mata*) imprisoned by the rulers, is strikingly shown through Gauri's response to the imminent assault: 'she looked very sad, and somebody had even seen a tear, clear as a drop of the Ganges, run down her cheeks, for she was of compassion infinite and true' (177). It is in the very crucial moment of confrontation between the villagers and the colonisers that Gauri appears in all her glory, like *Kamadhenu*, displaying her indestructible compassion and her entire motherly force beyond the boundaries of life itself:

> With the third move men pushed her up and she was on the top of the barricades . . . But their chief, the red-man, saw this and fired a shot. It went through Gauri's head, and she fell, a vehicle of God among lowly man. But they said blood did not gush out of the head but only between the forelegs, from the thickness of her breast. (180–81)

Particularly interesting is the way Rao introduces the reader to the Gandhian value of non-violence (*ahimsa*) depicted here as a means of liberation in the face of tremendous repression — undoubtedly a puzzling and inoffensive response in view of Western politics. Yet, it was capable of tapping the diverse energies and immense capacities of a large variety of people boldly grounded on the ancient philosophical and religious heritage of India. If, on the one hand, Gauri becomes through her peaceful revolt a tragic metaphor of Gandhian predicaments – one of the many martyrs of Indian nationalism – on the other it shows the distinctive capacity of a millenary civilisation to distinguish itself by offering to its population an experience between history and myth which eventually led the country toward its legitimate liberation.

To conclude, Rao's stories stand at a point at which tradition and modernity fuse and show the surfacing of the Indian anti-colonial consciousness caught between a traditional religious society and the new world-view instilled by the British Empire. It was an encounter-clash between history and popular folklore which could not fail to result in the mythical transfiguration of the Gandhian movement, thus illustrating an alternative strategy unleashed by the peasant community to counteract British colonialism. The three stories collectively reveal the realistic and metaphysical strands at work in Raja Rao's mind in which the events enacted upon the transforming stage of Indian nationalism appear to go beyond the surface of life and move closer to a sensibility unmistakably Indian. Less sophisticated than in his subsequent works, his rendering here of pre-independent India appears in its full strength by turning the new into the old and the present into the past, thus constantly revitalising and re-visioning its boundaries.

Notes

1 As far as the study of the national movement is concerned, the imperialist approach first emerged in the official pronouncements of the conservative colonial administrators, the Viceroys, Lord Dufferin, Curzon, Minto, George Hamilton and further put forward by V Chirol, Verney Lowett and theorised by the American scholar Bruce T McCully. The Marxist approach was laid down by R Palme Dutt and A R Desai. See Bipan Chandra et al., 17–23.

2 The first novelist who depicted the Indian struggle for independence was K S Venkataramani in his *Murugan the Tiller* (1927) and *Kandan the Patriot* (1932). The impact of Gandhian ideology is also found in the following novels: Mulk Raj Anand's *Untouchable* (1935), D F Karaka's *We Never Die* (1944), Aamir Ali's *Conflict* (1947), Venu Chitali's *In Transit* (1950), R K Narayan's *Waiting for the Mahatma* (1955), K A Abbas's *Inqilab* (1955), Nayantara Sahgal's *A Time to Be Happy* (1958), and K Nagarajan's *Chronicles of Kedaram* (1961).

3 'Starting out as a movement of the nationalist intelligentsia, the national movement succeeded in mobilizing the youth, the women, the urban petty bourgeoisie, the urban and the rural poor, urban and rural artisans, peasants, workers, merchants, capitalists and a large number of small landlords', in Bipan Chandra et al., 28.

4 Among the native Indian traditions of the Indian short story we find the ancient collections like the *Kathasaritsagara*, Gunadya's *Brihatkatha*, the Buddhist *Jataka* tales, the *Panchatantra*, Narayana's *Hitopadesa* and Dandin's *Dashakumaracharita*.

5 Raja Rao acknowledged Kafka's literary influence in his preface to *The Policeman and the Rose*: 'At that time there were also going on experiments with form. Kafka had broken the crust of realism and given fabled meanings to man's fears' (xv).

6 'I bow to thee, Mother' is the opening stanza of the Indian national anthem written by the Bengali novelist B J Chatterji (1838–1894). In addition, 'Mother India' (*Bharat Mata*) is the goddess of independent India, a Hindu cult in which all Indians are called sons or children of India and are expected to protect their mother. See Kensley, 178–96.

7 During the Indian national movement led by Gandhi, *ahimsa* (non-violence), along with *swadeshi* (self-reliance) and *satyagraha* (truth force) became the three powerful practices of his heroic civil disobedience to the British Government.

8 See, for instance, Narasimhaiah, 24–28; Belliappa, 199–201; M Mukherjee, 139.

Works Cited

Abbas, Kwaja Ahmed. *Inquilab*. Bombay: Jaico Publications, 1955.

Ali, Aamir. *Conflict*. Bombay: National Information and Publications, 1947.

Anand, Mulk Raj. *Untouchable*. 1935. Delhi: Arnold-Heinemann, 1983.

Belliappa, K. C. *The Image of India in English Fiction.* New Delhi: B. R. Publishing Corporation, 1991.
Bhattacharya, Sabyasachi. *Vande Mataram, The Biography of a Song.* New Delhi: Penguin Books India, 2003.
Chandra, Bipan, Mridula Mukherjee, Aditya Mukherjee, Panikkar K. N. and Sucheta Mahajan. *India's Struggle for Independence 1857–1947.* New Delhi: Penguin Books India, 1989.
Chitali, Venu. *In Transit.* Bombay: Hind Kitabs, 1950.
Cowell, E. B. ed. *The Jataka; or, Stories of the Buddha's Former Births.* Cambridge: Cambridge UP, 1895.
Desai, A. R. *Social Background of Indian Nationalism.* Bombay: Popular Prakashan, 1998.
Garg, Pramila. *The Freedom Movement in Indian Fiction in English.* New Delhi: Ashis Publishing House, 1993.
Hitopadesa. Trans. G. L. Chandiramani. Mumbai: Jaico, 1995.
Karaka, D. F. *We Never Die.* Bombay: Thacker & Co, 1944.
Kathasaritsagara. Trans. Radhavallabh Tripathi. New Delhi: National Book Trust, India, 1995.
Kensley, David. *Hindu Goddess.* Delhi: Motilal Banrsidass, 1998.
Mukherjee, Meenakshi. *The Twice-Born Fiction.* New Delhi: Arnold-Heinemann, 1974.
Mukherjee, Tutun. 'Of Other Voices: Mahasweta Devi's Short Stories Translated by Gayatri Chakravorty Spivak'. *English and the Indian Short Story.* Ed. M. Ramana and P. Sailaja. New Delhi: Orient Longman, 2000. 94–105.
Nagarajan, Krishnaswamy. *Chronicles of Kedaram.* Bombay: Asia Publishing House, 1961.
Nandy, Ashis. 'The Illegitimacy of Nationalism'. *Bonfire of Creeds.* New Delhi: Oxford UP, 2004. 153–233.
Narasimhaiah, C. D. *Raja Rao.* Delhi: Doaba Publications, 2000.
Narayan, R. K. *Waiting for the Mahatma.* 1955. London: Minerva, 1993.
The Panchatantra. Trans. Arthur W. Ryder. Mumbai: Jaico Publishing House, 1949.
Rao, Raja. *The Cow of the Barricades and Other Stories.* Madras: Oxford UP, Champak Library, 1947.
——. Preface. *The Policeman and the Rose.* By Rao. Delhi: Oxford UP, 1978. xi–xvi.
Sahgal, Nayantara. *A Time to be Happy.* 1958. Bombay: Jaico Publications, 1963.
Somadeva, Sattar. *Tales from the Kathasaritsagara.* Trans. Arshia. London: Penguin Books, 1994.
Three Novels from Ancient India: Dandin's Dashakumaracharita, Subandhu's Vasavadatta, Banabhatta's Kadambari. Trans. Vishwanath S. Naravane. New Delhi: Vikas Publishing House, 1982.
Venkataramani, Kaneripatna Sidhanatha. *Murugan, the Tiller.* London: Simpkin, Marshall, Hamilton, Kent, 1927.
——. *Kandan, the Patriot.* 1932. 2nd ed. Madras: Svetaranya Ashrama, 1934.

John Haynes

from YOU
for Afiniki Kyari

XVII

Rasheed has come on study leave. He brings
the taste of home, borkono, daddawa,
some of those little smoked fish coiled in rings
tail into mouth, that villagers from Hanwa
used to catch. As though under the water
now I walk the dried up river bed,
as steep banks slowly lift over my head.

For me, part of him *is* just this: the bush,
the sun as dark as a tomato, spokes
of big bike wheels along the paths, the hush
of kaftans as the farmers called their jokes
and greetings across that low sky, with hoes
on shoulders, and sometimes that motorcade
wailed far off like a spirit from the dead.

The river gravel now exposed in tapered
wedges getting finer at the tips,
the steep bank showing roots that went down deeper
than the plant grew up, my dry footsteps
clinking the pebbles, no wind on my lips:
as if I'd been allowed to walk beneath
the water just this once and yet still breathe.

borkono, daddawa: condiments

XVIII

What do I know about that land of his,
of yours, the bungled country where I found –
oh, all these findings, these discoveries,
these looted treasures stashed away in mind
to be brought back and labelled with the sounds
of English words whose meanings I don't know –
an ignorance? That's what I have to show.

Oh how socratic is the wood-carved head
which I unwrap as if from waterproof
like Livingstone, and put next to our bed
still as a soul. I have to keep it, love.
Such contradiction has to be enough
although it's not, I know. Nor is your known
voice intimately far off in a phone.

Rasheed's as well, talking of Bessie Head
again from his MA analysis
out on the porch after he'd come and set
down rice bags in the kitchen, laughing, 'Presents!',
me not sure if they weren't something else
at first. Stones on the pages, and a kind
of English not quite mine to understand.

XIX

He brings news of the killings: so-called *tribe*
on so-called tribe, and all goes back to oil
and looters in high places, banks and bribes,
and dead fish floating in a petrol smell,
and no Osama there, not yet, for Shell
so-called Nigeria who's bidding's done,
out in the bush somewhere, just before dawn.

Thought of your sister in that house, the walls
around it with barbed wire along the tops,
your brother-in-law's rifle, the split skull
your nephew Charles had seen with wet brain slopped

Wasafiri Vol. 21, No. 1 March 2006, pp. 22–23
ISSN 0269-0055 print/ISSN 1747-1508 online © 2006 Wasafiri
http://www.tandf.co.uk/journals DOI: 10.1080/02690050500475476
Routledge Taylor & Francis Group

on dust. Then, '86 after they'd stopped
the quelling of the students on the campus
a thinning mist, the faintest sting of gas.

Still there, are they, yards from the office, bullet
pock marks in the wall with felt tip O's
around each one, the total counted? Protests,
speeches, loud hailers, then Kill and Go,
Farida shot still in her shower robe
as she went back along the balcony
towards her room. FREEDOM! DEMOCRACY!

Kill and Go: military police

XX

Rasheed was editor in chief. He knew
them face to face, of course, Ken Saro Wiwa
who was done because of Alli who
had nursed this grudge, Abacha who was murdered
by the CIA – Call-girls, viagra,
poison, agent Coleman... How sheltered
I am, this teacher, due so much respect.

This is safe England where shysters like Blair
mix easy words and pictures, some, at least,
part true to tell us of a country far
away and strange with different customs, feast
days, and a wicked King whose wicked secrets
hide so deep down in the tale we haven't
found them yet. They keep us innocent.

We drive him all the way back to Heathrow:
a line of babban rigas for Abuja,
stacked up excess bags. Before he goes
he bends to give Tristan and Laraba
'something'. He waves. He goes into Departure
as we turn back and try to find the car,
then change, then A3 against spaceless dark.

Babban rigas: traditional flowing Hausa robes

XXI

I gave him cash, sterling, to give to Joe,
who runs the English office still, and eats
meat once a week these days and is supposed
to buy goats now that he's been made a chief
but can't afford to. Swivelling on his seat
he'd swivel back with any doc I wanted
from that filing system in his head.

I studied it, this Africa, it's use
of English in its poems, in Ikebe
Super Pidgin. I wrote to dispute
the thesis put forward by Ngugi
wa Thiong'o when he seems to say
that English words plug Africans with English
thoughts, surely quite unmaterialist . . .

I did a little bit. Got Awam in,
and Jenks, and Mbulelo, kept the VC's
buddies out, began a mag, got Pidgin
on the syllabus. Though none of this
would outlast Aliyu's return to be
true head again, and send out the Department
car to Sabo to collect his rents.

Ikebe super: literally 'large bum', popular tabloid magazine

XXII

Ninety-eight, we came back. There was Joe
grinning and pointing at the bucket on
the floor to catch the drips. Down south Okpewho,
Soyinka, Achebe, Biodun,
'Molara, Femi, Kole, they've all gone
where they can work, The States, South Africa,
UK. Our HOD's now bloody Emma!

Flight of the scholars. No more annual
conferences held in Ibadan now
nor Calabar where you came once when still
on NYS, and we walked with Okello
to the jetty and that clanking grew
into a blurry shadow on the mist
that for a moment was the Heart of Darkness

steamer on the Penguin book (A row
of them along the shelf behind Joe's head),
the river and the blur of primal Congo –
where the white man trekked to his meet id,
Achebe wrote, Joe's townsman, whom I met
once in that room, which maybe Joe was thinking
as he smiled back, with the bucket plinking.

NYS: National Youth Service, done – in an area of the country they don't come from – by all students after graduation

Achebe: Chinua Achebe, Nigerian novelist, author of *Things Fall Apart*

Nayantara Sahgal in Conversation

Shirley Chew

Nayantara Sahgal was born in 1927, in Allahabad, the second of Vijayalakshmi and Ranjit Pandit's three daughters, and niece to Jawaharlal Nehru, the first Prime Minister of India. She attended missionary and local schools in India and, from 1943 to 1947, Wellesley College, USA. She has held Fellowships at the Radcliff Institute, the Woodrow Wilson International Centre for Scholars, and the National Humanities Centre. During the 1980s, she served as Vice President of the People's Union for Civil Liberties in India. A novelist and political journalist, she has published nine novels and seven works of non-fiction, a body of writing which, even as it keeps pace with developments in India and the rest of the world, is informed by many of the ideals that had fuelled her country's struggle for freedom in the years she was growing up. The first of her novels, A Time To Be Happy, *appeared in 1958, and the most recent of them,* Lesser Breeds, *in 2003. Among the prestigious literary awards she has won are the Sinclair Prize for Fiction and the Sahitya Akademi Award, both for* Rich Like Us *(1985); and the Commonwealth Writers' Prize (Eurasia section) for* Plans for Departure *(1986). Her non-fictional works include two volumes of autobiography,* Prison and Chocolate Cake *(1954) and* From Fear Set Free *(1962); a political study,* Indira Gandhi: Her Road to Power *(1982); a collection of essays entitled* Point of View: A Personal Response to Life, Literature and Politics *(1997); and, co-authored with E N Mangat Rai,* Relationship: Extracts from a Correspondence *(1994). She has edited* Before Freedom: Nehru's Letters to his Sister 1909–47 *(2004). In 1990, she was elected Fellow of the American Academy of Arts and Sciences; and, in 1997, she received an Honorary Doctorate from the University of Leeds. In 2002, Wellesley College conferred its Alumnae Achievement Award upon her for 'bravely confronting authority in defense of the world's largest democracy' and her 'critical and courageous examination of gender, class and race (which) reaches far beyond India and resonates throughout the world'*

Nayantara Sahgal

Shirley Chew Nayantara, one feature your novels have in common is a strong sense of history — more particularly, of Indian history, though that could be tantamount to saying world history. For example, *A Time To Be Happy* is concerned with India in the early years of Independence; *Storm in Chandigarh* (1968) with the partition of East Punjab along linguistic lines; and *Rich Like Us* the so-called Emergency. The title of your most recent novel, *Lesser Breeds*, is a phrase taken from Kipling's poem, 'Recessional', and points yet again to your commitment to Indian history and Indian politics. In what way, or ways, is this new novel different from the earlier works?

Wasafiri Vol. 21, No. 1 March 2006, pp. 24–29
ISSN 0269-0055 print/ISSN 1747-1508 online © 2006 Wasafiri
http://www.tandf.co.uk/journals DOI: 10.1080/02690050500475492
Routledge Taylor & Francis Group

Nayantara Sahgal Well, perhaps you could say it is angrier, because it's a kind of summing-up of the history that I've been writing about. In a sense that earlier history of India charts a movement — towards Independence, then coming out of it, then establishing an identity as a people, as a country, as a civilisation. And yet, what we have come back to, almost, is 'square one', given that the global situation and the emergence – I should say, re-emergence – of the West in its new incarnation, as it were, of world ruler, makes every other history and civilisation marginal. I know that's putting it very simplistically but, roughly, the novel is a kind of despairing observation of that fact. And in that sense it is different because there isn't any optimism in it, particularly at the end where the main character realises that the period of struggle, when non-violence was the weapon, was a kind of passing moment in history and, for a great many reasons, did not survive. And, indeed, doesn't seem a useful weapon to contend with what is happening in the world today.

SC Yes, though the narrative of imperialism in *Lesser Breeds* is so cogently worked and elaborated that it comes across as something powerful – as you say, 'angry' – rather than a 'summing-up'. There is a tougher indictment of British rule in India than in your other novels, and our attention is drawn in no uncertain terms to the brutality of the Raj and the exploitative basis of British economic imperialism. Furthermore, the novel makes clear that, already in the 1930s and 1940s, there were intimations of the crises which Iran and Iraq are facing today. Can you say something about the inception of this novel? When did you start thinking about it? Was it after September 11? Or did it have an earlier moment of inspiration?

NS No, it had nothing to do with September 11. I had been thinking about the subject for a long time but as two different stories, two novellas — a story that happened in India based on non-violence and another that took place in America, starting in 1943. And then it occurred to me that what bound the two stories together was the concept of 'lesser breeds': the fact that it was not only confined to India, that we were not the only people marginalised and denigrated, and that there were obviously 'sufferers', as it were, in other parts of the world. What bound us was this notion imposed upon us of being 'lesser breeds' for whom the most elaborate and sophisticated punishments in history have been reserved. And the very first thing that forcefully impressed this upon me was Hiroshima. I was still in college when the atom bomb was dropped, and it seemed to me even then that, compared with the terrible devastation which resulted, and the vaporisation of countless numbers of people, the war with Germany had ended like a whimper earlier in the year, in May 1945. Hiroshima could never have happened to a white enemy. So I think it was then that the notion of 'lesser breeds' became a powerful image in my mind. Even the fairy tales one read at the time seemed to be saying the same thing about 'lesser breeds' and I think I quoted one of them in the novel where the victor gets two more beautiful wives, or something like that, and the vanquished, who is this black slave, has his arms and legs tied to four horses who are then whipped off to the four corners of the earth. So there is this difference in treatment, whether in myth or in reality. All of these things had been working in my mind for a long time and it just seemed to me that the two ideas I had for two separate stories could be brought together into one novel divided into different parts.

SC *Lesser Breeds* shows a number of interesting temporal shifts and turns in the narrative so that while the first section is concerned with the 1930s, there is constant harking back to the Salt March at the start of the decade; and then, in a passage in italics, we are propelled into the 1980s where Nurullah, one of the main characters, is being interviewed by Pete Ryder, an American student researching on 'non-violence and its soul force'. In deciding to put the two separate stories together, you must have been faced with specific problems relating to structure and form?

NS They were quite hard to tackle, which is why the writing took me a much longer time than it would have otherwise. And basically the novel starts much further back than 1930. The heart of the story is the exploitation that took place at the level of the countryside where there are two things to be considered: first, the peasant in that part of India, the province where I grew up, was someone indebted and deeply impoverished and without hope; and second, the same location was where recruiting had regularly taken place for the armed forces, particularly in the First World War. The soldiers were then sent off to European battlefields and those who survived came back to their tiny peasant holdings to find they had been turned off the land, because it had been taken over and they had no way of redressing the matter. And so it was a combination of two things: the peasant situation in the countryside in that province and the Empire's demand for soldiers to fight its wars. The protest which broke out in the countryside among the peasants was not organised by any political party, although the Nationalist Party, which was the Congress, did help and provide leadership for the *kisan* movement, the peasants' struggle.

To elaborate a little. An empire needs men to die for it, not its own people necessarily, but its subject peoples. Indians, as you know, were sent all over the world to fight for the British Empire, and they went, expecting every time to get something in return in the way of greater powers in the legislature at home, greater representation in government; but every time they found the British more unwilling to yield up power. For example, no Indian was allowed to command the army and, in one of the italicised portions of the novel, you will see that, while the British kept saying India would of course get independence when it was fit to defend itself, the catch was that Indians would never be fit to defend themselves because they did not have their own commanders, they were not allowed to be promoted beyond the rank of Major. That then was one of the causes of the national movement countrywide, which used non-violence as a weapon in a sustained way for the first and probably only time in history.

And yet, ultimately, what forced the British to leave was perhaps not the non-violence struggle at all, nor the conscience of the British, although both of these things might have played a part, but the fact that in the Second World War there was something like one million Indians in the army. They had fought on all the modern battlefields of Europe, they knew how to use their weapons, and it was no longer safe for the British to remain in those circumstances. That is really, I think, the underlying thread through all the different periods of the story. Does that answer . . .?

SC Yes, to an extent. But it's not just the Raj and imperialism your novel is criticising, is it? Some of the Indian characters are surely objects of satire? Perfectly 'nice people', and altogether serious about the task of resisting oppression and colonialism, they also appear to lead rather frothy lives, and spend their time playing party games like 'murder in the dark' or 'musical chairs' to the tune of 'O Silvery Arizona Moon'. Is that part of life as it was lived in India in the 1930s and 1940s? Take Mr Ghasvala, for example. Here is a cultivated and intelligent man, a wonderful host, yet he is also a supporter of Mussolini, does not blink an eye when Abyssinia is invaded, and obviously admires Hitler greatly. So I find the society you've depicted puzzling. Are these people meant to be the 'mimic men' colonialism produced?

NS Now there are two very different points here. First, there is Mr Ghasvala who, like many of his educated generation, is what I think of as 'mimic people', because their lives were patterned on the British way of life — they had been British educated, for one thing, and Mr Ghasvala was an Oxford man. Their aspirations leaned towards the West, they thought British rule a very good thing for India, and they followed the British lead in all political matters, including international matters. In those days, as you know, the British were pursuing an appeasement policy towards the growth of Fascism. Nationalist Indians were appalled by this and spoke out against it early on. The British were to change their minds, as you also know, but only later. So the 'mimic men' were part of that Western oriented scene, which existed in India at a certain level at the time.

The other point you raised about the games played at the party, that is something else, a way of overcoming the awkwardness of guests who have perhaps never been in a drawing-room. The National Movement had brought together all classes of people, most of whom were not accustomed to the Western style of living. Nurullah, you will recall, thought eating with knives and forks a very queer custom and took a long time to get used to them. And then only with the help of the cook who had served in a regiment and knew how places were laid, and what was used, and all that. But party games helped people relax. You could all play 'musical chairs', you could all play that game 'how green you are'. They were, of course, games I played as a child at children's parties so I put them in the book as a way for people to come together and be sort of relaxed with each other, even though they were all from different levels of society and different kinds of background. I wanted to reflect something of what the National Movement represented. It was classless, it cut across region, sex, language, religion, everything. It brought people together.

SC Yes; and I suppose that, disconcerting though the party games may be or dancing to the 'jhik-jhik rhythm of the moomphally song', they also throw into relief the tough, uncompromising side of the Movement. I have in mind Bhai's retort when he is asked why, having been in India so long, the British shouldn't be allow to stay: 'Why not let them stay! My dear, we can't afford them!' This is then followed by a brief but pointed analysis of the economic exploitation of India under the Raj. So the reader gets the effect of one narrative tone played off against another.

NS One word about that song 'The Peanut Vendor', a piece of Latin American music which was popular in my childhood. I remember my father and my mother used to dance to it for fun in the drawing-room, and it was a different kind of dance because it was the rhumba, not the staid foxtrot which the old Parsi ladies were teaching the little girl Shan to do. My father, who was a most wonderful man, gave me a glimpse for the first time of a different kind of music, one which, although it also came to us via the West, was full of joy and vitality, and which we didn't know anything about. There was clearly something else beyond the British circuit of ideas, fairy tales, and dances, and that's why 'The Peanut Vendor' appeals to Nurullah, you know. It has its own rhythm, its own has life.

SC On the subject of non-violence, *ahimsa*, which so absorbed Nurullah and Pete Ryder. One hears critics, Indian and non-Indian alike, questioning the relevance of Gandhi's ideals, or Nehru's, to present-day society. Does that particular question lie behind the narrative strand on non-violence in your novel? And what, at the end of the day, are we to make of the debate on *ahimsa* between the two men?

NS The anti-Nehruvian/anti-Gandhian debate has gone on in the last few years in India largely because of the rise of Hindu fundamentalism, and the fact that a fundamentalist party then came to power and has gone to the extent of trying to turn Hinduism into a sort of monoculture which it has never been and certainly isn't in modern times. And I don't think it's a debate which can take root (that's my own belief and I hope I'm right), because modern India has been built really on three different strands, if you like. I mean there was British liberalism, there was Marxism, there was Gandhism, all of which brought forth a very powerful mix, not just since Independence, but from the beginning of the century, the time of the Russian Revolution, and right through the struggle for freedom. I think the secular base of Indian politics was established upon those influences. And secularism is also part of the Indian psyche from the fact that Hindus and Muslims have lived side by side for centuries. We've never wanted a melting-pot for a country, you know; a salad bowl is more the thing, where identity and difference are honoured. And those elements are in the very soil of India, if you like. The other thing is that I don't think the political tradition itself can be easily disposed of — in fact, the recent election results are proof that most Indians believe in it.

SC Critics writing on your novels have been known to identify your characters with political figures in India, Nehru being an obvious example. Yet you killed off Nikhil who may be regarded as a Nehruvian character in *Lesser Breeds*?

NS I did that to show how justice was meted out during the war, where civil liberties of course didn't apply — in fact, human rights did not exist until long, long after the Second World War, when, I think, Mrs Roosevelt became a campaigner and, ever since then, we've heard of nothing else! But, until I was an adult, there was no such thing as human rights on the map. During the war there were, in India, Defence of India Rules and under those rules – DIR such and such a number and so on – the punishment was, I think, flogging, imprisonment or death for offenders. Now, in 1942, India had offered to support Britain in the war in exchange for independence at an agreed date after the war. Britain chose however to jail the nationalists instead, and it was in despairing response that outbreaks of violence took place all over the country and one of these was the derailment of trains carrying military equipment. So, in the novel, while Nikhil is not responsible for derailing the train, he is held morally responsible for his followers. And though he has refused to commit himself to violence at any stage, he is executed to show that in wartime there is no difference between real and moral responsibility.

SC And about Shan, Nikhil's daughter. Is there something of yourself and your personal experiences in the portrayal of this young girl who has to be re-educated, as it were, in order that she may look at things – history, for example – from a different, an Indian, perspective?

NS Yes, Nikhil wants Shan to unlearn, as it were, what she has been taught in the convent school since the difference between anything and everything is the way you see it, it's the point of view. That is partly why Shan is sent to America. And, yes, I went to America at the same age and, certainly, I saw it as a strange new world. But, unlike Shan, I wasn't as curious about dating habits [laughs].

SC Can I ask you to say something more about 'An Island Called America'? As an erstwhile colonial, brought up largely within what you've called 'the British circuit', I find that middle section of *Lesser Breeds* a little hard to follow at times.

NS Well, making America part of the story was important for many reasons, and one of them was to connect this section up with 'lesser breeds', that is, with the title and the main thread of the whole story. When I went to America at the age of sixteen, one of the people I met was the Japanese sculptor, Isamu Noguchi, who became a great friend and mentor, and taught me a lot about art. And there was also Paul Robeson. I remember being told that, although Paul was a brilliant student, he couldn't get admitted to a university except on a football scholarship, something of that kind. So those two personal memories went into the making of the two characters, the black American and the Japanese, who have both to face the consequences of being 'lesser breeds' — in the case of the black man, much more horrifically. The Japanese becomes a great artist in the end. And that is a comment on the fact that, though decimated, Japan rose from the ashes. I had these two things specifically in mind.

SC At the same time, characters like Edgar Knox and Pete Ryder are enlightened, highly intelligent, and committed to justice and equal rights.

NS There was a whole breed of American journalists at the time who studied India, wrote about it during the war, advocated, if not independence, then the move towards independence. Among them were Vincent Shea and John Gunther and Edgar Snow, and it was from the last of these that I took the name Edgar, thinking of a name for my character. And then my Edgar Knox became an even more committed advocate of freedom than Edgar Snow because, as I indicated or implied, he might even have written the statement Prime Minister Mossardeq sent to President Truman at the time of the battle for oil in Iran. He fought on the side of all attempts to resist imperialism in the 1950s — Vietnam, Suez, and so on. There's hardly anything more wonderful, I think, than America's civil society and the freedom it holds out to every citizen. I hope we will be able to do the same in India. Having said that, we have to remember also that in the novel America branded the character Edgar Knox 'dangerous and virtually disappeared him', that prejudice does exist, and horrors prevail.

SC Yes, and we could say it's the horrors we seem to be witnessing more and more these days. One recurrent subject in your fiction and non-fictional prose is the cultural plurality of India, the result of its many-layered history. You find different ways of projecting this, most often through landscape, through your delineation of, say, the Gangetic plain, as in *Rich Like Us* or *Mistaken Identity* (1989). In *Lesser Breeds* it is Nurullah's background that is fascinating — the way he is adopted and brought up to be a Muslim in order that, later, nobody could lay claim to him.

NS Nurullah, as you said just now, was born to Hindu parents and made into a Muslim to protect him so that he wouldn't be reclaimed by anyone from that earlier family. But it is very usual to find this kind of situation. Kabir was another example — the poet who was born to Hindu parents but brought up by a Muslim weaver and became a weaver himself; another is Sai Baba, not the present one that you hear about, but the original Sai Baba who was a Muslim fakir, lived in a mosque and was worshipped by Hindus and people of all religions. There is a temple to him down the road from my house in Dehra Dun, where he is revered as a great saint by Hindus, including fundamentalist Hindus. So it's very much part of the tradition, and Nurullah himself was, in a sense, the result of the fact that Hinduism and Islam are blood brothers. We've lived together so long we belong together, we are in the soil. And in his case, you will recall that, though he reads and studies the Koran, and worships five times a day, he takes Ammaji to the Ganges for her sacred bath on religious festivals. He even goes so far as to have a dip in the Ganges himself, wearing a dhoti. In other words, Muslims and Hindus, we are each other's history and there's no separating us.

SC To move sideways a little. In the first of your two autobiographical works, *Prison and Chocolate Cake*, you describe a moment when, watching the people coming along to greet and adore Jawaharlal Nehru at Anand Bhawan, you became yourself 'one of the anonymous faces outside, gazing with complete belief and affection at the man who stood before them. The little girl behind the window was on the wrong side of it, she should have been out in the garden with those others with whom she felt a strange and sudden kinship. It was a miraculous accident that she lived in the house with Jawaharlal'.

One reading of this passage is the obvious one — that, in your admiration for your Uncle, you also wished to be taking part in honouring him. Another is that, even in your early years, and despite your privileged position, you felt a strong kinship with the people which put you in what we might call an 'in-between' situation. To what extent does such a double awareness inform your writing on the whole?

NS Yes, well, my great love and admiration for my uncle was very much a part of my growing up years and is still very much a part of myself. And yet, as in that scene which you described, one felt even then that there was more to life than the four corners of that particular house, that one is connected, by a kind of heartbeat almost, to those people outside. It didn't mean that one had to fling oneself immediately into a life of political activism or anything like that. Indeed as a child I couldn't, in fact all my life I couldn't. Before Independence, I wasn't old enough to be arrested and be sent to jail. My older sister was. Of course, had the struggle gone on, I too would have become part of it. I remember asking my Uncle – this was after Independence – if I should do something, like become a Member of Parliament, get into politics? 'On no account. You love to write, and so why don't you write?' he replied, and went on to say that, if *he* really wanted to write another book, he would have to go to jail again, you know, to find the solitude and the opportunity. 'I haven't the time for it now. You have the time, so why don't you use it in writing?' In other words, he advised me against entering directly into politics. But the heartbeat connection has always been there and all my books have a political setting or theme, and my real character, you might say, is India in a way.

SC An inevitable question, who are the writers who have influenced you most strongly?

NS I always find that awfully hard to answer. Because, you know, influence is something that begins before you're even aware of it and I suppose that, in that sense, the folk tales and stories from the *Ramayana* and the *Mahabharata* which my great-aunt told me were an influence. Some of those stories are always there at the back of my consciousness. I would say my uncle's writings, though they were not fiction, were also an influence. They enabled me to see the world from a point of view different from what I was taught at school. I read his *Glimpses of World History* when I was a child. Written in jail without the aid of reference books, it was a panoramic survey, a wonderfully vivid account of so many stories about the past, and was regarded by some critics at the time as being better than H G Wells's *Outline of History*. Then there was the contemporary Hindi poetry and prose I read when, for political reasons, I was put in a local school in Allahabad and had to catch up with the other students who had been learning Hindi for years. They were profoundly influential, again in a way I can't point to exactly, but they made a great impression on me by removing certain barriers between me and my surroundings. They showed me I was part of the province I lived in, like the writers themselves. And, of course, English novels were an influence. I remember being sort of devastated by *Jane Eyre*, and this happens still when I re-read it and some of Dickens. And much, much later, I read a lot of Graham Greene and Iris Murdoch. I read too many Iris Murdochs, perhaps, and became extremely cerebral at one point and needed to get back into touch with emotions, which I think I did with *Rich Like Us*, *Mistaken Identity* and *Lesser Breeds*.

SC You said once, with some scepticism, that Indian writers writing in English and who live abroad are chiefly concerned with representing India to the West. They are not affected by the 'raw winds assailing India', or, which is more important, by the 'texture of daily life' in India, the 'nitty-gritty'. Is that still your view about Indian writers in diaspora who seem to be claiming a lot of attention in the West these days?

NS Migrant writing today is the most visible writing on India and I think it is a special genre. I think it needs to be separated from Indians writing about India, whether in Indian languages or English, who are not migrants. This is because they do obviously live in different worlds. What I said earlier still applies — that if you're not exposed to what is going on daily, you're not going to be able to write about those nitty gritty aspects of life. On the other hand, you are exposed to what's going on where you are and, after all, writing is about facing up to those actual experiences, and dealing with them at every possible level. So I would not say that one writing or the other is better or worse. They are different and I think they do need to be treated as two different genres of writing in English, which have just this thin connection of India between them.

SC One last question which will take us back to where we began, to the political commitment and that lived sense of history which have always inspired your writing. Are you planning to write a novel about the impact and influence of Hindu fundamentalism in recent decades?

NS I have thought about it, yes, and I think it would make a very good subject for a novel. But, as with all these intense periods of history, the problem is how to present the subject so that it comes through vividly as a human situation. And yes, I am thinking about it.

SC Thank you.

The Saint Who Resurrected a Goat

Sampurna Chattarji

Paya soup
Goat trotters simmered for eight hours in an aromatic broth
Nalli-ka-Salan
Shanks of baby goat in delicately spiced gravy, served with Khimiri bread
Gosht Biryani Nehari
Meat and Basmati rice slow-cooked, and served, in clay pot
Malpua
Fried sweet pancakes with honey and pistachio

What a strange mix of indelicacy and good taste, Supriya thought as she watched the food critic place their order. The beautifully designed raw silk cover on the menu. Inside, the finest hand-made paper, and in flowing letters, the names of the dishes so painstakingly detailed for foreigners. All around them, the simple, unaffected décor that only a great deal of money and an excellent art director could have assembled. The glowing recesses in the walls, framing saffron-shaded lamps. A hint of blue. So discreet was the effect that it almost wasn't there. Yet take away the light and the shade and the subtle washes of colour and the whole place would fall apart.

And in the midst of such refinement, they would proceed, calmly, to eat a baby goat. Wasn't there a more tactful way of saying it? Young. Tender. Anything but that. She didn't want it. But it was too late now. Rajiv had sent the waiter away with a terse instruction about the wine. French wine before a Hyderabadi meal. Seemed incongruous somehow.

'Well! That takes care of the most difficult part of the evening! Now, we can relax!'

Rajiv was the proprietor-editor of *Haute Cuisine*. Supriya had known him since college. Both slightly wild, both studying Mass Comm at Sophia's. Supriya had gone into TV. And Rajiv into food. There was nothing he loved better. Starting as a rookie writer subbing for other well-known writers, he had gone on to launch his own, highly successful magazine. Supriya wrote and directed her own, vastly popular serial for teenagers. The two of them, successful adults, fast friends, almost lovers once, now eyed each other with a growing sense of alarm.

Something was not quite the same. Supriya had begun to find Rajiv's all-knowing air both supercilious and faintly comic. Why did he take himself so seriously? Had he forgotten his days of slumming it, eating oily egg bhurjee off a cart near Churchgate late nights after college? He wore his success with something disquietingly like smugness. He had arrived. And what was worse, he had begun to realise that she found him tiresome. Tonight for example, he was trying to be humble. For her sake. Ah well. The wine had arrived. A Médoc. Brilliant. It would help her forget about the goat.

Somewhere in Mahim, near Makhdoom Baba's shrine, lived Augustus Andrade. He had always lived there, a devout Catholic family surrounded by equally devout Muslims. On holidays, his friend Irfaan and he went to the worst Hindi movies imaginable. *Havas Ke Shikaar. Daaku Aur Dain. Rangeeley Raat.* Irfaan owned the egg shop on the main road. House of Eggs. Sometimes, he kept quail in little cages, selling them to the odd car-owner with an appetite for the tiny bird.

Now Augustus was what one would call a Chhupa Rustum. No one who looked at the dark skinny boy with his bits of bristly beard, his hollow cheeks and his oversized spectacles would even begin to imagine how well-read or well-informed Augustus was. He read everything with a devouring zeal. His sister Alicia – a pretty, sassy thing, as confident as her brother was not – said his reading sucked all the juices out of him and made him all thin wrist and jutting jaw. She probably had a point. When Augustus read, all the energy in his frail body seized the written word with a kind of demonic intensity. The words poured into him and stayed there. Transfixed in a brain that stored *everything*. The first ever Catholic actress to star in a Hindi film. The reason why Brahma is not worshipped by

Wasafiri Vol. 21, No. 1 March 2006, pp. 30–33
ISSN 0269-0055 print/ISSN 1747-1508 online © 2006 Wasafiri
http://www.tandf.co.uk/journals DOI: 10.1080/02690050500475773

Hindus. The date on which *Apocalypse Now* premiered in Bombay. Polonius's farewell speech to his son Laertes. He was fantastic. He made no discriminations. For him good writing and bad had no meaning. Everything was important. Everything needed to be remembered. His brain – photographic, merciless and all-embracing – teemed and hummed with facts.

Irfaan knew his friend was a bit peculiar, but that never got in the way. Irfaan had his eye on Alicia who scorned him. Augustus had his eye on Bliss, the plump Rodriguez girl who was the sole reason he went for Novena on Wednesdays. He sat behind her in church and prayed for her to notice him. After months of agony, he took Irfaan's advice and proposed to her at Aunty Ivy's son's wedding. The look Bliss gave him was worse than mere rejection, it was a look of such pure whole-hearted disgust that it cured Augustus of romance forever, at least until another plump version of bliss came around.

Meanwhile he had his *Stardust* and *CineBlitz*, his film industry journals, his latest John Grisham, his leatherbound Tolstoy from the Don Bosco library where he worked, his third volume of *The Book of the Thousand Nights and One Night*, his musty hardback of Hindu mythology from the Asiatic and his Hindi porn magazine from the road.

'Ay Undey, coming?' Irfaan called up the dark steps where Augustus lived in a tiny room with his widowed mother Celestine, his sister Alicia (who had lately acquired a job as a steno and a number of good Goan-boy proposals) and his unnamed brother who drank himself into a Corex stupor every night.

Irfaan thought it was funny that his best friend's surname collapsed into the word that summed up his entire career. Undey. Eggs. Augustus hated being called Undey but it made him glad too in a way. At least he had one friend who felt strongly enough about him to fondly mutilate his name.

'Coming!' he yelled and tucking a paperback between his shirt and his vest – you never knew when a spare moment might crop up – he raced down, not drinking the tea his mother had just made.

Outside, the plump goats wandered around. They were being fattened for Bakrid.

Irfaan was getting impatient. In his hand were tickets for *Ek Shaitaan, Ek Haseena*.

The food was divine. But he wouldn't let on right away. Let the restaurant stay on tenterhooks until the article appeared. All of Mumbai's rich and famous read Rajiv Chawla's 'Flavour of the Month' before planning their dinners and engagements. This place merited a straight 5. The ambience is good, the service is good and oh the food! Divine.

'Well, do you like it?' he asked Supriya who was looking flushed after two glasses of wine.

'Uhhuh,' she said, not meeting his eye. She seemed to prefer the Khimiri to the tender meat that simply sang on his tongue.

'You ok?' he asked her. What was up with her these days? So cold. Maybe it was a mistake not inviting her husband as well. He had meant to but Supriya had said that Rajeev wouldn't be interested. Funny how her husband had the same name, only spelt with a double 'e'. It confused some of Supriya's old friends. Those who knew her husband was Rajeev but hadn't met him thought *he* was that Rajeev! It had happened on occasions like this one. Meet Rajiv. Oh, Rajeev! At last we meet! No, no, this isn't him. This is Rajiv Chawla.

Ouch.

They ate out often, Supriya and he. Whenever he had to test a new place, he called her up. Rajeev always declined. Supriya always accepted. She was as keen on food as he was. Had been. In fact, her comments had stopped being as astute and astonishing as they used to be. She would have made a damn good food critic herself. To his own uncertain pleasure, he had often found some choice phrase of hers creeping into the article he happened to be writing about the place he had last visited with her. He told her, 'Soups, I'm taking the words out of your mouth!' and she merely laughed and said, 'You mean stealing them! Go ahead. Just make sure you pay me — in kind!' and so he had, meal after expensive meal. If a place was awful he always made up to her by taking her to a place they both liked. His treat — personal, not office account.

And now here she was, toying with her spoon as if he had inflicted some frightful chore on her.

'So, what're you going to feature in the first episode?' she suddenly asked, as if suspecting the drift of his thoughts.

'What? Oh. Haven't decided really. I was thinking, maybe we can just flip the whole concept on its head!'

'Haute Cuisine eats Humble Pie?'

Maybe he was imagining it, but she wasn't merely teasing, she was being mean.

'Don't be so sarky, Soups. I mean something different. The search for the perfect taste needn't always start from the inside of places like *this*! It can start elsewhere, *anywhere* where the food is good, authentic and unspoilt by the need to please everyone!'

Supriya smiled. Sounded like the old Rajiv. A glimmer. Starting next month her channel would launch *Haute Cuisine* on TV. Something on the lines of *Floyd in France*, only less bizarre. Rosemarie, Head of Programming, had asked her if she'd be interested in directing that as well. No, she'd said. *It's My Life* took up all her time and creative energy and besides, she didn't want Rajiv Chawla eating into her notion of happiness at work.

'Ya ok peace. It's possible. Where'll you start?'

'I dunno. Some place without trappings — ' His fingers flew dismissively at the ambience he planned to give a 5. 'Somewhere where only the true aesthetes will go – in search of something as elusive as a *taste* – not caring if the sofas are Italian or the water Evian! That way you eliminate all the wannabe foodies, the ones who only want to be seen in the right places when all they really crave is a perfectly folded napkin and a delirious hodgepodge of bad taste.'

'Gosh Rajiv! You'll lose your audience! What's wrong with you? Or worse, those happy unknown joints will lose both their anonymity and authenticity. Your Page Three types will arrive in hordes and next you know — '

'I know I know, don't tell me. But I'm going to do it anyway. At least launch it like that — the Hidden Haunts of Haute Cuisine!'

'That sounds impressive enough! Go for it!'

And Supriya raised her glass to her old friend. The biryani was being served, and Rajiv's face was a study in sheer anticipation.

The Mahim cops all believed in Makhdoom Baba. He was lucky for them. Havaldars who prayed at his shrine got promoted, had male children or caught enough traffic offenders in a day to line their pockets for a week.

But he had not always been a saint. He had been — a law officer. Lean and incorruptible, he had, even then, way back in the fourteenth century, been something of a miracle. He lived with his mother and was – according to all reports – a good son. One night, his mother called out to him for a glass of water. By the time he reached her bedside with it, the dear old lady had fallen fast asleep. Next morning when she opened her eyes, she found him still standing by her bed, glass of water in hand, so keen was he to satisfy an ageing mother's thirst. Touched by his devotion, his mother had blessed him. He quit being a law officer and became a travelling mendicant, moving across the country with his desire to do good. It was to Mahim that he came back and died but not before he performed the miracle that would make him a saint. He had restored a dead goat to life.

'What?' Augustus had asked Irfaan, not believing his ears. 'Why a *goat*?'

'Why not?' Irfaan had said. 'Is not a goat as worth saving as anyone else?'

Perhaps, but coming from Irfaan's lips, that sounded ludicrous. The only concern Irfaan had ever shown for that poor four-legged beast was that it should be tender, young and delicious. Since when was *he* moved by the sanctity of a goat's life?

No, the whole thing defied logic. Not that Augustus minded. He took it, like everything else, as simply a memorable fact, worthy of being repeated to anyone who would listen. Like Alicia who carried it to office to share with the other Catholic stenos over lunch. And like the food critic who had stopped at Irfaan's to buy quail and had been totally nonplussed to see Augustus sitting on a wooden crate, reading *Larousse Gastronomique* as if it were the most natural thing for an egg-seller's friend to do.

Augustus remembered with pride the shock on the man's face when he saw what he was reading. Where did you get this, he asked, as if suspecting theft or some unmentionable foul play. At the Strand Book Fair, Augustus had replied, precisely. Got it for a substantial discount. I should imagine so, said the man. You a student? No sir, merely a learner, Augustus had said in his best pedantic manner. The man had raised his eyebrows and paying for the birds, had looked at him very oddly before leaving.

A quick bit of research soon unearthed the man's identity and next time he came around, Augustus had prepared his little titbit for the gourmet guru. His story on Makhdoom Baba and an invitation to visit Bohri Mohalla with Irfaan and him. Mr Chawla had reacted with that same odd look to the story but had responded positively to the invitation.

Four-thirty sharp the next morning, he had picked them both up from the deserted street outside House of Eggs and they had gone to Bohri Mohalla to taste the joys of Abdul-Aleem's Nau Handi. Augustus remembered with some amusement the look of distaste that had crossed the great man's fastidious features when he saw the mouldy green walls of the tiny hole where the skull-capped old owner sat, ladling out plates of nalli-nahiri to ragged men sitting at filthy tables smelling faintly of goat's blood and stale fat. A dark, disreputable air hung around the place like an unwanted aroma. Outside, on a tiny cart, another old venerable skull-capped man sold naan-khatais and lamba pau, which the boy ran and got for the three of them to dip into their gravy. As the Gucci-jeans-clad gent tasted his first mouthful of the meats that had cooked all night, his look of discomfort had been replaced by something close to ecstasy. He had eaten and eaten, plate after plate, wiped clean with hunks of flat pau and he had sworn it was the best meal he had ever had. He would write about it. He would make the place famous. Abdul-Aleem had lost none of his natural gravity at the prospect of becoming a legend and had said, gravely, 'Sir, you come with old friends of mine and are therefore my friend as well. I look forward to seeing you again.'

Ma-shallah, Mr Chawla had said and shaken their hands and not protested when they declined a ride back with him. They never saw him again, not even enquiring for quail, which had since then been officially banned and which Irfaan hid at the back of the shop for his regulars.

Augustus had only one regret about the whole episode. He had never had a chance to ask Mr Chawla what he thought of the story. Was resurrecting a goat enough to make one a saint? Now he would never know.

'I've finally made up my mind.'

'What, you're leaving Rajeev?'

'Ha — don't *you* wish! No, giving up meat.'

'You're joking. You're a born meat-eater.'

'No I'm not. Not any more. I've lost the taste for it. It doesn't feel right. Surely one can survive without eating baby goats. God, it makes me sick just thinking!'

'You drank too much.'

'Did they *have* to write baby goat?'

'OH! Is that what's been eating you all evening? Oh Soups! Don't get sentimental! Goats are reared to be killed. It's not like you're depriving the world of some rare endangered species! People eat monkey brains and lizards and puppies for god's sake. You just ate a kid goat, Soups. Chill. Why, in Guatemala they eat — '

'Stop it!'

'Listen. Let me tell you a story.'

And then he told her. She listened, trying to subdue the rising nausea that was probably the effect of having drunk both wine and liqueur on the same evening. In any case, she shouldn't have drunk anything at all. When he finished, she said, swallowing hard, 'Ya so? What's your point?'

'Why did he do it, Soups, think! So it could die again — the proper way! The goat, my friend, was born to be sacrificed. A natural death would be blasphemy. This man proved it. It's all part of a timeless ritual. The human being, with the sharpened knife and the keen hunger, and the goat — being fattened for the feast!'

Supriya just looked at him. He had clearly lost his marbles. In any case, she'd reached home. She could get out without letting on that, now, it was he who was making her sick.

'Bye Rajiv. I get off here. G'night.'

He looked abandoned. She turned and gave him the slightest wave. She had meant to tell him about the baby she has just discovered was growing inside her. But really, it was better that she hadn't. After all, the only thing he was really interested in was food.

She crossed the road, small and slender in her long black skirt.

He sat behind the wheel, red-eyed, slightly corpulent, and watched her go.

The Fulcrum of Instability

Salman Rushdie's *The Ground Beneath Her Feet* and the Postcolonial Traveller

Sara Upstone

In a recent lecture, postcolonial critic John Erickson has referred to what he has termed the 'nomadic thought' of the postcolonial novel.[1] Such usage immediately draws our attention to the ways in which it is the movement of the migrant that increasingly comes to define not only the postcolonial diaspora, but also a wider phenomenon: that the attitudes to crossing, exchange and cultural encounter that the postcolonial traveller embodies now speak for a way of thinking; a nomadic way of approaching the world. Following from Westwood and Phizacklea's belief that 'the spaces between nations . . . are not yet spaces of belonging . . . but are in the process of being created from the myriad diasporas and migrations', the journey may be seen as an abstract location distinguished from the places of arrival and departure, which means that, freed from the concepts of nation and national identity, new interactions of meaning may take place during its process (40). One of the most potent, and indeed controversial, attempts to seize this possibility for new concepts of belonging may be found in the work of Salman Rushdie. I would like to assert that Salman Rushdie's fiction should be read as epitomising not only these possibilities of nomadism, but also the contradictions that are evident in such a position. For Rushdie's body of work may be seen to encapsulate the journey's contradictions, whether it is his first novel *Grimus* (1975), that is examined, or his more recent, *Fury* (2001).

There are acknowledged dangers in the utilisation of such a nomadic discourse. In particular, the way in which a myth of nomadism has, in the past, not cemented freedom for those it is attributed to, but has rather been used against them in order to justify territorial expansion and the disenfranchising of particular groups. A notable example of this exploitation has been the case of Australian Aborigines, once exoticised as 'nomadic' in order to fuel British settlement, then denied status because 'they were not divided into nations with fixed localities', the space universally available because 'the Aborigines had made no use of the land' (Reece 170, 169). In her recent book on travel metaphors, Caren Kaplan has highlighted the dangers in the use of nomadism more generally, noting how 'Euro-American recourse to the metaphors of desert and nomad can never be innocent or separable from the dominant orientalist tropes in circulation throughout modernity' and that 'further historicization of terms is required' (66). Postmodern theory's concept of the nomad as a subject of endless freedom simplifies the patterns of movement and return that nomadic culture in fact encompasses; its generalisations inevitably obscure the cultural traditions, and indeed possible oppressions, that construct marginal positions.

It is therefore worth noting that to take up the discourse of nomadism is to take up a strategic position in which free movement – and an associated suggestion of free thought – is utilised as a political strategy, rather than to equate oneself with those who practise nomadism as a cultural custom in a way that would essentialise a particular group. Deleuze and Guattari exemplify this strategic use of the nomad motif, associated by critics such as Marcus Doel with a 'nomadic thought' related to the construction of a unique poststucturalist space (Doel 35). Deleuze and Guattari illustrate the intensely political nature of taking up such a position, casting nomadism as an interrogation of power structures and a celebration of multiplicitous identity. This is a particularly attractive idea when viewed from a postcolonial perspective; indeed, for Deleuze and Guattari it is nomadism more that anything else that is anti-colonial in nature. For nomadism is a movement against that which the colonist would halt, because 'it is the vital concern of every State not

Wasafiri Vol. 21, No. 1 March 2006, pp. 34–38
ISSN 0269-0055 print/ISSN 1747-1508 online
http://www.tandf.co.uk/journals DOI: 10.1080/02690050500475807
Routledge Taylor & Francis Group

only to vanquish nomadism but to control migrations' (Deleuze, and Guattari 385). It is the multiplicity of the nomadic space that represents the resistance to traditional order, to territory and to control. When we move, we challenge the identity of the state; when we cross boundaries, we challenge the colonial control of territories. Such an articulation of the power of what often seem like chaotic, unstructured and meaningless movements not only challenges colonialism, it also challenges the lack of meaning so often attributed to discourses of fluidity. Placed therefore in the hands of the contemporary postcolonial traveller, free movement is no longer simply a post-modern 'game' (Harris 27). Instead, it is a strategy of resistance as empowering as any conventional assertion of belonging.

Misreadings of Rushdie's motivations and the way he represents the postcolonial condition are misreadings of the discourse of nomadism that he employs. Nowhere is this discourse more evident than in *The Satanic Verses*. Here, the message is that the traveller is not the exile, dreaming of return, yet neither is he the traditional migrant, who 'can do without the journey altogether; it's no more than a necessary evil; the point is to arrive' (94). Rather, he is – as if you haven't guessed it by now – the nomad, who is 'rootless as the dunes'. Yet the second clause of Rushdie's sentence must not be neglected: the definition of the nomad is quickly corrected; not rootless, 'rather rooted in the knowledge that the journeying itself [is] home' (94). It is a complex negotiation of fluidity and fixity that creates Rushdie's sense of self here, and neither extreme is entirely welcome.

Thus on one hand, Rushdie's novels recognise the relationship between cultural exchange and colonial discourse. They acknowledge the fact that, through the journey, adventure facilitated colonisation, and that, for the migrant, the reverse journey from periphery to centre may be fraught with danger and riddled with prejudice. Yet, coterminously, Rushdie's novels also present the traveller as having a significant role in undermining such discourses, seizing travel precisely because of its colonial connotations in order to strike at the heart of colonial discourse. In presenting this dual faceted experience, I would suggest that nomadism, and more explicitly its physical expression through the journey of the migrant traveller, works for Rushdie as a fulcrum. Indeed, his own experience of his journey to Nicaragua recounted in *The Jaguar Smile* suggests such a function, what he describes as 'a moment, but, I believe, a crucial and revealing one, because it was neither a beginning nor an end, but a middle, a time that felt close to the fulcrum of history, a time when all things, all the possible futures, were still (just) in the balance' (13). In this way, the journey truly is a fulcrum, fulfilling its meaning as noted in the Oxford English Dictionary as 'the point against which a lever is placed to get purchase'. For it is through such journeys that the postcolonial novel gathers the force to return to other spaces and re-make them, a physical experience but also a metaphor for the spiritual and psychological nomadism required to grasp the shifting sense of postcolonial space in the modern world and its impact upon identity, journeys which embody a search for strategies of resistance and survival.

It is in these terms that I would like to read Salman Rushdie's recent novel *The Ground Beneath Her Feet*, not as a post-modern free-play that neglects the violence of cultural encounters and the diaspora, but rather as a postcolonial text that utilises movement and nomadism precisely to confront and challenge this violence in its most pervasive and aggressive forms. The journeys presented in *The Ground Beneath Her Feet* are the most prominent in Rushdie's fiction to date; it is a novel of travel which interacts with both postcolonial issues and aspects of post-modern culture. Under the direction of the narrator Rai, the central characters of Ormus, Vina and indeed Rai himself seem to typify the negativity of a homeless, fast-paced, global media world of which the continual traveller is undoubtedly a major part. Vina and Ormus form an international rock band, Rai is a photographer, and all three live their lives through movement, travelling on planes from one unfamiliar destination to another; their dwellings, if they can be said to have any, are the aircraft and the hotel room. Yet as travellers are transported upon planes named the *Mayflower* and are described as 'Pilgrim Children' it is clear that the colonial undertones of travel and exploration are an important undercurrent to the post-modern movements conducted by Rushdie's characters: movement that sees them as both echoes of colonial exploration but also, as Pilgrim Children rather than Pilgrim Fathers, those who must live with the legacy of colonisation. Rushdie's novel is emphatic in stressing that travel can still be an exclusion in the era of this legacy, this postcolonial age, and that the hierarchies of travel have been perpetuated long after the end of British rule in India in 1947. This makes the early movement of Rai, Ormus and Vina *not* a post-modern norm but an exception and, indeed, makes movement itself into a political act. When Vina flees Bombay, Ormus cannot follow, and Rushdie's words clearly highlight the implicit critique:

> Back then it wasn't easy to travel if all you had was an Indian passport. Inside this passport some bureaucrat would laboriously inscribe the few countries you were actually allowed to travel to, most of them countries that had never crossed your mind as possible destinations. All the rest – certainly all the interesting places – were off limits unless you got special permission, and then they would be added to the passport's handwritten list by another bureaucrat, with the same handwriting as the first. And after that there was the problem of foreign exchange . . . I offer this brief lesson in nostalgia economics to explain why Ormus Cama wasn't on the first plane in pursuit of his great love. (178)

Such a great struggle to achieve the journey may make it understandable that Rushdie so often celebrates freer access to movement. Yet the implicit hierarchies involved in travel are also felt more locally, so that it is clear that it is not only the travel of the migrant that is traumatic, but also the access to movement one has once one has settled. As a child, Vina may be able to fly to India from the United States because of a US passport, but within America she faces prejudice that threatens her potential to travel. Her mother and step-father have to go to the school to secure her place on the school bus, to explain that Vina and her sister's, 'darkness was not Negro darkness, they were Indians from India and didn't need to be discriminated against, they could ride on the bus along with the regular kids' (105).

In such a way, Rushdie suggests that it is a fusion of real inequality and mental turmoil that combine to make travel for the migrant a frightening experience. Indeed in *The Ground Beneath Her Feet* it is evident that it is the psychological dislocation, the impact of travel on identity as much as the injustices perpetrated by others, that Rushdie may really be seen to want to emphasise. The logistics of travel are a whirring hive of chaotic activity serving to disorientate; being 'drugged by flight', 'the airplane terror and doubt' means that 'Ormus Cama's head starts pounding' (253, 354, 268). For despite their continual movement and re-invention of themselves, there is a shadow that Rushdie's trio of major characters cannot outrun, regardless of the distance travelled, referred to in the text as 'the noisy pain of the compulsive wanderer', a 'Disorientation: loss of the East' of which Rai is clear he is, of the three, the only survivor (360, 176). There is no certain ground, no stillness of home or firm sense of place to provide solace and relief from their hyper real existence. This is not only reflected in Rushdie's use of the theme of music, so that, 'Later, entering that world of ruined selves, music's world, they will already have learned that such damage is the normal condition of life' but also again in Rushdie's magical realism, which creates a world in which certainty has been removed, a world where there are other dimensions, and 'the maps are wrong' (352).

Ironically, it is here, in the wake of all this tumult, that I think the great possibilities of Rushdie's narrative arise. This is because, for Rushdie, while the violence of migration is always condemned, the chaos isn't always entirely a bad thing. Yes, it causes confusion. Yes, it may mean that 'only the show was real' (559). But it also means, because of this, that when you have lost your identity, when you *cannot* go back, you can get *something* back: that you can find meaning in the journey and make it, rather than the nation state, the basis of your existence. The very newness of this is terrifying, but it also removes the opportunity for further loss, and allows you to celebrate your hybridity as a wealth of cross-cultural experience. In *The Ground Beneath Her Feet* Rushdie goes further than ever before in support of such a proposition familiar too in his earlier novels. For the novel is a privileging of the journey *qua* journey, never-ending. No longer, as in previous works, does even death hinder this process: the reader is immersed in a world that 'is not cyclical, not eternal or immutable, but endlessly transforms itself, and never goes back', and, as a result, personal journeys are left indefinitely unfinished, held in suspended animation by deaths that refuse to yield conclusions (145). Thus, though the character Vina dies, her life, its journeys, are endlessly repeated, and indeed take on a new life of their own in the television media that continues to celebrate her music. This is affirmed at the level of the narrative structure, a narrative continually replaying with altered significance, acknowledging, 'We have been here before' continually throughout the novel (464 etc). Even Rushdie's analogies support such process: a democratic movement forwards and backwards through literature in which hierarchies are razed, as Tolkien and Fitzgerald come to illuminate the classical myth of Orpheus and Eurydice; itself translated into a valorisation of popular music and television. The nature of Rushdie's nomadism is so important that it is not confined to the journey: the very structure of Rushdie's novels, and the characters he populates them with, continually affirm the hybrid and non-linear structure of nomadic movement.

Claiming that this is what should be aspired to in this transnational, post-modern and postcolonial world is, on one level, the apolitical throwing away of homeland that Rushdie is so often accused of and yet, in combination with the recognition of oppressive journeys and the anti-colonial power of nomadism that I have noted here, it may also be read in very different terms: as Ormus's father confirms: 'the only people who see the whole picture . . . are the ones who step out of the frame' (43).

Movement and uncertain identity are enshrined in Ormus's belief that 'I don't have to choose . . . I don't have to be this guy or that guy . . . I'll be all of them', the creation of a new hybrid identity which is characterised by a feeling of independence; for there is a sense of possibility that means, 'if you are Ormus Cama, if you are Vina Aspara, whose songs could cross all frontiers, even the frontiers of people's hearts, then perhaps you believed all ground could be skipped over, all frontiers would crumble before the sorcery of the tune' (303, 55). Thus the dichotomous factors upon which Rushdie's fulcrum turns are revealed. While constant travel makes Vina and Ormus's band something with no national or racial identity, it at the same time allows the group to represent everyone as potent statements of cross-culturality. It is the space between these two extremes, a fulcrum of instability refusing to turn in either direction, towards denigration or celebration, that Rushdie's journeys occupy. They are the spaces in-between binary opposition where 'periphery and the center . . . seemingly no longer applies' (532). For Rushdie, the journey is always double-edged, an experience 'swung moment by moment between elation and despair' (7). Even in Rai, the most reluctant of travellers despite 'a name that travelled easily', such a paradox is always present (18). He reveals that 'a kind of India happens everywhere . . . But if I'm honest I still smell, each night, the sweet jasmine-scented ozone of the Arabian Sea' (417). Indeed it is ultimately Rai who comes to express the dual importance of the journey most succinctly, in a voice which could be used in itself to sum up Rushdie's view: that, 'there is *thrilling gain* in this metamorphic destiny, *as well as aching loss* . . . which kicks in *only under extreme pressure*. When we are faced with the immense' (emphasis added) (441, 461).

Rushdie does not deny the problems in such movement, you may go 'too far', and, indeed, if on offer, what you ultimately wish to end up with is still a sense of home; Rai's desire to 'stand my ground, right here' (55, 575). Yet in a world without firm meaning, Rushdie suggests it is through movement that identity is forged, creating the ground beneath our feet as Rai accepts that 'footprints are the only fixed point in the universe . . . made real, step by step': not the migrant, but the nomad; not abandoning belonging but rather finding it in unfamiliar places, creating 'a new fixed thing' not in opposition to translocation, but as part of its process so that what emerges is an unconventional, and provisional, resolution (268, 461). In its hybridity, the nomadic postcolonial journey, which is focused not on beginning or end, but on process, forms an important opposition to the gridded and tabular nature of colonial space and mapped journeys. This latter kind of space is represented in fiction such as Defoe's *Robinson Crusoe* as the story of a traveller who, 'haunted by the footprints of the other, is driven to a singular obsession: he draws circles, constructs fences, erects walls in an endless pursuance of boundaries' (Islam 2). Yet it is also a feature of real colonial travel, where the mapping of territory played a crucial role in defining the colonist's rights to the land, creating an artificial division which would later create the unstable nations of the postcolonial world, most notably, for Rushdie, the partition of India.

This enterprise has been emphasised by critics such as John Noyes, Paul Carter and Mary Louise Pratt. In his study of South West Africa the former highlights in great detail the 'strategies for mapping universal principles' that define imperial possession of territory, centred upon the enshrining of colonial order through sight and writing (Noyes 164). In his study of Australia Paul Carter attempts to tell a spatial history in which land is 'written-over, criss-crossed with explorer's tracks, gradually inhabited with an network of names . . . blazed with boundaries' (xx–xxi); Pratt, too, complements these works with her comprehensive focus on one particular element of such a process, that by which 'imperial eyes passively look out and possess' (7). However, Noyes's study is of particular significance, in that it reveals the inherent instability in such a process that might be exploited by the colonised citizen. Noyes reveals that the order instituted by the colonialist is a fallacious – and ultimately unrealisable – attempt to obscure the freedom of movement on which colonisation actually depends:

> The acquisition of land in the name of a writing requires the establishment of borders and ensuing subdivision. This in turn leads to an ever increasing segmentation and fragmentation of space on almost every level . . . And this fragmentation brings with it the necessity of crossing, a constant violation of the boundaries it has created. The colony must, however, present itself as a unity, not only for the purposes of ideology, but also (and perhaps this is a more important consideration), for the purpose of communication — its very ability to function as a colony. . . . A restoration of the totality of experience which the capitalist fragmentation of space is constantly threatening and which appears as a specific attraction of colonial space in comparison to European space. (162)

There can be no better acknowledgement of this chaotic reality – no better unravelling of colonial order – than Rai's own description of his movement:

> Suppose you've got to go through the feeling of being lost, into the chaos and beyond . . . You stepped off the edge of the earth, or through the fatal waterfall, and there it was: the magic valley at the end of the universe, the blessed kingdom of the air . . . It feels better than 'belonging' in your lungs. (Rushdie, *The Ground* 177)

For Rushdie it is only through facing the oppression that is the legacy of colonialism, the flux of the cross-cultural and transnational postcolonial journey, that you find creative possibility. Within this context, Rushdie's choice of subject may be explicitly connected to the promotion of a nomadic way of life. For who is the metropolitan nomad, if not the popular musician? Such figures increasingly cross boundaries, not only within same-speaking nations, but beyond them, as western musicians play in China and, more recently, Latin American artists have found success in the United States and Europe. Indeed, it is entirely fitting that Rushdie's own lyrical composition in the novel – from which its title comes – has been appropriated by international rock band U2 for their film soundtrack *Million Dollar Hotel*. For U2 are the nomadic face of rock music *par excellence*, a multinational media force that extends far beyond their Dublin roots and whose lyrics include their own nomadic message. More significantly, they also espouse the real potential behind such an ability to transect conventional identities that extends beyond the joys of free creative expression. As Ormus and Vina declare themselves potent statements of cross-cultural identity, able to represent everyone as 'the exaggerated avatar of their own jumbled selves', so U2 have proved the viability of such an attitude and realised its possibility, providing a high profile and influential face for charities such as Amnesty International and Greenpeace (Rushdie, *The Ground* 339). Travelling through Africa to highlight AIDS with US Treasury Secretary Paul O'Neill, meeting Presidents Nelson Mandela and George Bush, lead singer Bono is seen to represent the popular voice of an international community; with an acknowledged power, hence his declaration: 'I'm not about entertainment right now, I'm about mobilizing people to change the world. I can't change the world . . . but we are engaging with people who can' (Bono np). As real-life versions of Ormus and Vina, the band's cross-cultural appeal – their own strategic nomadism – has resulted in important political influence.[2]

Presentation of the chaotic journey of the migrant or colonial citizen through the strategic use of the nomad suggests more than simply a hopeless situation as a victim; the movement of the central characters within a world of grounded possibilities, however problematic, provides a personal act of resistance. Refusing to ever succumb entirely to the loss of movement or the pain of restriction, Rushdie suggests that celebration and revision may make the journey an important political strategy, that the journey may be reclaimed so that its positivity is focused on, rather than simply its trauma. Presenting us with the journeys of postcolonial survivors rather than victims of colonisation: characters in *The Ground Beneath Her Feet* refuse to be indefinitely traumatised by the loss of home, and instead come to find some value in the hybrid identity that is so often a result of their movements. Thus what emerges is not a denial of the violence of migration, but rather a movement beyond it, in what is an important – if problematic – strategy of survival that allows the migrant to move forward into the future.

Notes

1 These comments were made by John Erickson as part of a conference paper on 'nomadic thought': 'Magical Realism and Nomadic Writing in the Maghreb', Genre Transformations and Narrative Ideologies, SOAS, 8 Nov. 2002.

2 U2's political activism is evident on the 'Hearts and Minds' section of their website: http://www.u2.com/

Works Cited

Bono. u2.com report. 27 May 2002. 30 Nov. 2003. <http://www.u2.com/>

Carter, Paul. *The Road to Botany Bay: an Essay in Spatial History*. Faber: London, 1987.

Deleuze, Gilles, and Felix Guattari. *A Thousand Plateaus*. Trans. Brian Massumi. London: Athlone, 1988.

Doel, Marcus. *Poststructuralist Geographies: The Diabolical Art of Spatial Science*. Edinburgh: Edinburgh UP, 1999.

Harris, Wilson. 'Literacy and the Imagination'. *The Literate Imagination: Essays on the Novels of Wilson Harris*. Ed. Michael Gilkes. London and Basingstoke: Macmillan, 1989. 13–31.

Islam, Syed Manzurul. *The Ethics of Travel: From Marco Polo to Kafka*. Manchester and New York: Manchester UP, 1996.

Kaplan, Caren. *Questions of Travel*. Durham and London: Duke UP, 1998.

Noyes, J. K. *Colonial Space: Spatiality in the Discourse of German South West Africa 1884–1915*. Reading: Harwood, 1992.

Pratt, Mary Louise. *Imperial Eyes: Travel Writing and Transculturation*. London and New York: Routledge, 1992.

Reece, R. H. W. *Aborigines and Colonists*. Sydney: Sydney UP, 1974.

Rushdie, Salman. *Fury*. London: Jonathan Cape, 2001.

——. *Grimus*. *1975*. London: Panther-Granada, 1977.

——. *The Ground Beneath Her Feet*. 1999. London: Vintage, 2000.

——. *The Jaguar Smile: A Nicaraguan Journey*. London: Pan, 1987.

——. *The Satanic Verses*. 1988. London: Vintage, 1998.

Westwood, Sallie, and Annie Phizacklea. *Trans-nationalism and the Politics of Belonging*. London and New York: Routledge, 2000.

Critical Imperatives

Notes on Contemporary Art Criticism and African Cultural Production

Anthony Downey

> A social and historical critique which does not consider the conflictual structure of its own discursive operations will only produce the constraints it is seeking to displace. (Weber 111)

'Africa Remix', the recent showcase of African art at the Hayward Gallery in London, prompted a number of mixed but largely positive critical responses. In the *Observer*, Emma Lindsey extolled the 'ground-breaking and electrifying work' (26) on show and encouraged everyone to see it. Elsewhere, and in a more mixed response in the *Guardian*, Jonathan Jones was impressed by the art in the show but equivocal about his own reaction to it. Towards the end of his article, Jones wrote 'but that's enough criticism. In the end, this is a subject I probably shouldn't even be writing about. What do I know? Racism is limitless' (22). The sense of bemusement in Jones's article is worth dwelling on here, not least for the fact that its disposition reappears in more 'critical' reviews of 'Africa Remix'.[1] In *Art Monthly*, Sally O'Reilly's review of the same show started with the above quote from Jones's article and went on to engage in its own series of caveats. 'It was not my idea of fun to review "Africa Remix" either,' O'Reilly wrote, 'and the idea would be horrifying, I imagine, to most European art critics especially those from European nations' (27). For O'Reilly, this ostensible conundrum is made manifest in a number of 'double binds' including, but not limited to, the manner in which postcolonial liberalism can often translate into 'colonialism itself when applied to interpretations of "the other"' (27). In the subsequent issue of *Art Monthly*, O'Reilly was taken to task on the letters pages for both an 'unreflexive' response to the show and the reiteration of a view of African art as somehow culturally (and hence critically) other (Jelinek 14). To *Art Monthly*'s credit – being one of the few journals in this country, alongside *Third Text*, to consider the question of art criticism and its purpose to be worthy of any enquiry at all – it allowed this discussion to continue into the following issue where Jones's take on the show was criticised for being 'intellectually cowardly' – a response, in sum, that merely re-codified a number of obstacles to formulating an effective critical response (LaFuente 17).

What Jones's periphrastic bout of rhetorical hand-wringing (perhaps inadvertently), and O'Reilly's equivocations, accentuate here is a nominal but all too systematic assumption that returns with tenacious frequency in debates about contemporary African cultural production: namely, African cultural production, because of its distinctive otherness, produces a critical response that is ultimately incommensurable with the object of its enquiry.[2] This incommensurability – the lack of an integral and categorical critical register – has been often rearticulated in terms of incommiscibility: Western art criticism and contemporary African cultural production do not necessarily mix well. To the extent that the latter point has a critical purchase, there is a need here for a qualifying distinction: hermeneutic incommiscibility does not equal incommensurability; on the contrary, it is precisely the difficulties involved that provide the imperative basis for enquiry. To argue otherwise is to not only abjure critical responsibility but coextensively rehabilitate a hierarchical economy of otherness that merely reinscribes the very tropes that critics – particularly those steeped in postcolonial theory – have been at pains to debunk. That we should have to note this at all is a further source of hermeneutic anxiety insofar as it belies an additional concern: if we have managed to identify (or at least engage with) the inequitable economy of difference that posited *inter alia* Africa as the 'other' of the West, and the African 'other' as the touchstone for the development of Western humanism, then to what degree have we engaged – if indeed at all – with the issue of how the apparent 'otherness' of contemporary African cultural production is the substantiative rather than interrogative prelude to critical responses. To what extent, that is, do we need to talk about how we talk about the art object. In the reviews noted above, my own included, I would suggest that what is being expressed, however nebulously, is the need for a series of critical imperatives: the demand, that is, that

Wasafiri Vol. 21, No. 1 March 2006, pp. 39–48
ISSN 0269-0055 print/ISSN 1747-1508 online © 2006 Wasafiri
http://www.tandf.co.uk/journals DOI: 10.1080/02690050500475831
Routledge Taylor & Francis Group

Yinka Shonibare (UK/Nigeria), Victorian Philanthropist's Parlour, 1996–97, mixed media (furniture and objects of different sizes), dimensions variable. Collection Eileen Harris-Norton and Peter Norton, Santa Monica, California.

criticism questions its own discursive function when it comes to writing about contemporary African cultural production and develops, in turn, a metacritical approach to the subject of art criticism.

Why, you may ask, does any of this matter? All art criticism should have a metacritical component to it and enquire into, however extraneously, what a critical response does to the art work and future interpretations of it. This observation is as valid for African cultural production as it is for cultural production elsewhere. However, the stakes are higher, I would suggest, when it comes to critical responses to African cultural production. When Edward Said articulated the structural and discursive mechanisms by which the West insinuated itself into the so-called East, he listed, amongst others, the practices and practitioners of literary, historical, philological, psychological, anthropological, and philosophical study as precursors to actual material exploitation. The 'East' had to be discursively produced if it was to be exploited, and the West's 'imaginative command' over that imaginary realm had to be secured through the production of knowledge. The tenacity of a view of the other as voiceless spectacle and entertaining exoticism – the corroborative object of enquiry rather than the subject of communication – was the manifest consequence of the West's 'imaginative command' over its (in this instance, African) others. In light of these historical incursions (not to mention their consequences), art criticism about contemporary African cultural production needs to be both critically conscious of its 'imaginative command' over cultural output and, perhaps more importantly, mindful of the sociopolitical and hermeneutic ramifications of such critiques.

Art criticism, as always, confers its own exegetics of inclusion and marginalisation — a discourse of containment that needs to be understood within the context of how the rhetoric of legitimisation and marginalisation subsidised discussions about the West and its 'others'. It is with these points in mind that the following article will offer an overview of the problems associated with articulating a critically commensurate response to contemporary African cultural production. In doing so, I will suggest some preliminary notes that seek to further encourage critical engagement without reifying concepts such as critical incommensurability, heuristic incongruity, and irreconcilable otherness. This is to imbricate contemporary art criticism within a wider sociopolitical discursive realm that indexes the concurrent impact of globalisation, multiculturalism, postmodernity, and the over-arching discourse of art criticism *per se*. This is not, however, a proposal for a methodological approach – a proposition that would be in danger of further prescribing the terms of debate – as much as it is an attempt to methodically outline the issues that would affect such a methodology. How, in sum, do we explain the apparent otherness of African art without reinstitutionalising an analogous rhetoric of otherness that merely trades on its neo-liberal conviction, multicultural sentiment, postmodern (dis)ingenuity, and the periodically triumphalist postcolonial recuperation of otherness.

Global Mandates: Art Criticism and Globalisation

Often viewed in terms of the sinuous lines of exploitation by which new markets are opened up, the extrinsic influence of globalisation is frequently theorised as a force acting upon the art network — a 'cause' of which the global reach of the art network is an 'effect'. In its avaricious and often rapacious appetite for the 'new', globalisation is consequently figured in negative terms whereby its exacting effect is understood to be not only producing the art object as a commodity fetish – that which must be had – but also reconstituting the 'local' and its indigeneity in the name of 'universal' appeal. The hermeneutic effect of this process is that cultural distinctions are being inevitably elided in the name of a strategic inclusiveness that thrives on the commodification (and inexorable elision) of difference itself. Despite the apparent indifference of globalisation to differences *per se*, other than in the activity of producing the other as a commodifiable (and therefore closely controlled) object in a free-market, neo-liberal economy, there is a distinction to be made in this minatory vision of globalisation as a rampant and indifferent spectre.

In their discussion of the 'new world order', Michael Hardt and Antonio Negri have persuasively argued that the sovereignty of nation states, contrary to the greatly exaggerated news of their demise, has taken on a new form under the guise of national and supranational institutions — a new global form that they sum up in one word: Empire. Within this new imperial order, communication systems not only legitimate the new world order but supply the very channels by which globalisation operates. Hardt and Negri write:

> communication not only expresses but also organizes the movement of globalization. It organizes the movement by multiplying and structuring interconnections through networks. It expresses the movement and controls the sense and direction of the imaginary that runs throughout these communicative connections; in other words, the imaginary is guided and channeled within the communicative machine. (32–33)

Contemporary art criticism, in this context, could be seen to be complicit with globalisation inasmuch as it transcribes the 'local' into a 'universal' – and therefore empirically 'available' – frame of reference. It is a process that, in its critically abbreviated manifestation, effectively 'flattens out' cultural distinctions. Art criticism – whether it be in the form of academic critique, commentary, or the belletristic – could be seen to produce one of the very channels by which the art market accesses 'other' artists. If we accept, for now at least, that globalisation is characterised by a programme of homogenisation, the question remains as to what methodology can iterate difference in the face of such an apparently consummate process without reducing difference to a series of essentialising and exoticising poses.

Admittedly, this is to perhaps place too much importance on the consequences of art criticism — the proliferating worldwide biennials are just as responsible for bringing heretofore 'unknown' artists to the attention of Western institutions. However, art criticism, and nowhere more so than when it is deployed in the service of lifestyle commentary, is all the more understandable today as both a form of communication and part of the vocabulary of the 'communicative machine' that Hardt and Negri identify. 'Language, as it communicates,' they continue, 'produces commodities . . . ' (33). Rather than rehash the notion that art criticism is no longer either critical or consequential, having long since been superseded by the marketing machines of commercial galleries, this is to suggest that it is indeed *critical* in the sense that it plays a role in an increasingly globalised art market: art criticism, that is, discursively produces the 'other' artist who is subsequently subsumed within the art market; it opens up, however tentatively, the very markets by which globalisation is sustained. To this end, both art criticism and globalisation could be seen to, on the most basic level, foster, regulate and administer difference – be it cultural, racial, social, or political – in order to further define mutual channels of influence.

This is not so much to make either a qualitative or indeed quantitative judgement about such criticism, as it is to accentuate my initial point: how we write about African cultural production has to be considered in a metacritical framework whereby the ethics of art criticism itself is put under the hermeneutic spotlight. Globalisation, and its sinuous lines of transaction, further accentuates the a priori need that we address how, to paraphrase Homi Bhabha, newness enters the world (212–35). This is all the more essential when the art market for African art, alongside the market for contemporary art as a whole, shows all the signs of continuing to grow exponentially, not least after substantial exhibitions such as 'Africa Remix' which, alongside London, took in venues in Dusseldorf, Paris and Tokyo. And this is but the latest manifestation of an increasingly prevalent theme in contemporary curating in the last two decades that must also include 'Tributaries: A View of Contemporary South African Art' (1985), 'From Two Worlds' (1986), 'Perspectives: Angles on African Art' (1987), 'Magiciens de la Terre' (1989), 'Contemporary African Artists: Changing Traditions' (1990), 'Africa Explores' (1991), 'Out of Africa' (1992),[3] 'Seven Stories about Africa' (1995) and 'The Short Century' (2001). This abbreviated list, moreover, does not take into account solo showings of African artists and their worldwide appearance in biennials and seminal exhibitions such as Documenta 11.

Whilst the politics of multiculturalism – a discursive framework, in one sense, for legitimating differences in a globalised world economy – has for the most part represented a favourable force for change, there is an increasingly prevalent view that reads the grand narrative of inclusion represented by multiculturalism as yet another increment in the institutionalisation of 'good' (legitimate) difference and 'bad' (illegitimate and therefore threatening) difference. It is against this backdrop that the discursive channels of influence traversed by multiculturalism can be seen to intersect with globalisation. To suggest as much is to invoke what Slavoj Žižek proposes to be the fundamental problematic that usurps multiculturalist claims to inclusivity: the apparent universalism, paradoxically, that lurks beneath its premise:

> The 'real' universality of today's globalization through the global market involves its own hegemonic fiction (or even ideal) of multiculturalist tolerance, respect and protection of human rights, democracy, and so forth; it involves its own psuedo-Hegelian 'concrete universality' of a world order whose universal features of the world market, human rights and democracy, allow each specific 'life-style' to flourish in its particularity. (41)

Zineb Sedira, Mother, Father and I, 2003, 3 DVD video projections, dimensions variable. Commissioned by Contemporary Art Museum, St Louis, Missouri. Courtesy of The Agency, London, and Galerie Kamel Mennour, Paris, © the artist 2005.

Hassan Musa (Sudan), Great American Nude, 2002, ink on textile, 204 × 357 cm. Courtesy of the artist.

Multicultural inclusiveness does not, Žižek argues counter to popular belief, challenge the cultural logic of global capitalism; on the contrary, multiculturalism, and its implied corollary, liberal tolerance, strategically produces the 'other' as a marketable form of identity-formation. Žižek further argues that, '[l]iberal "tolerance" condones the folklorist Other deprived of its substance — like the multitude of "ethnic cuisines" in a contemporary megalopolis; however, any "real Other" is by definition "patriarchal", "violent", never the Other of ethereal wisdom and charming customs' (37). In other words, the pronouncement of multicultural inclusiveness – its claim to realise a more progressive representational space that is legitimated by a non-totalising form of politics – is the disavowed, inverted, and self-referential assertion of superiority and should be seen as such. And herein lies the corrosive rub: how do you (re)write the terms of a critical debate, in conjunction with the re-territorialising urges of globalisation, that avoids merely repackaging difference within the neo-liberal, and invariably empty, wrapping of multicultural inclusiveness? In what could be seen as a form of rhetorical epenthesis, whereby an idea or caveat is inserted into the middle of an argument, there is a consistent demand for a metacritical approach in critical responses to contemporary African cultural production in light of both the politics of multicultural representation and the exigencies of globalisation — both of which intersect with one another, however inadvertently, in the presentation of 'otherness' and difference.

If we enquire into the nature of the discursive institutions that multicultural discourse instigates, then we must similarly enquire into how art criticism, in an attempt to answer to multicultural priorities, effects a similar institutionalisation of difference. This concern revolves around not so much how we write about culturally 'other' work as to what hierarchical structures such writing sets in place. Whereas multiculturalism, in respect of the visual arts, is largely concerned with how the other is represented, this is to investigate how the other (the art object) is translated into the rhetorical schema of art criticism. John Picton has put it thus:

> the anthropology of the colonial period promoted a way of writing about Africa characterised as the Ethnographic Present. This, in effect, denies both history and contemporary reality while encouraging the invention of a 'traditional' Africa that privileges certain social, ritual and visual practices at the expense of others. (118)

We return here to the valorisation of the local in the critical name of the universal and its corollary: the dehistoricisation of cultural production. As a critical observation, this is perhaps an obvious one to make in the context; however, we need to consider the obverse to this comment: the critical and habitual dehistoricisation of African cultural production has been subsequently refracted through a critical approach (postcolonial theory and criticism) that seeks to not only re-historicise but politicise such production – a process, as we shall see, that is not without its own distinctive challenges.

Postcolonial Theory and its Discontents

The tenacity of a view of the other as voiceless spectacle and entertaining exoticism was the manifest consequence of the west's imaginative command over its 'others'. Postcolonial theory was a productive, necessary, and indeed provocative intercession into this relatively uninterrupted empirical field. The hermeneutic benefits were many and do not need reiteration on these pages. However, it is worth noting that one of the foundational questions of postcolonial theory, addressed by Gayatri Chakravorty Spivak, was relatively simple: can the subaltern speak? The attendant concern here is what happens when we speak for the 'other' and, in the context of my immediate discussion, how art criticism, in its inevitable schema of legitimation, speaks for the apparent otherness of African cultural production. The problem is squared, so to speak, if we address the fact that in speaking for the other, or otherness in general, we are inevitably engaged in a process of prescribing meaning and – nowhere more so that when it emanates from Western institutions – a further hierarchisation of discourses about Africa. The connotative reverberation here is that the need to interpret otherness for a Western audience reinscribes the trope of African passivity that is often rolled out in defence of such interpretative incursions in the first place. We move here – albeit in tentative and highly provisional terms – towards an ethics of addressing and speaking for the other, whereby the other (a corporeal being) can be seen, admittedly with some conceptual leeway, in the objective terms of contemporary African cultural production.

The categorical dilemma here continues to rotate around the otherness of African art and who gets to speak for – categorise – and interpret that otherness. In this context, the authenticating voice of the critic can often result in a misplaced significance on the ostensible 'authenticity' of the artist or artwork in question. For Linda Martin Alcoff, the

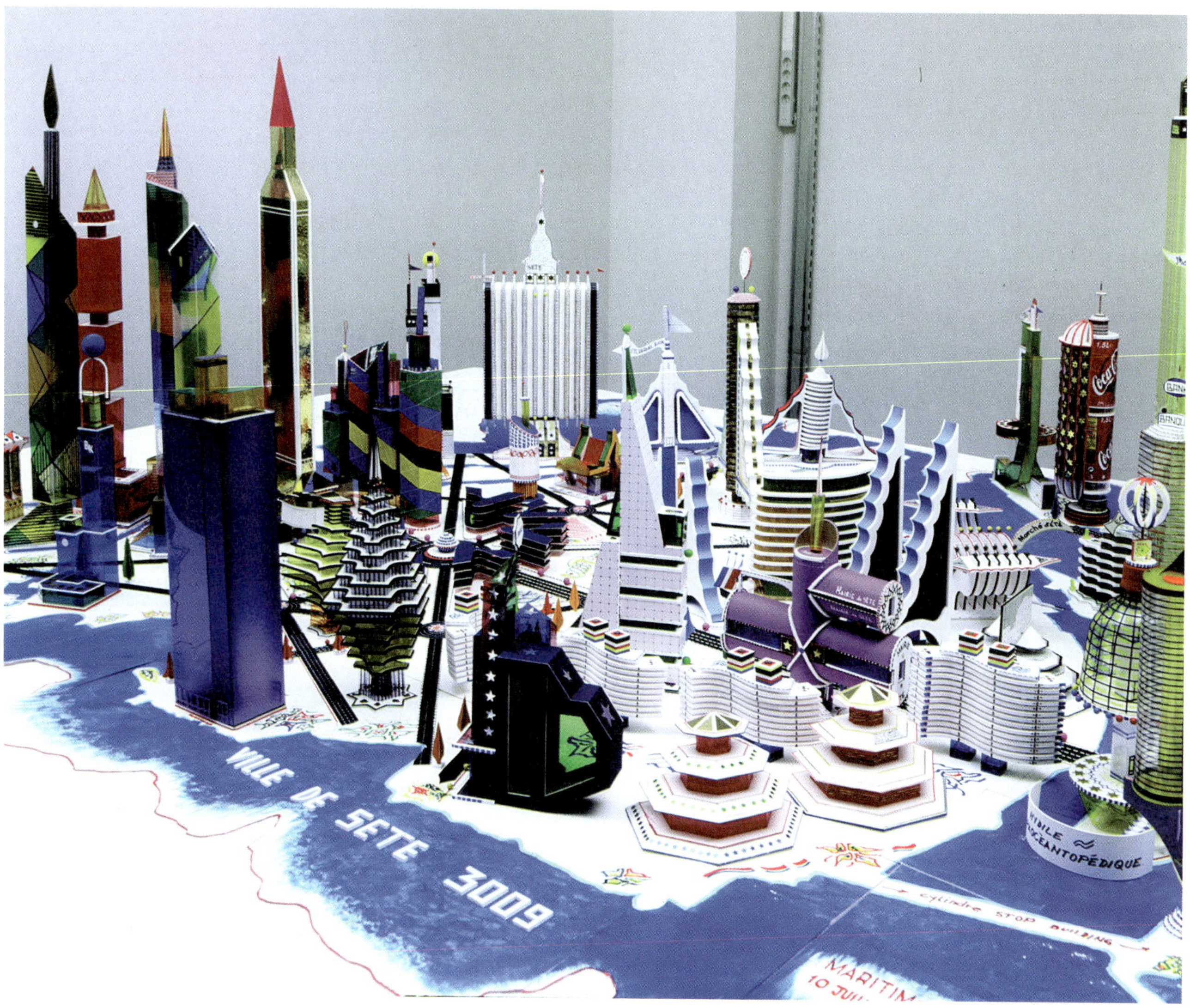

Bodys Isek Kingelez (Germany/Congo), La ville de Sète en 3009, *2000, paper, cardboard, paint, sequins, glue; covered by polyester in wooden frame, 210 × 300 × 89 cm. Collection Musée International des Arts Modestes, Sète, France.*

problematic of speaking for others generates a further misleading emphasis on the notion of authentication to the extent that 'persons from dominant groups who speak for others are often treated as authenticating presences that confer legitimacy and credibility on the demands of subjugated speakers' (Alcoff 9). The trope of authenticity, needless to say, has been much used and abused in discussions of both art and identity. The concern here, however, addresses the broader philosophical anxiety of interpreting the other and how African artists have often been made to wear, so to speak, their identities on their sleeve in a manner that would be both reductive and condescending if applied to a Western artist. The politicisation, or situating, of African cultural production, whilst preferable to its depoliticisation (and hence homogenisation through dehistoricisation), is nonetheless not without its own distinctive pitfalls. Although writing with literary production in mind, Robert J C Young's reading of the political mandate in cultural theory is integral to any consideration of the critical fact that African art be understood in a political, historical, socially-specific, and economically nuanced context – a context, in sum, that prevails against globalisation's apparent indifference to difference itself. Arguing for a more rigorous understanding of the trend towards political interpretations of cultural production in the last twenty years, Young notes that such criticism seeks to re-establish a connection between action – inflected in the context of this essay to specify African cultural production – and 'the world'. There is a similar tendency, I would argue, in contemporary critical – not to mention curatorial – approaches to African art: the latter, that is, must be seen to answer to both history and political (postcolonial) interpretations of the work. Young writes:

> Perhaps the current pressure for theory to deliver a politics itself constitutes a response to the reformulation by theory of the concept and operation of the political. As with the call for 'history', it can be used to reintroduce the very formulations that theory has been concerned to recast: the call of the political in itself seeks to reinstitute or reground the link between representation and reference that has been questioned by the semiotics of the past twenty years. If the representation of the literary text to the world becomes problematic, then the link can be reinvoked by the introduction of political criteria in criticism which re-establish at a stroke the supposedly lost connection with ethics, action, and 'the world'. (85)

This is to return to the discussion above and how the advent and development of postcolonial theory – in the promotion of a more critically rigorous and ethical approach to interpreting the otherness of the other – sought to mitigate the disjunctive correlates used to define African cultural production in ahistorical and depoliticised terms. However, the methodology that sanctioned such an undertaking was largely underwritten by so-called continental theory. The issue here is relatively straightforward: what, if any, are the problematics of deploying poststructuralist theory and its stress on the displaced and destabilised subject of modernity – a subject void of agency – in a debate concerning the need to historically and critically re-instate postcolonial subjectivities and the agency of African art(ists)? For Linda Hutcheon, the conjugation of poststruturalism and postcolonialism provokes a form of ideational retrenchment whereby

> the current post-structuralist/postmodern challenges to the coherent, autonomous subject have to be put on hold in feminist and post-colonial discourses, for both must work first to assert and affirm a denied or alienated subjectivity: those radical postmodern challenges are in many ways the luxury of the dominant order which can afford to challenge that which it securely possesses. (151)

I have no doubt simplified the issue here and it is equally possible to argue that the radical enquiry into the contingencies that endowed the Western subject produced precisely the epistemological conditions needed for the emergence of its 'others'. If I can nonetheless generalise for now, and pace Hutcheon, it is possible to argue that poststructuralism, deconstruction, postmodernism, and postcolonial theory, far from calling for a relativisation of value, truth, history, identity, agency, and the subject were addressing another issue: the ethics of representing otherness and the contingent responsibilities involved in speaking for others. The misgiving here is that for postcolonial studies this was a political, as much as a conceptual or theoretical, ideal. And this is where we run into problems. Whilst the thorny issue of art's relationship (representation) to the world (that which is re-presented) can be traced back to the tenebrous depths of Plato's cave, it has a further immediacy to it in a neo-liberal, globalised market where the mantra of 'freedom of choice' and a concomitant break with traditional cultural affiliations is the predominant ethos within contemporary art. In such a rubric a continuous break with the past is advocated through a series of ironic gestures and a (formal) freedom of expression. The 'political' in this paradigm is not so much frowned upon as it is adumbrated by commercial modes of exchange and a mode of critical engagement that flirts with commentary rather than engagement. The political is not only seen here as a maleficent spectre waiting to bring the cogs to a grinding halt, but it is often seen as the realm of, for example, the African artist who has yet to make the postmodern leap into the vacuum of self-referentiality and the free-for-all 'play' of signification. In this context, African artists are made to answer for, or address, African history and be political in a manner that we would not necessarily expect of a 'Western' artist. Ontological insecurity is effectively replaced by an ontological determinism and this is just as reductive, I would argue, as the dehistoricisation of African art. Contemporary African artists and art, in this instance, are in danger of becoming a sounding board (or test-case) for critical theory — forever the object of information rather than the subject of

Antonio Ole, Townshipwall No. 10, 2004, 16 parts, mixed media, (found materials), 180 × 120 cm each. Courtesy of the artist, photo: Lothar Milatz.

communication. Art criticism is equally in danger of being enmeshed in a hermeneutic tautology, producing in art works the very concerns it set out to 'discover' in the first place. The attendant issue here entertains a simple and decidedly paradoxical paradigm: to what extent has African cultural production, rather than challenging our expectations and the critical cohesion of contemporary critical and curatorial theory, come to represent a reductive obligation to both?

Cultural Incommensurability and the Myth of the 'Ineffable'

One of the key issues that needs addressing when we consider how the 'other' – be it in cultural, literal or metaphorical terms – is re-presented is the extent to which categorical imperatives effectively prescribe rather than encourage discussion. There are two ways in which this is done: the general, though largely unstated, idea that the exigencies of African cultural production are largely 'unknowable' and, closely associated with that point, that any such writing must somehow have a privileged 'insider' knowledge of African art. These two points open up a veritable plethora of associated issues. To suggest, for one, that we cannot write with perspicacity in respect of African art, because of its supposed otherness, is to merely reinstate the scenario of Africa's irrevocable 'otherness'. This is indeed both a reprehensible and singularly shoddy response — an effective abnegation of critical responsibility that misses the point: the so-called ineffability of the experience of an art work and the concomitant difficulty of transcribing that which is (at least nominally) a visual experience into a literal language, is the *a priori* obligation of art criticism. This is indeed a hoary and decidedly capacious chestnut and it is beyond the remit of this discussion to fully explore the genealogy of such debates. However, it is suffice to say that the very notion of 'ineffability' in and of itself would appear to be yet another apotropaic (and highly nuanced) strategy for not engaging with the object — a process of 'turning away' from the responsibility of a response. Pierre Bourdieu, commenting on the issue of ineffability, has pointedly asked 'why so many writers, so many philosophers take such satisfaction in professing that the experience of art is ineffable . . . and why they are so eager to concede without a struggle the defeat of knowledge' (xiv). As in so many cases where the ethics of criticism *per se* is an issue, Bourdieu is principally concerned with the remit of the literary field; nevertheless, his point focuses a distinction that needs to be made here: following on from the poststructuralist proposition that literary criticism is written in the same language as the object (literature) of its enquiry, there is ultimately no absolute distinction to be had between literary and critical discourse. This is obviously not the case for the so-called visual arts, where art criticism is not, for the most part, expressed in the form of visual art — although such a development might sharpen the minds of some commentators.

These remarks take us away from the original question and yet engage a similarly inflected point: why are so many critics ready to concede conceptual defeat in the face of interpreting and criticising contemporary African cultural production, and, in turn, resort to a version of its inherent 'unknowability'? Furthermore, the claim of 'unknowability' can be readily countered by simply noting the vertiginous propinquities involved in contemporary African cultural production and so-called Western art production. In its deconstruction of the discursive ploys by which Western humanism and colonial discourse constructed the African 'other' as the apparently irrevocable (and ultimately irredeemable) other, postcolonial theory has made a significant and lasting impact on how we consider not only Africa, but the 'West' and its categorical compulsions. However, if we have (however successfully or unsuccessfully) deconstructed the discursive economy of otherness that subsidised colonisation, then there is an ongoing demand that African cultural production is seen for what it is: imbricated with, and at times predicating, Western art history and its 'modernity'. It is with such points in mind that Rasheed Araeen has observed that part of the conundrum surrounding identity politics can be addressed 'when we accept the fact that the other is no longer Other'. For Araeen, this acceptance is recognition of how the West's so-called 'others' permeated 'modernism and have redefined it through its own logic of innovation and historical breakthroughs' (7; see also Hassan). Many African artists are as much a product of the Western academy as they are of African institutions and a significant number of artists in 'Africa Remix', for example, live in the West; however, the ostensible incommensurability of African art production has been often premised upon the misplaced idea that African artists are somehow atavistically joined at the hip to Africa in both conceptual and geographical terms. It is a notion, Okwui Enwezor has observed in respect of African artists living in the so-called Western metropoli, that effectively excludes African artists from the 'sites of normativity' which, in turn, produces a far from satisfactory critical response when it comes to their output (245). Where a response is forthcoming, it is articulated in terms of how the artistic production of these 'displaced' and diasporic artists is figured as an 'aberrant production of a denativised imagination or to an inferior mimetic exercise in futility' (245). Enwezor's remarks, and Araeen's, are preliminary observations in two provocative essays that further signpost the fundamental problematic with which we started: what method, to paraphrase my epigraph, can we employ here to analyse the object of our criticism that concomitantly avoids reiterating the critical configurations that we are attempting to repudiate. How, in sum, do we explain the apparent otherness of African art without reinstitutionalising an analogous rhetoric of otherness that merely trades on its neo-liberal, multicultural and critically informed (and periodically mis-informed) credentials? To ask such a question is to evoke yet another: how does the West negotiate its colonising tendencies, engendered in a new global imperial form that Hardt and Negri have termed 'Empire', and repudiate the predictable co-option of non-Western art into a self-validating discourse in which it becomes yet another derivative footnote to Western art history? And how, in sum, can the critical imperative of art criticism both agitate for and instigate such a seismic shift without reinscribing the very tropes that engaged criticism has been at pains to debunk? How we interpret African art, finally, is an ethical undertaking riven by the politics of criticism and the demand that we rethink how we engage with ostensible difference, the otherness of the 'other', and the critical imperatives implicit in such an undertaking.

Notes

1 In reading broadsheet reviews against more 'art critical' responses, I am not setting up a hierarchy of response between the two — both have an obligation to responsibly acknowledge the object of their enquiry. It is arguable, however, that a broadsheet – with its sizeable readership – is more 'influential' in the sense that its discursive influence is more widespread.

2 I should also, at this point, put my cards on the table and note that I reviewed 'Africa Remix' in the pages of this journal, and I too engaged in a similar bout of rhetorical and critical throat-clearing. See 'Curating Africa: 'Africa Remix' and the Categorical Dilemma'. *Wasafiri*. No. 46, 2005.

3 The latter was the final incarnation of a show that began as 'Africa Hoy' in 1991, which became 'Africa Now' before finally settling on 'Out of Africa' for its final showing at the Saatchi Gallery in 1992.

Works Cited

Alcoff, Linda. The Problems of Speaking for Others' *Cultural Critique* 20 (1991–92): 5–32.

Araeen, Rasheed. 'A New Beginning: Beyond Postcolonial Cultural Theory and Identity Politics' *Third Text* 50 (2000): 3–20.

Bhabha, Homi. 'How Newness Enters the World: Postmodern Space, Postcolonial Times and the Trials of Cultural Translation'. *The Location of Culture*. London: Routledge, 1994. 212–35.

Bourdieu, Pierre. *The Rules of Art: Genesis and Structure of the Literary Field*. Cambridge: Polity Press, 1996.

Enwezor, Okwui. 'Between Worlds: Postmodernism and African Artists in the Western Metropolis'. *Reading the Contemporary: African Art from Theory to the Marketplace*. Ed. Olu Oguibe and Okwui Enwezor. London: Institute of Visual Arts, 1999. 245–75.

Hardt, Michael and Antonio Negri. *Empire*. Harvard University Press: Cambridge, MA, 2000.

Hassan, Salah. 'The Modernist Experience in African Art: Visual Expressions of the Self and Cross-Cultural Aesthetics'. *Reading the Contemporary: African Art from Theory to the Marketplace*. Ed. Olu Oguibe and Okwui Enwezor. London: Institute of Visual Arts, 1999. 215–35.

Hutcheon, Linda. 'Circling the Downspout of Empire'. *Ariel*. 4.20 (1989): 148–159.

Jelinek, Alana. 'Black and White'. *Art Monthly* 287 (2005): 14.

Jones, Jonathan. 'Africa Calling'. *Guardian*, 9 Feb. 2005, 22.

LaFuente, Pablo. 'Back to Black and White'. *Art Monthly* 288 (2005): 17.

Lindsey, Emma. 'Shout of Africa'. *Observer* 13 Feb. 2005, 26.

O'Reilly, Sally. 'Africa Remix'. *Art Monthly* 286 (2005): 27–28.

Picton, John, 'In Vogue, or the Flavour of the Month: The New Way to Wear Black'. *Reading the Contemporary: African Art from Theory to the Marketplace*. Ed. Olu Oguibe and Okwui Enwezor. London: Institute of Visual Arts, 1999. 114–126.

Spivak, Gayatri Chakravorty. 'Can the Subaltern Speak? Speculations in Widow Sacrifice'. *Marxism and the Interpretation of Culture*. Ed. Cary Nelson and Lawrence Grossberg. London: Macmillan, 1988. 271–313.

Weber, Samuel. 'The Intersection: Marxism and the Philosophy of Language', *Diacritics: A Review of Contemporary Criticism* 15.4 (1985): 109–118.

Young, Robert. *Torn Halves: Political Conflict in Political and Cultural Theory*. Manchester: Manchester University Press, 1996.

Žižek, Slavoj. 'Multiculturalism, or, the Cultural Logic of Multinational Capitalism'. *New Left Review* 225 (1997): 28–51.

Lou Smith

Voyage Through the Grey

Sometimes it was if I were back there and as if England were a dream. At other times England was the real thing and out there was a dream, but I could never fit them together.

Was everything reduced to shades?
The sea no longer a myriad blues
but *grey-brown, grey-green*
and you
seeing England through a haze
low-lying cloud
covering your thoughts
light seeping through
as water
seeps
through
cloth

The days were no longer bright
and rain fell in whispers . . .

As you walked the streets
of stone bruised blue
did you imagine the spring flowers coming into bloom?
What were your reasons to stay?

The cold, a numbing
like the hollowing
of a tree trunk
cutting back
until the sap
runs clear
as the years
are erased
severed stumps
in soft groundfall

There is more white than black in this grey

*It's funny how parts of London are as empty
as if they were dead.*

Is warmth in the sunshower of autumn leaves,
floating, as memory hovers

*There was no sun, but there was a glare
on everything like a brass band playing.*

The cold, bitter,
like the first taste of winter greens
rocket and stinging nettle tea
of skin made pale

It is always the smell
that is left,
the smell that brings
thoughts back

of yellow flesh
of ackee, frying

Passages in italics are quoted from Jean Rhys. *Voyage In the Dark.* Middlesex: Constable, 1934. London: Penguin, 1984.

Exile

Grey, the down
that grows
upon the melancholic body,
like a hatchling unable
to stand
or fly away

Wasafiri Vol. 21, No. 1 March 2006, p. 49
ISSN 0269-0055 print/ISSN 1747-1508 online © 2006 Wasafiri
http://www.tandf.co.uk/journals DOI: 10.1080/02690050500475864
Routledge Taylor & Francis Group

New Writing and Nigeria

Chimamanda Ngozi Adichie and Helen Oyeyemi in Conversation

Aminatta Forna

Chimamanda Ngozi Adichie was born in Nigeria in 1977. Her first novel Purple Hibiscus *was shortlisted for the Orange Prize in 2004 and won the Commonwealth Prize for best first book in 2005. Currently a Hodder Fellow at Princeton University, she travels between the USA and Nigeria. She is working on her second novel called* The Heart of a Yellow Sun *set in the period of the Biafran war.*

Helen Oyeyemi was born in Nigeria but moved to London when she was four in 1988. She is a final year student at the University of Cambridge. Her novel, The Icarus Girl, *published in 2004, was written while studying for her 'A' levels and received great critical acclaim. She has written two plays,* Juniper's Whitening *and* Victimese *and is working on her next novel, which is about African-Cuban mythology. The two writers talk here with writer and journalist Aminatta Forna.*

This discussion took place at the 2005 British Library conference *Think Africa: African Visions 2005 — A Festival of African Literature, Culture and Politic* organised by the Africa Centre in association with the British Library, the African Books Collective and the Africa Book Centre, supported by the Arts Council.

Aminatta Forna We're here today to talk about African writing. I want to begin with a question that is concerned with the whole concept of African writing and the African writer. This idea of an 'African writer'... I'll start with you Chimamanda, is this something that you respond to? Do you find it helpful?

Chimamanda Ngozi Adichie I don't know that helpful is the right word. Being labelled an 'African writer' is something I am uncomfortable with but also proud of. Proud because it's a heritage that I embrace; uncomfortable because it's a loaded term and often one that's given to you by somebody else. If it didn't come with baggage, then it would be fine, but it does and because of that there is some discomfort.

AF What about you, Helen? How much time have you spent in Nigeria?

Helen Oyeyemi Oh gosh. Well, I came over to Britain when I was four but I have many memories of Nigeria from that time. When I was about twelve we went on holiday to Nigeria every year until I was sixteen — so not very much time spent there at all, but enough for it to make a very vivid impression on me, in contrast to London, which sometimes seems quite grey and quite compact, whereas whenever I go to Nigeria everything seems to expand.

But, as far as being an African writer is concerned — Chimamanda's definitely right about there being a tradition that's embraceable and that's a great tradition. In a lot of ways I think it helps to put your writing in context — because there are concepts you can talk about, and use, from African literature in your own writing, that other people who have read African literature will then understand and be able to get their heads round. But it does also pigeonhole you because when you walk into bookshops you often see a lot of great Nigerian or African writers being put into categories such as 'Black Interest' or 'African Interest'. How are people going to discover them? You know, how are people going to know that they're interested in these writers if they're being put under sections like this? That is annoying.

AF And yet both your books seem to have these scenes that come out of that African experience as well as the sense of cultural dissonance — with the character of Eugene [in *Purple Hibiscus*] who seems to have one foot in the colonial era, one foot in the modern era; and Helen, with Jessamy

Wasafiri Vol. 21, No. 1 March 2006, pp. 50–57
ISSN 0269-0055 print/ISSN 1747-1508 online © 2006 Wasafiri
http://www.tandf.co.uk/journals DOI: 10.1080/02690050500520511
Routledge Taylor & Francis Group

who grows up between two cultures. Chimamanda, where did the character of Eugene come from?

CNA I wish I knew. It's important for me not to think in terms of themes, because I'm interested in writing realistic fiction set in the Nigeria that I know. I tried very hard to keep it as true to what I've observed and sometimes what I've imagined. The themes emerge from that, organically — so Eugene really developed, not so much from my desire to show the theme of a colonised mind, as from my desire to portray a man who, in many ways, represents many men that I know and have observed in Nigeria. So he came originally from that desire to write realistic fiction. Of course he then turns out to also exemplify the incongruity of colonialism.

AF Interestingly, both of you have a character in your books, a grandfather, who seems to represent an 'old' Africa. These characters seem closer to the traditions of Africa. Helen, when you created the character of Jessamy's grandfather, to whom she becomes so close, what were you thinking of?

HO Basically, in Jess's world she has nobody practically that she can speak to and that she can communicate with — I guess I wanted there to be a safe person and a safe place for her in Nigeria. Her grandfather is quite traditional but I think that just ties in with him being of his time and . . .

AF Just an old man?

HO In Nigeria, yes. Yet I was thinking more about his relationship with Jessamy and how he could be a safe house for her.

AF The other thing that strikes me links to a book I read recently, Tsitsi Dangarembga's *Nervous Conditions*, written some years ago. She has this character who is nervous, uncomfortable in her own skin, and both of you have characters who are somehow not quite located in themselves. Do you think that's a coincidence? Chimamanda?

CNA Yes, absolutely. But I think the 'nervousness' in *Nervous Conditions* is quite different from that in *Purple Hibiscus*.

AF Tell me how.

CNA Well, in the sense that Kambili's 'nervousness', if we can actually call it that, is less to do with cultural dislocation than with growing up in the shadow of a father who you both love and fear in an incredible sort of way, and not quite having a voice because you haven't been allowed to. There really aren't two cultures so to speak because she finds her voice within the same culture, in her family as well, just a different branch within the same family. I think *Nervous Conditions* has a lot more to do with the main character, Tambu, not being quite sure where she fits in with her society. This is a problem I don't think Kambili has.

AF Though Kambili is torn between her father's principles, his ideas about European-ness and Christianity, and wanting to be closer to her grandfather. At school she doesn't quite know where she fits in, does she?

CNA But at the same time she is what I like to call an African Catholic. She believes in a Christian God and in some ways probably believes that that God is white. She wants to have both, that is the point. My belief is that it's possible to have both.

AF These different perspectives are more comfortable in her than they are in the father, aren't they?

CNA Yes.

AF He's the one who seems to be torn apart by it, as part of that older generation. Helen, with your character, Jessamy, the transition is occurring in her own generation. It's she who is navigating Nigeria and Britain in a different kind of way from Tambu in *Nervous Conditions* or Kambili in *Purple Hibiscus*, but is it not the same sort of theme?

HO I think it is similar because there's a whole vein of black womanhood today that isn't necessarily being exploited; there is not very much talk nowadays about issues of 'nervousness' and illness affecting black women particularly in transition stages, and I think there's something very real there that people are beginning to tap into.

AF One of the things that Dangarembga has said is that she was inspired to write by the fact she had never seen herself in literature and she wanted to see herself there. Does that have resonance for you?

HO Definitely. I remember just reading lots and lots of books with white protagonists etc, and then coming upon *Yoruba Girl Dancing* by Simi Bedford and just going, wow! And being completely knocked out by it. I mean, it wasn't so much that it was me, but it was a world that I could see myself in and inhabit. That was amazing and inspiring.

AF Chimamanda?

CNA Oh yes. My *Yoruba Girl Dancing* equivalent was Chinua Achebe's *Things Fall Apart*, or Camara Laye's *The African Child*; and later, Flora Nwapa. For me it was this glorified shock. My God, people exist in books and they're African, they eat yams, you know? I started to read and write at a really young age and I was reading lots of books with white people in them, so I assumed that books by nature had to have white people. When I started to write stories everybody was white, and in my case it was really funny because I was writing about what I did *not* know and had never experienced. I was writing about people eating apples and I

Helen Oyeyemi

had never tasted an apple and — so when I read *Things Fall Apart*, *The African Child*, and then Nwapa, it just opened the world for me. I thought I *can* write about people who speak Ibo. That gave me permission to become what I think I am now as a writer.

AF How has your book been received in Nigeria? Do you know?

CNA I do know. This *is* a Nigerian edition, by the way... published in Nigeria, printed in Nigeria and affordable in Nigeria, which is very important for me. It's been widely circulated in a country where for a while we haven't been reading fiction. People seem to be excited by it, and the responses have ranged from people sending me really nasty emails – why did you portray that father character like that? – to people hugging me on the street. So it's a range. But for me it's exciting and...

AF Passionate.

CNA Yes. And that passion for me is the most important thing.

AF I must admit, there's been this extraordinary canon of literature coming out of Nigeria. Is that...

CNA Because we're the best?

AF Yes.

CNA I'm sorry! I'm not sure it's unusual. I suppose it might be unusual because we've had people reading and excited about literature in the 1960s, and then we had the slump which many people like to attribute to our economy, and that might really be true. Now it seems that we're coming up again and — and, you know, I'm not a prophet so I really don't know what's going to happen in the future, but I'm very excited because there's so much talent in Nigeria and now it seems people are going to have more and more opportunity to see that talent.

AF It could be a new dawn. Helen, do you know how your book was received in Nigeria?

HO It hasn't been published in Nigeria yet. It's going to happen soon.

AF But they ship them over presumably?

HO I don't know that anybody's read it in Nigeria. I don't really know that. I don't anticipate people being as excited about it as, say, *Purple Hibiscus*, because the book is very dual in nature. It grabs stuff from all kinds of mythologies and also it's quite diasporic, set both in London and Nigeria, and it's not perhaps that relevant there — I would be surprised if a Nigerian person read it and found themselves firmly located in it. However if a second generation Nigerian or somebody else in my position read it, they might say OK, I can kind of dig this.

CNA I think people are excited about Helen's book in Nigeria. I don't know that they necessarily have to have read it. The book might not be available or may be really expensive when you convert it to Naira, but people are excited about it. People know about Helen in Nigeria without having read her book and they claim her.

AF Yes, we have few enough heroes in Africa. People usually do get hold of things, and if they need to they'll photocopy it. In the market is where I suspect you'll find it! What did your family make of it?

HO Well, because I hadn't told them I was writing it, when I rolled up and said, 'Hey, I've got a book contract', they didn't believe me at first. And then –

AF They thought you were a fantasist.

HO Yes, and then they said 'Are you sure?' and aren't you...

AF Studying too hard?

HO Yes. I had told them I'd been writing an essay but when I showed them the contract and talked about it, it was 'Oh well, we always knew that you'd do this', 'You've been reading all the time', 'This is destiny'. They just accepted it and were really proud.

AF OK, let's open the questions out to the audience.

Audience I just would like to say there *is* a lot of excitement about Helen Oyeyemi's book in Nigeria. When I was there recently a major bookshop in Victoria Island was stocking at least two different editions. Perhaps the reason Helen doesn't know how it's being received is because publishers in Britain have not tuned themselves as yet to the Nigerian or the African market? So, maybe this is an issue.

AF Do either of you want to respond?

HO There's not really anything to say.

Audience I have a question for Helen. How has your book been received by the Nigerian community in London and by other Africans living here?

HO Well, that's a really difficult one. My parents' network of friends got their hands on the book practically the day it came out. They seemed to see it as a kind of advertisement for why *not* to emigrate to England, because — Jess's Mum is this Nigerian woman who comes to England and marries this white guy and has this kid who's so mentally disturbed, and I think they see emigration as a kind of tension that in some respects isn't worth it. It also reflects on their own experiences of having come to England, and there are of course all sorts of issues there that they find with it.

Audience I know you said Chimamanda that you don't actually concentrate on themes, but there's an underlying portrayal of colonialism in your book and I just wondered, given that, how would you define 'colonial' and, more importantly, how would you define 'postcolonialism'?

CNA These are terms that are problematic. When I say I am not interested in themes, it doesn't mean I am saying my book doesn't illustrate these themes, I'm saying that I don't start from a place of set themes. I start from my characters and the story, and if 'colonial' and 'postcolonial' then become attached to my work, perhaps it's because the reality I describe *is* colonial and postcolonial. And what do these terms mean? I have no idea. I think for me 'colonial' means that I grew up speaking both Ibo and English; that I have family members who say things like 'Oh, when the British were here things worked . . .'. That's 'colonial'. 'Colonial' is that my entire education was in English. 'Colonial' is really that I don't know what Nigeria is in some ways, that we have this incongruous boundary that has brought people together who I am not sure should have been together in the first place. Colonial means so many things. I don't have an academic definition for you but I'm sure many textbooks can give you that.

Audience I wanted to ask if you ever felt overwhelmed or intimidated at any point by the wealth of Nigerian writing that's already out there? Did you feel, gosh, if I start writing

Chimamanda Ngozi Adichie

won't my themes have already been covered? Did it at any point make you think of not continuing?

HO I don't feel particularly intimidated by it because I don't see myself as ever trying to reach that standard. I see myself as trying to write what I can write and do what I can. I feel more intimidated by other things. One writer that really grabbed me early on and almost killed me was the poet Emily Dickinson. I read her stuff and I was just overwhelmed . . .'oh my gosh, how am I ever . . .'. As a literary figure, she is huge and intimidating to me, because of how sophisticated she is in putting across her inner life. She uses symbols to describe her life and to describe her spirituality in ways that are so complex that I'm still trying to unravel them, three, ten, a hundred million readings later. Any great writer will scare the hell out of me!

AF Did you grow up reading African writers?

HO Not really, I came upon them from about the age of thirteen, so they didn't 'get' me so hard as some others.

AF And what about you, Chimamanda, were you intimidated?

CNA No I wasn't. I did grow up reading African writers. While I love writers from different parts of the world, there's something special and different for me in reading good African writers. It's that shock of recognition. I find it nurturing rather than intimidating. So when I work it's Achebe that I'm more likely to want to re-read or Flora Nwapa. I'll read somebody Nigerian sometimes just to nurture my writing. I didn't really make the choice to write — I like to say that writing chose me, I didn't really sit down and say I'm going to be a writer. Because of that I will write anywhere and because of that as well I can't afford to become intimidated by what others have done before me.

AF Who do you read now, Chimamanda?

CNA I read everyone. Right now? I'm reading Romesh Gunesekera's novel *Heaven's Edge*. I loved his novel *Reef* so I got this one.

AF Helen, what are you reading now?

HO I'm reading this book and I can't pronounce the name of the writer because she's Swedish, but it's called *April Witch* and it's a Ray Bradbury-esque book about a woman who is paralysed. She can't speak, but she can go outside her body, and she visits her sisters and tries to influence their lives. It's really cool.

AF Yes, that keys in to the sort of thing you also explore. You presumably wrote your book in your bedroom, while you were supposedly studying for 'A' Levels?

HO Yes.

AF Chimamanda, did you write in Nigeria or in the States or neither of them?

CNA In the States.

AF You don't feel the need to go over and write in the location you're describing?

CNA Not with this book. With the book I'm working on now I did spend a lot of time in Nigeria, this year and last year, because I needed to be there. But *Purple Hibiscus* is very much a nostalgic book and I think it became what it is because I wrote it outside Nigeria. If I had written it in Nigeria it would have been a different book. I was horribly homesick and it was the middle of a New England winter... never pleasant. Often I actually feel the need to be away from the Nigeria I'm writing about. I need a certain detachment to write, to see it clearly.

AF There's certainly a wistfulness in the tone of *Purple Hibiscus*. Was that because you were out in the freezing cold of North America?

CNA Yes, but also because the tone was intended. I did want it to have that.

AF Helped, if you like, by where you were?

CNA Yes.

Audience I'm interested in the writing process. I wonder if each of you could tell us how you went about writing your first books?

HO Well, my book started as a short story, so I didn't know that it was going to be a novel. Whilst writing it, I thought the most important thing was not to get scared, so I told myself it was a short story that just kept getting longer. I had a character called Tilly Tilly from short stories I'd already written, so I was pitting her against another character and just trusted the plot to come out of that tension between them. Basically I had no idea what was going on. I just wrote and wrote a lot.

AF How long did it take?

HO Seven, eight months.

AF And how are you approaching the current one?

HO Nervously! I thought it best to put my head down and not think of it as the second novel. I was reading a book of Cuban legends and I started to see Yoruba words in there, but they'd been attributed to the wrong things, like the Yoruba word for shoes was given to clothes. Nevertheless I saw it was an attempt to try and maintain Yoruba culture in Cuba. I was fascinated by that. So I looked it all up and was off straight away into another story.

AF And Chimamanda, how did you approach writing *Purple Hibiscus*?

CNA Before I wrote *Purple Hibiscus* I'd written a really bad novel, which I thought was hip and cool! It was set in the US, and everybody was nicely Americanised but it was just very contrived and forced. So I put it away and then this one came. When I'm working on a book, I'm not conscious of the creative process, it just happens and then afterwards you have to reflect and invent answers to questions such as this because you have to be useful! I really don't have a plan — I'm not one of those writers who say I write from nine o'clock until noon and have a certain painting on the wall. I don't. I write when it comes and the process depends a lot on what I am writing. I really didn't need to do much research for *Purple Hibiscus*, I let it come out organically because I don't like to plot my work. I find the minute I start to plot it, it just goes flat. I started with Kambili. What I did know consciously was I wanted a character who was voiceless, because that would make it possible for me to tell the story in a way that would leave a lot of things unsaid, which is how I wanted to write it. But then the rest I just let go. I didn't know how it would end, I didn't want to know until I got there, because for me the writing process is the discovery of what will happen.

With the book I'm working on now it's a very different process, because I have done a lot of research. I've so many notes which are overwhelming and there are times when I've just thrown my hands in the air and have no idea what I'm going to do with the notes. But I also find that for this second book I've had to plan a bit more. Of course I've left the ending open because the minute you tie things up before you start, it's no good — at least not for me.

AF I'd like to ask both of you about voice in your books. Helen, you chose a very young child, Jessamy, only eight years old, which is actually quite a tricky voice to do. Did you have to work hard on it or did you have the voice all ready before you started?

HO Well, eight was a good year for me, I remembered it very well and all I had to really do in practice was subvert my experience of my good year into Jess' bad year. It was quite easy for me to revert to the juvenile voice — except there were times when I felt I needed to say more and I had to restrict myself. There were times when I wanted Jess's Mum, for example, not to appear as such a horrible person, but I just had to leave this, because it was written from Jess's perspective. I had to keep the grown-up figure quite shadowy.

AF And what about you Chimamanda, with Kambili, who is voiceless — you had to create a voice for a voiceless person. One of the things that has been said a great deal about *Purple Hibiscus* is that the novel's concern with this wistful, very subdued voice makes the dramatic events become even more shocking in contrast. Did you have to hold on to a very clear idea of that voice or was it something that was already there?

CNA This is one of those invented answers again. The voice was already there. When I was writing her I wasn't thinking about the fifteen-year-old voice, I was thinking about *this* particular fifteen year old. Because often when people impose reality on fiction it worries me: they say, 'oh a fifteen year old wouldn't sound that way', but I'm thinking about a particular character who has had particular experiences. I knew I was writing about weighty things. I was writing about religion, about fundamentalism and politics. I didn't want these issues to overwhelm the story. I felt that maintaining this voice which would keep things really, really subdued would really be the best way to do it.

AF Helen said that sometimes she had to keep control of the material, she couldn't use words, expressions, thoughts that an eight year old wouldn't have. She had to think about the portrayal of the mother that she might have liked to shift but she had to keep writing from Jessamy's point of view. Do you consciously hold on to that voice all the way through or does it sometimes slip?

CNA I think you realise it slips in the re-writing and editing process, because what I remember very clearly is that there are times when, not necessarily Kambili, but the other characters would go into long lectures on Nigerian politics and history and educate the reader. Those had to go because they just...

AF They didn't work?

CNA That's right. As far as Kambili's voice is concerned — I really don't know. I think, because I started with this voice in my head, most of the time I stayed with it. I don't remember ever having to rein her in but I did have to do this with some of the other characters who were giving lectures.

AF *Purple Hibiscus* is in the first person but you Helen actually wrote in the third person, didn't you? Did you ever think about doing it in the first person?

HO No.

AF You just started in the third and off you went?

HO I think if I had done it in the first person a lot of the things that happen would suddenly be put beyond question, a lot of the ambiguities of the book and the subtlety would be lost. This is because you could conclusively say all the things that are happening to Jess mean that she's mad. I think with the third person you can put a little bit of distance, a sort of membrane between these kinds of events and the reader's perception of them.

Audience Do you both as first novelists feel hampered by the fame the other two books have brought?

CNA Yes. I mean, how can you not be aware that people are waiting for the second book and that they're unsheathing their knives? I've often been told I should do a sequel to *Purple Hibiscus*. I imagine that lots of people want another *Purple Hibiscus*, and what's coming after is not at all like it. I'm convinced that everybody who loved *Purple Hibiscus* will hate *Heart of a Yellow Sun*, but then I'm hoping that the people who hated *Purple Hibiscus* will like *Heart of a Yellow Sun* — so there is hope!

AF Helen, do you feel overwhelmed?

HO Not really. I think it's because I'm still in the process of developing a style. So the second novel is an opportunity to try and flex my fingers a bit and see what else I can do rather than being simply another statement by the writer Helen Oyeyemi. I don't feel like that at all.

Audience This is a question for Chimamanda. I was interested in your comment about reading in Nigeria — the idea that at a certain point fiction reading stopped there. You seem be hinting that now reading fiction has gone up again, and I believe you've related that to the rise of Pentecostal Christianity in an article you wrote for the *Guardian* some time back. I'm always struck in Nigeria that where newspapers are sold, there's always a huge crowd of people around there *reading* the newspapers. Also there are books being sold everywhere, from the backs of cars on the streets . . . so there is a lot of book *selling* going on. I wondered if you could relate that to your earlier comments?

CNA There is a lot of book *selling* going on. I think the question is about what sorts of books are being sold and bought and by whom. I wish I had one grand answer. I don't. There are a number of reasons and it's very complex. I think our education system is part of it, the economy is part of it. Before you can afford to buy books to read for pleasure you need to have disposable income, which is something in decline in Nigeria. Our government plays a role. If you have a president who says some disciplines are not useful particularly in terms of the social sciences and the humanities, that really doesn't send a positive message. I think also the rise of this New Age Christianity plays a huge role. So people who buy books and who can afford to buy books will buy books like *Breaking the Spiritual Bond*, and *Two Hundred Ways to Make One Million Naira in Five Months* and that sort of thing. It's very worrying. There's something very literal about that kind of reading and very utilitarian: what *use* can this book be? What can I get from it today to help me now and here? When I was back home I did a number of book readings and often people would say 'Oh, you wrote just a novel'. The significance is that it is nice but it's just fiction which says a lot about where fiction is placed in that society. It's a huge and complex subject, very worrying — but I'm also hopeful, because people like my publisher who produced this book, and who has also just done the novel called *Everything Good Will Come*, people like him do recognise there are still those who want to read quality fiction in Nigeria and who will read it if you make it affordable and available.

Audience This question is for Chimamanda. I first read *Purple Hibiscus* in a reading group that we run at my library. Everyone thoroughly enjoyed it whatever their background. One thing that was very interesting to me was how you mix two languages in the novel, because I felt that you threw in a lot of Ibo words into what was an English novel really. Who inspired you to write in that way, because it's quite unusual. Have you read other books that do this?

CNA I have read books from Asia and Africa that mix languages, but the reason I did that was simply because I wanted to. I wanted to remind the reader that you're reading conversations between characters who are mostly *not* speaking English. If they are speaking English, they are also speaking in a mix of both, which is the reality for many languages in Nigeria today. I often find unconsciously I'm speaking Ibo but English words slip in all the time. So I wanted to remind the reader that these are characters who speak in a mix of both languages, who really make sense of their world through the lens of two languages rather than one.

Audience Chimamanda, are you worried about the rise of new religious movements in Nigeria and the rest of Africa?

CNA I am deeply worried about modern religion and about the state of the world. I think it's important if we care about Nigeria and Africa and the future. We have to engage with religion because it's a huge force. I think it is shocking in debates that go on to invoke God in spaces where really God has no business being invoked. There's a problem with people telling you constantly how 'born again' they are, how close to their pastor they are, when we actually should be talking about why pensions aren't being paid etc. I believe religion can be a force for incredible good, but I have a problem with the *brand* of religion that seems to be exploding in Nigeria now. In Lagos there's a church in everybody's backyard and poor people are giving their money to pastors who then buy private jets . . . Nobody sees the horror of it, because it's all in God's name, covered if you like by God. I think that is very worrying and it's something we should talk about more in Nigeria rather than covering up this kind of corruption in Jesus' name.

Audience I would like to ask if there are themes of being an African woman, or specifically a second generation African woman that you try to explore in your work?

HO Well, when I started *Icarus Girl* I basically thought it was going to be about an eight year old girl and her imaginary friend. I didn't expect that in the writing of it I wouldn't be able to shake off things like gender and ethnicity. I was actually really surprised that it suddenly became this saga of identity, because it's not the sort of thing that I usually talk about to my friends. It's not something that I externalise or think about very much, but in my writing it was suddenly there. I guess it must be a preoccupation, because it's springing up in the second novel as well. So even though I don't consciously go for these themes, these things do affect me and come out in the writing.

AF What do you think Chimamanda?

CNA My feeling is much like Helen. I don't sit down and say I'm going to write women's fiction. However, I am a woman, I care about women's issues, and there are many to care about. When I write I suppose they come out, but what I found myself very conscious of trying *not* to do was to not impose my politics on my fiction. If I did, all my books would have strong women who were proud and independent. However, I realise that in reality this is not the case; it's very important for me to write truths that I can relate to. Because of that I am interested in writing about women who are weak, who are not independent, who make poor choices . . . this is the reality of their lives.

Audience This is a question for Helen. I just wanted to ask, given that you wrote your book when you were doing your 'A' levels, how did you have time to do it?

HO It was a crazy time. I still think of it as fun, but it was stressful. I had teachers demanding homework and practically chasing me around school — it was like a cat and mouse game bound to end in dread. I think I just prioritised the book, which in retrospect seems quite scary, because I also had this offer to go to Cambridge. I had to get three As but I also wanted to write this story, so I did.

AF Helen is at Cambridge now so what does that tell you about what she got? Three As. Well done. That's it. My thanks to Helen Oyeyemi, Chimamanda Ngozi Adichie and to you the audience, thank you very much indeed.

Who Will Bury the Dead?

Victor Ehikhamenor

I'd just lowered the yellowish wick of my kerosene lantern to go to bed when the sky opened. I knew it was going to be a long night of restlessness. My father was about settling to his mud bed too. The zinc roof over our head's was rusty with tiny holes like stars all over it. In no time at all I scurried into the only dry corner of the leaking bedroom in my grandfather's big compound. My father did not seem to mind; he only shifted a bit here and there, but remained lying down.

Black soot like chewed tobacco started dropping on the mud floor and on my body. I wiped some of the soot off my exposed leg, leaving dark smudges on my skin like dry faeces. I could not wait for the day my father would finally finish his cement brick house behind my grandfather's mud house, so that I could be saved from getting wet inside the old house I was born in each time it rained.

The heavy downpour silenced the owl that had been hooting since early evening. My grandfather's rubber trees were heard falling as if a lunatic was lumbering them with a new *usala* chainsaw.

Thunderous wind howled and lightening brightened our semi-dark room through the cracks in the door and window in quick violent succession. I knew in the morning some weak and rusty zinc corrugated roofs would be hanging atop the trees like giant Chinese farmer's hats.

The entire village was beaten to a still quietness never before experienced.

'A great man has departed ... this is not an ordinary rain.' My father declared into the grisly night, as he too could not sleep.

'Aba, how can you tell?' I asked my father, who was now sitting on the edge of the mud bed trying to resuscitate a dying fire that warmed the room.

'Can't you hear the thunder ... it is full of anger ... it has come to escort someone great to the ancestors and people should beware,' he replied.

I concurred. My father knew things like that. All the traditional signs and wonders were on his fingertips. Myths were passed down from generation to generation by word of mouth. From father to son, mother to daughter.

When the rain was subsiding I heard my mother open her door, taking out the big earthenware pot we used for drinking water, to gather some of the rain water.

Her sudden scream of '*Uwesan o o*' jolted my father from our discussion. My mother had a way of screaming the name of my village, *Uwesan*, in the face of danger, as if the name would save her life. I heard her thanking the gods for not making her fall in the slippery terrace while trying to place the water pot in a proper corner to gather drinking water.

'Get inside woman ... this is no time to play around ... have you taken leave of your senses?' My father called out to her. My father's stern voice made my mother know it was no time for a woman to be messing around in the night rain; she hurriedly placed the pot in its *ukpeda*. I heard her cursing the local government that had refused to install public taps in my village or fix the broken ones installed in the sixties. She quickly shut the door and latched the lock.

We had enough drinking water, and she would go to Afuda river to wash our clothes if need be. No need to kill oneself in the precarious rain.

After my mother entered her room, I thought about my father's explanation of the thunderous rain and wondered who the dead one could be among the village old men I greeted on my way to and from St Joseph Catholic College. My mind ran through the entire village streets scouting for the dead ... could it be Tenga the old man with a matted white beard, who dragged a swollen leg caused by elephantiasis?

Wasafiri Vol. 21, No. 1 March 2006, pp. 58–63
ISSN 0269-0055 print/ISSN 1747-1508 online © 2006 Wasafiri
http://www.tandf.co.uk/journals DOI: 10.1080/02690050500475898
Routledge Taylor & Francis Group

The old man always had snuff bottles and cans playing orchestras in his swollen pockets. Or was it Oyamedan who never failed to show up at dinnertime in my grandfather's house?

Tenga was the likely one; he was always coughing and spitting dark phlegmatic liquids like the residue of a piglet's afterbirth. No, it couldn't be either of the two . . . they were not great enough to make the earth shake and uproot trees. They were ordinary farmers with annual meagre harvests. They do not even command respect from their wives, let alone to talk of the gods honouring their departure with an earth-shaking thunderstorm. My search for whom to award the night of thunderous rain lulled me into a restless sleep. I started dreaming of angry looking soldiers flooding my entire village and making everyone frog jump. We were holding our ears, both young and old and we were not told our transgression. It was the following morning that Ukordion, the official village messenger came to our house to tell my grandfather that Enogun the blacksmith had joined the ancestors. My grandfather had to be the first to know as the *odionwele,* the head of Uwesan village elders. It was my grandfather who appointed Ukordion as the village's chief messenger. Ukordion was a man nature had not blessed with size; he was the height of an eight-year-old boy. His owlish oval face made him look like a neckless gourd. He did not have enough lips to cover his teeth or maybe his teeth were too big to stay in his mouth. His frontal denture protruded like a big bush rat's. It made him seem as if he were perpetually laughing. But he was a man who knew his job, and relished doing it. Ukordion was also the town crier who announced new edicts and bylaws to the villagers after the elders had decided such matters.

That morning he had a smirk on his face as he delivered the message to my grandfather that Enogun had died the previous night. His morbid elation was because of his entitlement to the heads of the goats and cows that would be killed during Enogun's burial ceremony. Tradition required that all the heads of any sacrificed animal belonged to him as the chief messenger.

The village was buzzing with excitement like a fired up beehive. Though some of the villagers lost their thatch roofs and zinc roofs to the previous night's rain, they couldn't care less and were in festive mood. Enogun by my village standard was a wealthy man, not because he was the only blacksmith in the entire Uwesan village but because his son was a 'big man' in Lagos. No one even mentioned the fact that he had five daughters married in various cities and towns.

None of the villagers remarked that he was the blacksmith that made hoes and cutlasses for the entire farming village of Uwesan. Enogun's craft as a blacksmith was well known, even to children.

When I was in primary school, I took an old rusty nail to him like every other kid on my street. As I entered his workshop, I met Isesele his apprentice, pumping the huge bellows; the orange coal fire was billowing with a smooth bluish flame. Inside the hot fire was a nearly completed hoe head. I greeted him and watched as his old sinewy biceps danced flabbily. The huge mattock he wielded fashioned the hot metal to a sharp hoe atop a thick anvil. The sound of metal hitting metal could be heard miles away, it was a calling voice to the villagers to bring their hardware for Enogun to hammer. Sweating profusely, he beat the hoe into submission. Enogun's black body glistened with ripples of black beads of sweat. He looked like he had oiled himself with Vaseline and jumped into a murky river. His long hands made folks call him *Otanbhabor*, 'the one with long hands'. His legs were also very long, sitting in a low stool made him looked like a giant bow in an archer's grip.

Enogun put the nail I gave to him on the beautifully burning embers. I watched his face go cadmium red from the reflection of the fire, his eyes were biddy and brownish from the excessive heat. He had a face the length of a baby pumpkin, lined with folds of wrinkled skin. His eyelashes were going gray; he was an old man who kept working because he loved his profession, not because he needed the money. Isesele the apprentice increased the pumping of the bellows with a rhythmic *fukufuku* . . . *du-omonanor* . . . *fukufuku* . . . *du-omonanor*. The air from the pump titivated the flame and turned the nail into a bright red metal, ready to be shaped into a different functional tool. He removed the bright red nail and pounded it until the nail flattened into a knife. He threw it into a bucket of dirty water; a hissing sound of the hot object cooling in the water resonated like a cobra ready to do damage to its prey, and the ensuing smoke enveloped the tiny thatched workshop. It cooled in no time, and he dipped in his long coal-stained right hand and retrieved the new knife. He handed it to me and said:

'Greet your grandfather for me, and tell your father his hoe is ready.'

I couldn't wait to get home that day to test my new penknife on a big avocado or orange. It was my first tool as a young boy.

Enogun was also the high priest of the god of iron, Ogun. This was so because he worked with irons. Who else would understand the fierce god of iron if not Enogun? He was responsible for sacrificing dogs at the Ogun shrine. The shrine comprised of all the used metallic objects he could lay his hands on . . . from old hoe-heads, cutlasses without wooden handles, pincers and old pliers without handles. The shrine was set up at one corner of the workshop. According to myth, the god of iron did not drink any ordinary blood, except the hot blood of dogs. When Ogun was angry worshippers would sacrifice dogs to him, through Enogun the priest. The neck of the dog would be slit in one fell swoop with a sharp *ematon*, and the severed oesophagus would be directed towards the shrine, with all of the blood drained onto all of the irons, as if they were taking a cool shower. The head of the dog and its perplexed eyes would be left on the shrine overnight. By morning it would have disappeared, Ogun had come overnight to claim its sacrifice.

None of these civil duties mattered when Enogun died; the villagers were only interested in the burial ceremony that would be made grand by his rich son from Lagos.

Okuta Enogun was the only man that went to university from my village. He went to the one in Lagos, back in the days when government gave young graduates cars and jobs to start their new lives. He was the richest son my village had in Lagos; the others were mere messengers or day labourers. The gods smiled on the son of Enogun, as some villagers would say.

One Christmas, he brought two new Peugeot 505 cars. This was a rare brand of Peugeot; we were used to the very old 404 like the one owned by Mr Roman in the next village. Some old men who rode in the car said it had the harmattan inside, referring to the air-conditioning.

Me, Kisofa and Asene my friends thought he was going to leave one for his father, but he went back to Lagos with the car. We heard him saying the roads in my village were too bad for such new cars, that he would talk to some of his friends in government to fix the roads. But that was before the coup that removed his politician friends from power and killed some of them.

Potholes continued to take over the roads, even the pickups and *bolekeja* that transport *garri* traders to and from Uromi market baulked at the gaping potholes. The military government had long abandoned the big cities, not to talk of the villages like mine. Yet, the villagers said Okuta would talk to the big men in government in Lagos to fix the bad roads for us because they did not know that power had shifted.

Okuta plastered and repainted his father's old mud house, making it look like a brick house. He replaced the rusty and brownish leaking zinc roof. Okuta's wife bought new lace and a George wrapper for her mother-in-law from Liverpool, England, which she wore to women's meetings every Sunday. Enogun and Adiza his wife were rich and were way above the average Uwesan villager. They were the closest to royalty; everybody wanted to be their friend.

The biggest thing Okuta did for his father was putting electricity in his father's house. He bought a generator and fluorescent lamps. These were the only lights at night in my village apart from moonlight and kerosene lanterns. At night Enogun's house became the magnet that attracted the villagers like bees to nectar. Men, women, children and insects flocked there to see the light. His small black and white Grundig TV that the villagers referred to as *ekpeti omen*, box of noise, was the major attraction. Though the transmitted images from the black and white TV were grainy, there was a multitude of village boys and girls, men and women watching whatever programme the Nigeria Television Authority had to offer. The old men and women could not really understand what was being broadcasted if it was not traditional dance. When the 9 pm news came on, they lost interest because it was in the 'white man's language' as they would say. The only adult that understood the news was Emos the owner of Property Provisions Store. Me, and my secondary school friends understood the news too, but small boys were not allowed to interpret the 'white man's language' when Emos was around. He boasted that he too attended Government College during the first republic, and he could have gone to university in England if not for farm work forced on him by his father.

In the morning when the news of Enogun's death had spread like heated oil in the sun, the villagers knew it was festival time. Free food for seven days and seven nights was expected. Instead of the locally brewed *ogogoro* gin, Okuta would bring Star and Gulder lager beer from Lagos. Instead of the smelly SM and Gold Leaf cigarette manufactured by the Nigerian Tobacco Company, he would bring the scented Rothmans of Pall Mall from London or Marlboro and Camel from America.

Tenga, the-white-bearded man, was particularly happy because he relished Gordon's Aromatic Schnapps made in Sango Otta.

Emos was bubbling because partygoers would buy extra sweets and candies from his store and children would buy *goodie goodie* candy and *blow blow*. If he was lucky and Okuta ran out of drinks, he could finally sell the Guinness stout bottles, which had gathered red dust over the years like unclaimed goods in the wharf. His store was about to become the commercial nerve centre of the entire village.

Uwesan women started bringing melon, *ugu* leaves, *ogbonor* seeds, cray fish and dry *bonga* fish for Adiza the new widow. Some women had already started cooking and the aroma of cooked *egusi* soup and pounded yam wafted through the air and lodged in our noses. Men kept taking bundles of big yams to the late Enogun's house. In my village, death drives away stinginess and brings people together. The villagers fed themselves better when a man died than when he was alive. His son from Lagos will repay us, the donors kept saying. Amala the taxi-driver took a full gallon of scarce black-market petrol to Enogun's house for the generator. There had been a scarcity of petrol all over the country as usual, and the generator in Enogun's house had not worked since the last time Okuta brought jerry cans of black market petrol from Lagos. Amala concluded that Okuta would bring even more this time and replenish his emptied stock.

All Uwesan elders were present in Enogun's house at about 10 am. By then the sun had emerged from the cocoon of a clouded sky like a newly hatched chick. The fourteen elders that made up the highest council in the village welcomed the relief of the upholstered chairs in Enogun's parlour. Okuta brought the big 'full cover' chairs from Lagos one November afternoon.

The meeting was to decide whom to send to Lagos to break the news to Okuta of his father's death. While the meeting was going on inside the house, young adults sat on long benches under the kola nut tree in front of Enogun's house. Some sat on old cement blocks which Okuta had bought to build a new kitchen extension for his mother. Others sat on the bamboo bench in Enogun's workshop, while another set of villagers sat under the big pear tree on the side of the house.

I sat close where I could hear older adults analyse the upcoming festivity.

'Which kind work Okuta dey do sef?' a man called Awilo asked.

'Na government contractor for Lagos,' answered Emos the storeowner.

Only Emos could answer such questions, he had been a friend of Okuta right from their childhood. Also only Emos read newspapers like *The Daily Times* and *The Observer*, and knew what was going on in the cities. Though he was Okuta's age-mate, he ran errands for Okuta like a small boy whenever Okuta visited the village. He paid Emos in the form of used clothes and oversized shoes. Rumour had it that Okuta helped in opening the Property Provisions Store for him, so he could feed his family with the proceeds. But business was always slow in the village; the only provisions villagers bought were cigarette and OMO detergent soap, and sometimes bread when there was flour in the country to produce bread. And the rest: stuff like sardine, Blue Band butter, Bournvita and Tate sugar gathered dust for months, way past the expiry date.

'Emos, you think say brother Okuta go come with many big men from Lagos . . . like last time when im papa become elder?' queried Takwa, an ashy man with a hawk-like face.

'So you can get drunk and shit on your trousers like you did last time?' Emos shot back at him sarcastically.

About five years ago when Okuta came to celebrate his father's initiation into elderhood, Takwa got so drunk he urinated all over himself.

'Who do you think they will send to Lagos to tell Okuta?' Amala the taxi-driver wanted to know.

Everyone knew the answer to that, even Amala knew. But there was always a little rivalry between him and Emos because he too was half-educated, read old newspapers sometimes and knew Okuta when they were students. No one answered him, because we all knew it was only Emos that knew how to get to Okuta's house in Lagos. Amala could not go beyond Benin City with his coughing old Datsun Laurel taxi. I knew Amala secretly wished he were the one that would go to Lagos. But Emos' celebrity status had already skyrocketed when Enogun died. All questions were directed at him. The villagers had found a new information conduit in the person of Emos.

The elders' meeting was finally over, and Emos hovered around like a vulture waiting for disembowelled cow entrails. Oko-Edion, a younger elder with a chiselled face like a mask carved out of Masonite approached Emos. He adjusted his half-torn dashiki to cover the straying sweat-stained undershirt. He brought out a bottle of snuff, tapped it with his right thumb and opened the bottle like a scientist in a lab. He tilted it, did a mental measurement and dispensed an exact amount on his left palm; with his right thumb he pinched half and piled the fine brown tobacco into a flared up nostril, the left one first . . . and then the right. His eyes went teary red like a flashlight with dying batteries. He pulled out a white-turned-brown kerchief from his right pocket and dusted his nose that looked like twin rabbit holes. All the while Emos was transfixed like a waxed object, waiting patiently for Oko-Edion's theatrics of snuff taking to be over with.

'*Vae Emosi* . . . *comu* here . . . the elders want you to go to Lagos . . . tell Okuta his father don go join our ancestors.' Oko-Edion was weaving back and forth like a nylon bag caught in a whirlwind, mixing his broken English with the native tongue of Uwesan. The *ogogoro* gin was controlling his balance, and he had little or no say over what his body did.

'And the elders want him to come immediately . . . immediately as the first son . . . he must come at once without delay . . . *umahon* . . . you hear me . . . tell him if he does not come quick the elders will go ahead and bury his father . . . we can not let an elder be late in settling with his ancestors.' Emos was nodding his head profusely like a broken doll-baby.

'You hear wetin I talk so?' Oko-Edion queried Emos for the tenth time.

'*Mehonmin* . . . I hear you sir.'

Oko-Edion dipped his right hand in a side pocket that was half torn and brought out rumpled naira notes and handed them to Emos.

'*Ekakhornin* . . . how much be that?'

Emos quickly spat on his index finger and rubbed it against his thumb to get a good grip and started counting the money quickly. He counted the money really fast and announced

'Three hundred naira *owaen*.'

Three hundred naira would take him to Lagos but would not bring him back. He needed no return fare because he would ride back with Okuta or one of his drivers in an air-conditioned Peugeot 505. Emos was greatly envied by the other villagers, especially Amala the taxi driver.

'Go come,' Oko-Edion concluded in broken English and walked to a private corner like a masquerade on stilts and started passing water.

Emos knew the urgency of his message. He ran to his house like a man chasing a stubborn goat to be taken to market. He changed from one tattered trouser to a fairly better one. He held the trouser with a rope in place of a belt and folded the bottoms. He had on an oversized chequered long sleeve shirt. He did not pack any overnight bag; what he wore was enough for the overnight journey. Okuta might even give him new clothes; after all it was Okuta who gave him the ones he was wearing to Lagos. He had to walk to the next village to catch a taxi or motorcycle to Uromi where he would find a taxi to Lagos.

As Emos disappeared through a narrow path, Oko-Edion climbed the final stairs and went inside to join the rest of the elders who were starting another gallon of *ogogoro*. The hot local brew would keep the body warm till the cold beverages from Lagos arrived. As the alcohol began to spread in old bloods, aging mouths began to thaw into old rhythms. Songs were heard from Enogun's compound. Someone had gotten a big gong and samba from Abella's house. Abella was the chairman of the village's *asonogun* dance group. He too would benefit from Enogun's death, because his dance group would perform on wake keeping night, alongside musicians from Lagos.

Some villagers believed because Okuta lived in Lagos, the musician would be King Sunny Ade; others argued that it would be the new juju music sensation Shina Peters. These musicians cost plenty of money. But money was like water to Okuta. His regard for the Nigerian naira was very minimal. Some said he would not even spend naira to pay the musicians; he would use the almighty American dollar like they do in Lagos. Big men in Lagos no longer spend the local currency; it was either the American dollar or the British pound sterling. Emos once said one dollar was equivalent to 130 naira. The villagers were amazed and completely lost in calculating how many years of saving would buy them ten dollars.

'Where does he get dollars from ... has Okuta been to America before?' Kisofa wondered out-loud.

'Haba! He can always buy dollars in the streets of Lagos!' someone answered.

Enogun could not have chosen a better day to go meet the ancestors. He died on a Friday night and there was no school the following day, which was a Saturday. There was no farming either; this gave me the opportunity to keep vigil with Kisofa, Asene and other village youths in waiting for the feast to kick off fully. Though we ate rice cooked by the village women, it was not satisfactory enough until the first born of Enogun arrived. Night met us at his compound.

The *tutu tutu* sound of the generator and the smoke coming from it did not bother any of us.

The fluorescent lamps outside had started attracting insects never before seen. Moths, pale coloured butterflies, fire flies, green-and-yellow grasshoppers, crickets, termites; they all gathered to enjoy the bright light.

Children caught and released harmless insects. Boys stood near girls, and girls recoiled from the boys' lurid overtures. Women started pounding on large mortars with very long pestles, while others broke melons and fermented cassava for *fufu* in big aluminium buckets and earthenware pots. Some of the women were tipsy with some gin they had mixed with Coke, Sprite and Fanta.

Some women washed Adiza's dirty clothes, while others helped move plates around and re-arranged cluttered earthenware pots and buckets. Adiza would not wear an ordinary black cotton shirt as mourning clothes; she would wear black lace ... some women coming down from the street gossiped openly. The nobles don't mourn like the peasants, another woman said.

As the night metamorphosed into a deep dark purple beyond the luminescence of the fluorescent bulbs, weaker insects started dying from too much excitement with the light.

I too decided to go home and save some energy for the next day's activities. I bade Kisofa and Asene goodnight.

I took a narrower and shorter path towards my house and left behind the greyness of a distant light. As I moved further into the unlit path, my dark shadow started submerging into the night becoming one huge darkness. The faraway sound of songs and gong became one, and trailed behind me like cheap perfume. I could only hear the *goen ... goen ... goen* of the big gong, without making sense out of the words in the accompanying song.

As I hurried home, the flip-flop sound of my Hausa slippers scared large bats out of an Obadan tree, their sudden flutter scared me and broke me into a jerky run. The path to my house was dark, and ghostly images began to play kaleidoscopic games with my senses. Fireflies flickered momentarily like twinkling stars, like meteors they disappeared. My grandfather's house was the last on the northern side of the village, there were no houses after ours; the only dark silhouette behind our house at night were shadows of rubber trees, palm trees, and one tall obeche tree which had become the home of weaver birds in the day time and hooting owls at night.

I heard the owls hooting and I quickened my footsteps. The hooting of owl was a bad omen in the village, it gave me an eerie feeling as if acid was pouring down my spine.

When I was about six years old, the hooting of the owls was so overbearing that grandpa had to come out with his dane-gun and shot one down, which silenced them for a while. Later that week grandpa's entire cocoa plantation was infested by black-pod disease. He never shot any owl thereafter.

As I climbed the steps to open our front door, the distant sound of the gong was wavy in a hypnotic lull. The travelling of its sound relied on the strength of the night wind. The sound eventually blended into a million voices of twilight insects. As I shut the door, I heard nothing but the deep throated snore of my grandfather; he was too old to buy into the fanfare of Okuta's wealth or Enogun's death. He had sent my father to represent him and my mother was among the women commiserating with Adiza.

Emos was supposed to arrive from Lagos on Sunday. And that night was when Enogun would be laid to rest. And there were going to be celebratory gunshots. That would mark the final farewell to Enogun, a great man, a thoroughbred blacksmith and the chief priest of Ogun.

None of that would commence if Enogun's first son were not around to put the first dust on his father's grave.

On Sunday morning after I came back from mass, the festive ambiance that enveloped my village could only be compared to that of a new yam festival. There was a gentle hazy smoke, which came from nowhere in particular. Men became more tolerant with their wives and children. Tales and folktales were told and retold with new embellishment. Men dug deeper into their pocket not for snuff bottles or dry kola nuts, but for extra money to buy drinks.

Everybody was waiting for Okuta to arrive. Abella had contacted his dance group members to cancel all travelling plans for the next seven days. It was going to be their biggest outing for the big men coming from Lagos, naira would rain and dollars would flow. Even the sons and daughters of the village who lived in not so far away cities like Benin City, Ibadan, Sapele and Warri were already arriving in long dresses. News of death travel fast like a broken wind. They came to show compassion and celebrate with Okuta the successful son of Enogun. Other men from neighbouring villages started pouring in like mini-tributaries floating into a bigger river. Takwa was already drunk with giddiness. Awilo the village comedian had people doubled up with laughter under the kola nut trees. Children played and got dusty in the red sand, making them look like clay effigy.

Farmers only went briefly to the farm to check traps and see if they had caught any bush meat to be used in cooking at Enogun's burial ceremony. More women from neighbouring villages brought soup ingredients to Adiza. Young girls plaited and added extra colourful beads to their long braided hair; all in preparation for the arrival of Okuta so the burial ceremony could begin in earnest.

Takwa was the first to sight Emos when he went to urinate near the bush path. He ran inside to break the news to the elders. Many thought it was the alcohol that was bothering him.

If Emos was back from Lagos, how come there were no cars blaring horns and revving engines?

'*Kpaaa! Emenmen* worry eh . . . it is madness that is worrying you,' Oko-Edion shouted and shooed Takwa out like a seditious dog.

Emos came in full view like a picture from a negative, trekking with a newspaper tucked under his armpit. His face had lost the pageantry and lustre it went to Lagos with. The big trousers he was wearing seemed bigger than when he left, and the oversized-chequered shirt hung loose on his left shoulder making him look like a scarecrow. He looked pale and tired and very unkempt. His dishevelled beard was not a sign of someone who had been to a big man's house in Lagos. As he got closer, it was obvious he was holding *The Guardian* newspaper. Which meant he actually got to Lagos, because only Lagosians bought *The Guardian* newspaper.

He trudged with steps full of reluctance as if he did not want to get to Enogun's compound. Did he walk the ten miles from Uromi to Uwesan? We wondered.

Why did he look so tired and worn out? What was wrong? Did he not meet Okuta? Or has he changed his address? That couldn't be, people hardly moved in Lagos once they rented a place. My aunty once told my father that accommodation in Lagos was not a bone to be cracked with milk teeth. She had been using the same Ebute Meta address since I was born.

Emos went past the puzzled faces of Amala the taxi-driver, Awilo the comedian, Takwa the drunk, and other waiting faces and went straight to the elders who were still talking loudly amidst songs and drinking.

Speculations and rumours quickly filled the air like the smell of rotten egg. Everything kicked into slow motion like the steps of Emos. We stretched our ears like ostrich necks . . . craving for the news from Lagos.

As Emos entered the parlour, the songs and noise subsided, praises and encomium took over. We knew you would come safely and peacefully, some of the elders chanted. They were too drunk to note that he did not come with Okuta or they thought Okuta was outside parking his cars. Through slightly opened windows we strained our ears; we could not hear Emos' report too clearly. He was speaking in a tired and exhausted low tone like a farmer whose entire barn had been raided by thieves.

Suddenly there was a loud scream. It was the voice of Adiza, wailing.

She ran out barely clothed and flung herself on the ground outside the compound, in full view of the waiting crowd.

We were shocked, but more puzzled about what had transpired inside Enogun's parlour. She could not be mourning her husband who had been dead for two days then. She did not cry the first day, why all of a sudden now? We wondered.

'My Okuta o . . . My Okuta o,' she kept wailing uncontrollably.

People wondered why was she calling Okuta's name instead of her dead husband's. Her friends and some elders that were not drunk came out and gathered her like spilt washed clothes, and huddled her inside.

Emos came out and opened *The Guardian* newspaper he had folded under his armpit. On the front page was the picture of Okuta Enogun, the wealthy businessman who had been accused of sponsoring a failed coup in Dodan Barracks, Lagos. The botched coup took place on Friday night, the same night Enogun died.

No-one heard about any coup in the village, singing elders had replaced the TV in Enogun's house.

Ten other soldiers and Okuta were under arrest in an undisclosed location in Lagos; only the senior members of the junta were allowed to see them. Okuta was the only civilian among the coup plotters. His wife and two children were also under arrest. Emos kept reading the newspaper to no one in particular.

All the villagers put their hands on their heads as if they were about to start frog jumping. Slowly, we started filing away from Enogun's compound with long faces, like a column of ants sensing the smell of a hazardous insecticide.

'A good woman in a good country' or The Essence is in the Pumpkin

Alexander McCall Smith's Mma Ramotswe Novels as a Case of Postcolonial Nostalgia

Christine Matzke

The first time I heard of Mma Ramotswe and her No. 1 Ladies' Detective Agency in Botswana was through a colleague and friend of mine who herself had been recommended the books by a very well-known couple of South African social anthropologists based in the United States. A coincidence, for sure, but then perhaps not quite, especially when I noticed other colleagues in my discipline, African Studies, picking up the books and reading them for their 'loveable' characters and 'heart-warming' qualities, myself included. The author, Alexander McCall Smith, born and brought up in Zimbabwe, then Rhodesia, before moving to Scotland for his university education, had himself spent a good number of years in Botswana, working on the country's criminal law and helping set up the national law faculty. Now it seemed, he was making a fictional 'return' to a country he was obviously very fond of (Frost np; Anon np). I am by no means suggesting that McCall Smith had an expatriate audience in mind when he set out to write the books, or a public predominately comprised of western-based African studies scholars (one living in Botswana actually disliked the series intensely); but it is undeniable that our 'specialist' reaction mirrored that of the general reading public. An overview by Elfi Bettinger of the reception of the series confirms that there has been ample praise for these 'wise' and 'charming books', said to celebrate the 'moral certainty, warmth and compassion' (Frost np) of a continent and its 'gentle, dignified African simplicity' (Bettinger np). On second thoughts, however, it appears a rather sanitised version of Africa we are presented with, and Botswana, for that matter.

So far, six novels have come out in rapid succession: *The No. 1 Ladies' Detective Agency* (1998), *Tears of the Giraffe* (2000), *Morality for Beautiful Girls* (2001), *The Kalahari Typing School for Men* (2002), *The Full Cupboard of Life* (2003), and *In the Company of Cheerful Ladies* (2004).[1] All of them centre on the formidable figure of a 'traditionally built' Motswana woman detective, Precious Ramotswe, whose infallible intuition makes up for her lack of experience in solving the queries of her anguished clientele. Surrounded by two equally upright, though sympathetically imperfect, characters – her long-time fiancé Mr J L B Matekoni, proprietor of Tlokweng Road Speedy Motors, and her diligent secretary-cum-assistant, Mma Makutsi who is later promoted to Acting Manager of the garage and eventually sets up her own business, the Kalahari Typing School for Men – the figure of Mma Ramotswe has propelled the series to the top of contemporary bestseller lists. Five other characters complete her microcosm: two motherless

Wasafiri Vol. 21, No. 1 March 2006, pp. 64–71
ISSN 0269-0055 print/ISSN 1747-1508 online © 2006 Wasafiri
http://www.tandf.co.uk/journals DOI: 10.1080/02690050500475922
Routledge Taylor & Francis Group

Masarwa children who Mr J L B Matekoni 'acquires' in a futile attempt to resist the pushy matron of the orphan farm, Mma Potokwane; and two rather hopeless apprentice mechanics whose main preoccupation is girls rather than gears and hubcaps. All in all, as Bettinger has pointed out, 'there is zero crime, little mystery and only short suspense' (np), with cases ranging from tailing unfaithful spouses to sorting out sullen maids and other 'more domestic matters' (McCall Smith, *CCL* 37).

Despite these 'precious little happenings' (Berlins np), as one quick-witted reviewer has put it, the figure of Mma Ramotswe has become immensely successful in the literary world. Indeed, she nowadays seems to be having another life beyond the pages of the books, in the worlds of counselling and advertisement. In April and May 2005 the BBC World Service announced one of its radio programmes as the 'The No. 1 Listeners' Detective Agency', with 'an office deep inside the BBC's Bush House' – pun obviously intended – 'waiting to investigate the issues that are bothering you'. On the website of Random Publishing House Mma Ramotswe now presents a seemingly 'interactive' agony column (np); and she has also started to market McCall Smith's other works of fiction. A new edition of African folk tales, *The Girl Who Married a Lion* (2004) (some previously published as *Children of Wax*, 1989), not only announces McCall Smith as 'the bestselling author of The No. 1 Ladies' Detective Agency', but also features a 'A Letter from Mma Ramotswe', prominently publicised on the book cover. While McCall Smith introduces these tales in a vein reminiscent of the critical tenor in which his detective series has been reviewed – 'part of a universal language which can speak to people across human frontiers' (ix) and which 'speak to us from the African heart' (xi) – Mma Ramotswe initially strikes a more melancholic tone in her foreword. She 'writes':

> When I hear these stories they make me sad. That is not because they are stories of sad things that have happened, it is because they remind me of the Africa of my childhood and of all the good things that there were then. Everybody feels a little bit sad when they think of their childhood, because the world we knew then seems so far away.... But then you hear these old stories – the stories that you heard so many times – and suddenly everything comes back. You are there again, sitting with your aunt outside her house, and it is quiet, and the sky is empty and the sun is on the land. And you think: I am a lucky person to be here, to be listening to these things that happened in another place, just round the corner, in the days when the animals could speak. And the sadness goes away and your heart is full again. (xiii–xiv)

It is this immense sense of nostalgia, and the attempt at (re-)creating a wholesome world, that not only pervades the above introduction, but also the No. 1 Ladies' Detective Agency series; and it is at this aspect that I want to look here. It is an attempt at mapping out a nostalgia which curiously seems to amalgamate both 'colonial' and 'postcolonial' longings, and is so unlike any expectations readers might have when picking up a work of postcolonial crime fiction, or African crime fiction for that matter. It is also, as I will demonstrate, a nostalgia that at times gently mocks itself by means of subtle, or fairly obvious, irony.

I will first look at very general notions of crime fiction in relation to postcoloniality, followed by a note on postcolonial nostalgia, before reading selected aspects of the texts. Of particular interest is the return, and partial re-signification, of the Mother Africa trope venerated in early nationalist fiction, mostly as the custodian of 'tradition', 'Africanness' and identity; and the wistful projection of social and political order onto the protagonist's ample figure. While the generous female form is again deployed as a vast iconographic repository, the series markedly differs from the nationalist symbolism of early African literature by projecting a humorous, somewhat naïve, re-codification of gendered power. Women are portrayed as the driving agents, not the powerless icons, of an African society, but they are non-confrontational and do not really threaten the given order. I will argue, however, that this is one of the series' deliberate strategies of postcolonial nostalgia in its invention of a 'good', 'peaceful' and politically correct milieu.

Crime Fiction and Postcoloniality: A Case of Riveting Resistance?

Recently Postcolonial Studies have discovered the crime novel as a worthy area of exploration;[2] while crime fiction enthusiasts have noticed the postcolonial detective as a genuine alternative to investigators from the mother countries of crime fiction, Britain and the United States. Several recent publications, such as Ed Christian's *The Post-Colonial Detective* (2001) or *Sleuthing Ethnicity* (2003) by Dorothea Fischer-Hornung and Monika Mueller, attest to their growing appeal, as does the increasing number of detective fictions with a postcolonial setting or a 'postcolonial' investigator.

To put it in rather simplified terms, 'postcoloniality' often invokes concepts of subversion and challenge to western mainstreams or other 'master narratives', to which the 'periphery' 'writes back' or which it is making a clever attempt to 'subvert'.[3] A recent call for papers on 'Postcoloniality and the Detective', for example, points out that 'postcolonial criticism has powerfully analyzed the ways in which the "epistemological dominant" ... of modern narrative meets with *richly layered resistance, ambivalence*, or *mimicry* in the colonial environments it presumes to survey or represent' (emphasis added) (Pearson, and Singer np). For Christian too, postcolonial literature is linked to the struggle of marginalised peoples 'against cultural hegemony and assimilation and neo-colonialism' (1), with 'diversity' and 'hybridity' generally being celebrated. While perhaps a narrow, though certainly prevalent, point of view, the rise of the postcolonial detective hence suggests the appropriation of a popular genre to investigate questions of power and authority within a postcolonial context and against potential projections of a (neo-)imperial West; or of community, beliefs and identity constructions in a postcolonial environment, including gender and race relations.

Given that crime fiction can be a highly moralising genre in which social stability and order cannot only be interrogated, but also confirmed,[4] it is perhaps not surprising that the Mma Ramotswe novels do not at all fit into the anticipated pattern of postcolonial subversion and volatility. Instead of syncretic disorder and insurrection, we find personal and political stability. What we encounter in McCall Smith's No. 1 Ladies' Detective Agency series is not the disruption of 'typical' postcolonial dichotomies – tradition/modernity, empire/colony or 'the West' and 'the Rest' – but the return to an almost pristine, essentially righteous, African environment with a strong, though empathetic, sense of human 'good' and 'evil'. Whereas national and other seemingly stable categories are increasingly eroded in this transcultural, transnational day and age, Mma Ramotswe promises readerly respite from postmodern fragmentation and insecurities by offering wholeness for body, spirit and nation.

A Note on Postcolonial Nostalgia

This raises the question — what does nostalgia bring to the postcolonial crime novel? '*Nostalgia*', Fred Davis in his early study *Yearning for Yesterday* (1979) writes, 'is from the Greek *nostos*, to return home, and *algia*, a painful condition — thus, a painful yearning to return home' (1). Previously denoting a medical condition associated with melancholy, but also with patriotism, intellectual activity and, in Arabic, passion,[5] the 'nostalgic paradigm' (Turner 150) has taken on more psychological than physical connotations in contemporary western understanding. Bryan Turner, for example, identifies several aspects of nostalgia 'as a social and cultural discourse', such as 'a sense of historical decline and loss', a 'sense of the absence or loss of personal wholeness and moral certainty' – usually associated with 'a collapse of values' – and the 'idea of a loss of simplicity [and] personal authenticity' (150–51). Interestingly, Turner uses white colonial settler societies of the old Commonwealth as an example, which at the time of decolonisation idealised the 'motherland' as a place immune from such crises; and he associates 'post-colonial [*sic*] nostalgia' with representations in contemporary British culture that deal with 'the loss of imperial power and world influence' (154). In the No. 1 Ladies' Detective Agency novels, it is of course not so much the loss of imperial power that is being mourned – despite Mma Ramotswe's unabashed admiration for English (and other) royals[6] – but the loss of simplicity and moral values. More importantly, we find an exact reversal of fortune: the enthusiastic reception of the series suggests that the (former) centres of (imperial) power, where the author and most of his reading public are located, find enormous comfort in the gentle predictability and essential 'goodness' of the texts.[7] Instability, disorder and contingency are merely temporary phenomena to be rectified by the formidable protagonist, Mma Ramotswe, Upholder of Tradition and Values.

This readerly revelling in an imagined culture seems to point to what Linda Hutcheon has called 'a dissatisfaction with the culture of the present' (2), momentarily compensated by the invention of a Botswana microcosm rooted in a resourceful past. (Not all of Africa, the reader is quick to learn, has the same wonderfully reassuring qualities). Obviously, it is not a Botswana as actually experienced by its people, but as idealised and creatively imagined by the author through his protagonist. Whether this is related to McCall Smith's alleged, but unproven, romanticised memories of the place is not really an issue; the fictional nostalgia of Mma Ramotswe however is, as is, to a certain extent, the sentimental reception of the series. Both substantiate Hutcheon's claim that

> nostalgia is less about the past than about the present. It operates through what Mikhail Bakhtin called an 'historical inversion': the ideal that is *not* being lived now is projected into the past. (original emphasis) (3)

In the case of the No.1 Ladies' Detective Agency, it is not so much a past into which it is projected – though memories of the past play an important role in the construction of the narratives' modern-day realities – but into an 'Other' present. To quote Hutcheon again:

> The simple, pure, ordered, easy, beautiful, or harmonious past [the 'Other' present] is constructed (and then experienced emotionally) in conjunction with the present — which, in turn, is constructed as complicated, contaminated, anarchic, difficult, ugly, and confrontational. (3)

This construction – or projection – of a stable 'traditional' African social order is reminiscent of nineteenth-century encounters between the West and its colonies, when the latter's seemingly timeless 'traditional culture' occasionally served as reassuring antidote against the less desirable aspects of modernity at home (cf Matzke 248). It also shares similarities with the 'Enlightenment hankering after Oriental "harmony"' (Robertson 150).

But there is more to McCall Smith's novels than a simple comparison to colonial culture. Nostalgia has also been an aspect of modern African literature and cultural theory, particularly during the time of twentieth-century decolonisation. To some critics, for example, the *négritude* movement 'with its focus on the pre-capitalist, pre-imperial past, was the sign of a nostalgic search for a lost coherence' (Hutcheon 6);[8] similar observations can be made of the 1960s cultural nationalism of Anglophone East Africa.[9] One of its main proponents, the Ugandan Okot p'Bitek, vociferously condemned the alienation and 'apemanship' ('Pop Music' 3) of his contemporaries in their search for western/ised culture, and called for a return to their own values and 'roots'. His seminal prose poem, *Song of Lawino* (1966), is moreover a text against which the No. 1 Ladies' Detective Agency series can be very loosely read; in both we find versions of the Mother Africa trope, and in both we find plenty of pumpkins. Contrary to p'Bitek's earnest enterprise, though, McCall Smith allows for an 'ironic double vision': while well-known tropes are indeed summoned for sentimental projection, the gently mocking undertone undermines the seriousness of the texts and thus acknowledges the final impossibility of the nostalgic endeavour (Hutcheon 7).

Mma Ramotswe in Mother Africa Costume

This ironic viewpoint might be seen in the gentle parody of the tropes of social order and nationalism often found in the classical detective novel. For instance, Dennis Porter argues that '[d]etective novels provide reassurance, then, not only because they deal in identifiable good and evil... but also because they propose a world of fixed cultural quantities' (218). One of these 'quantities' are 'national cultural ideals' or 'stereotypes' that form an important factor in the genre's attraction. Porter notes that it 'is reassuring... to find one's expectations about the English, the Americans, and the French confirmed in one's reading' (217). Mma Ramotswe is, of course, nothing less than the quintessential Motswana, and she is very proud of it. In the No. 1 Ladies' Detective Agency series, McCall Smith plays with positive cultural stereotypes of her 'Africanness', and particularly with common – and commonly reassuring – images of the African woman linked to homeliness and maternity. The Mother Africa trope has a long and complex history in African literature, starting with the colonisers' mythologising of Africa as female, seductive and treacherous, its affirmative, often nationalist, reclamation in the African male literary tradition, and its subsequent re-signification by women writers from an African-feminist point of view.[10] Léopold Sédar Senghor, for example, was one of the most prominent *négritude* writers to re-employ the embodiment of Africa in the figure of a woman to refute colonial representations; Okot p'Bitek did likewise in his *Song of Lawino* to disprove western cultural influence (McLuskie, and Innes 3–4; Stratton 43). Here, the plump eponymous female narrator embodies tradition and authenticity, while rebuking Tina, the slender second wife of their husband, Ocol, for her modern, seemingly alienated ways. It is the pumpkin that eventually emerges as the ultimate symbol of time-honoured values and customs in Lawino's refrain, 'Let no one uproot the Pumpkin [in the old homestead]' (p'Bitek, *Song* 216). While early African writers thus recuperated their own identities in images of whole, and usually ample, African female bodies – Elleke Boehmer speaks of the 'continent-wide proportions' (233) that some characters were provided with – they nonetheless reproduced the binary mode of western Manichean allegories (male/female, body/mind, sensuality/rationality, etc) and did not attempt a re-codification of gendered power. Florence Stratton has developed two models to categorise different manifestations of the Mother Africa trope specific to the African male literary tradition, one known as '"the pot of culture" strand' which 'analogizes woman to the heritage of African values, an unchanging African essence'; the other '"the sweep of history" strand' in which women serve 'as an index of the state of the nation' (41).[11] Both strands reverberate in McCall Smith's Mma Ramotswe novels, though they are much more light-heartedly employed, and have been given a mildly gender-sensitive revision where necessary. Fundamental gender stereotypes, on the other hand, are never 'seriously challenged' (Bettinger np). None of this speaks for an earnest attempt at renegotiating contemporary African identities; all is non-confrontational and non-threatening and thus geared towards playful, reassuring entertainment.

From the very beginning we learn that Mma Ramotswe is an unusual lady, a single nearly middle-aged woman without dependants, but a respected member of the community for her integrity, poise and practical wisdom. Whatever she 'lacks' in terms of conventional 'African womanhood' – a spouse and (preferably plenty of) offspring – she gradually 'acquires' over the course of the first couple of volumes. Her relationship to both her fiancé and her children, however, is anything but ordinary, even though they all seem to be leading very commonplace lives. Mr J L B Matekoni might be Botswana's most capable mechanic and the kindliest bachelor — in many other matters he is inept and clumsy. Whether it is his impertinent housekeeper who takes the better of him, or the paperwork in his garage, things always improve when Mma Ramotswe delicately intervenes. 'There was nothing that Mma Ramotswe could not do — in his [Mr J L B Matekoni's] view, at least. She could run Botswana if only they would give her the chance' (*CCL* 164). Clearly, it is the women who are the most capable characters in the narratives; they are the ones who run detective agencies, orphan farms, or discrete typing schools for ham-fisted men, and they are the ones to sort out the more mundane matters of daily living. '"We need more women in public life," said Dr Maketsi [one of Mma Ramotswe's clients]. "They are very practical people, women. Unlike us men."' (*LDA* 196).

Unsurprisingly, then, it is Mma Ramotswe who eventually takes care of the children which Mma Potokwane, the pushy matron of the orphan farm, had forced on her soft-hearted fiancé. They are of Masarwa (or 'Bushman') origin, and one is wheelchair-bound and thus doubly marginalised in terms of physical disability and ethnic background. Mma Ramotswe, however, has 'no time for those who had raised an eyebrow when she and Mr J L B Matekoni had taken on these children' (*CCL* 156–57).

> There should be room in our hearts for all the people of this country, she said, and those people are our brothers and sisters too. This is their place as much as it is ours. (*CCL* 156)

In Mma Ramotswe's ideal Botswana, then, there is no place for racial or any other discrimination, even less so in her compassionate heart. (With the exceptions, perhaps, of Nigerians whose country, together with South Africa, habitually serves as the backdrop for vice and evil). In 'the best-run state in Africa' (*LDA* 152) everyone has a right to some happiness in their lives, and if there are troublesome mysteries, Mma Ramotswe is prepared to look into the matter. Indeed, she is more of an agony aunt than a hardened investigator, operating on decency, gut feeling and common sense.[12] And if a case proves particularly challenging, Mma Ramotswe retreats to homely, domestic matters in order to anchor herself; the drinking of bush tea and the preparation of the most ordinary of all vegetables:

> It was time to take the pumpkin out of the pot and eat it. In the final analysis, that was what solved these big problems of life. You could think and think and get nowhere, but you still had to eat your pumpkin. That brought you down to earth. That gave you a reason for going on. Pumpkin. (*LDA* 85)

Lest we forget: whether a symbol of tradition or the investigator's peace of mind, the essence is in the pumpkin.

In sum, there is nothing really 'mysterious' about Mma Ramotswe's way of life, but plenty that is wonderfully comforting:

> She was a good detective, and a good woman. A good woman in a good country, one might say. She loved her country, Botswana, which is a place of peace, and she loved Africa, for all its trials. I am not ashamed to be called an African patriot, said Mma Ramotswe. I love all the people whom God made, but I especially know how to love the people who live in this place. They are my people, my brothers and sisters. It is my duty to help them to solve the mysteries in their lives. That is what I am called to do. (*LDA* 4)

Such generosity of the heart can only find room in the generosity of an ample body, which Mma Ramotswe is nothing but very happy with: 'she was proud of being a traditionally built African lady, unlike these terrible, stick-like creatures one saw in the advertisements' (*LDA* 195). While her largeness occasionally provides comic relief – such as in the frequent contrast to her tiny white van, to which she is very attached, but which can hardly contain her ample figure; or the incident in which she nearly suffocates an intruder by lying on the bed he is using as a hiding place (*CCL* 17–19)[13] – the beauty of her body is never doubted. Nor, should I say, are its benefits. When one of her female clients is nervous about consulting her, she (the client)

> was soon put at ease by the comfortable, overweight figure sitting behind the desk. It was rather like speaking to a doctor or a priest, she thought; in such consultations nothing that one could possibly say would shock. (*LDA* 139)

Mma Ramotswe's father, the late Obed Ramotswe, had already noted that 'Precious was like her mother, who was a good fat woman' (*LDA* 28); and so eventually Mma Ramotswe turns into Everyone's Mother, despite her biological childlessness and the traumatic experience of losing her own at an early age. Readers will be quick to learn that the loving relationship between father and daughter is the true foundation of the protagonist's life and that his down-to-earth philosophy has become her personal yardstick. 'And what', she muses again and again when faced with yet another troubling issue, 'would my late Daddy have thought of him [it]?' (*MBG* 5). Obed Ramotswe's reminiscences make up a large part of the opening novel; he is the true linchpin to the novels' imagined Botswana and its evocative past. It is through her memories of him that Mma Ramotswe has a sense of self and of tradition, and it is these recollections which help her re-order her present realities.[14] For the Botswana of the here and now is very much different to the country perpetually remembered.

> There were many selfish people about these days. . . . Mma Ramotswe knew that this was what happened when towns became bigger and people became strangers to one another; she knew, too, that this was a consequence of increasing prosperity, which, curiously enough, just seemed to bring out greed and selfishness. But even if she knew why all this happened, it did not make it any easier to bear. The rest of the world might become as rude as it wished, but this was not the way of things in Botswana and she would always defend the old Botswana way of doing things. (*CCL* 2)[15]

It is the image of Africa as the welcoming, nurturing continent where people of all colours and creed can find a peaceful place to live which is constantly projected in the novels — an Africa which, for Obed Ramotswe, was his 'mother and. . . father' (*LDA* 17). It is also the image of a stable nation-state which, in the light of the problems of globalisation or internal security, allows a sense of socio-economic stability and political order. It is a fiction not only shared by the protagonist and her imaginary acolytes, but also perhaps by the implied author and his numerous readers. It is, moreover, an Africa treasured by many (former) expatriates, who might recognise themselves in another of Mma Ramotswe's clients. When an American lady returns to Botswana hoping to bring closure to a personal mystery, she recalls this sense of painful longing for her 'true-blue homeland':

> [Back in Washington] I missed Botswana, and not a day went past, not a day, when I would not think about it. It was like an ache. I would have given anything to be able to walk out of my house and stand under a thorn tree or look up at that great white sky. (*TOG* 32)

Perhaps this yearning belongs to what Dennis Walder has addressed as 'one aspect of cultural connection –

remembering – and in particular, the way memory may connect us across national and historical as well as personal boundaries' ('Remembering Rousseau' 423). It is this craving for an imagined (African) home – or better: *Heimat* – that breaches all boundaries in the texts; racial, national, and personal, real or imagined. As the American continues:

> I think that I can say that I had never been happier in my life. We had found a country where the people treated one another well, with respect, and where there were values other than the grab, grab, grab which prevails back home. I felt humbled, in way. Everything about my own country seemed so shoddy and superficial when held up against what I saw in Africa. People suffered here, and many of them had very little, but they had this wonderful feeling for others. (*TOG* 27)

While not everyone can have all their desires quenched, Mr J L B Matekoni finds fulfilment in the figure of Mma Ramotswe. At the end of the opening novel, in a scene which amalgamates colonial, revisionist, and very personal longings in what Bettinger describes as 'a conflation of femininity, landscape and Africa' (np) she finally agrees to become his wife. So over-determined is this postcolonial-nostalgic revision of the Mother Africa trope that it cannot be presented other than in kitschy (though tongue-in-cheek) Hollywood fashion:

> The sun went, and it was dark. He sat beside her in the comfortable darkness and they listened, contentedly, to the sounds of Africa settling down for the night... He looked at her in the darkness, at this woman who was everything to him — mother, Africa, wisdom, understanding, good things to eat, pumpkins, chicken, the smell of sweet cattle breath, the white sky across the endless, endless bush, and the giraffe that cried, giving its tears for women to daub on their baskets; O Botswana, my country, my place. (*LDA* 235)

Suffice to say that this image is not entirely unproblematic in its hyperbolic, if not gaudy interpretation. While eluding widespread representations of Africa as the 'lost continent', it contains the danger of demoting Botswana to a static, exotic setting while denying its social dynamics and cultural complexities.[16] The irony, however, with which these images are laced, helps create a distance to the texts' nostalgic projections and thus permits at least a modicum of critical awareness towards their improbability (cf Hutcheon 7, 9).

Ultimately, the immense popularity of the books suggests that they allow readers to participate in a collective fantasy which helps them temporarily escape their daily trials and tribulations (cf Frost np). As Janice Radway in her study on reading popular romance fiction concludes,

> real people can use the romance [or any other formula fiction] to address their unmet needs experienced precisely because that ideal relationship [or world] is made highly improbable by the institutional structure and engendering practices of contemporary society. (221)

And though we should ultimately be committed to global justice and social change, a temporary escape is not necessarily a bad thing — as long as we don't forget that the essence is *not* only in the pumpkin.

Notes

The author wishes to thank Wendy Knepper and Susanne Mühleisen for constructive comments on earlier drafts, and Dennis Walder for an inspiring exchange on nostalgia.

1 The novels will be abbreviated as follows: Alexander McCall Smith, *The No. 1 Ladies' Detective Agency (LDA); Tears of the Giraffe (TOG); Morality for Beautiful Girls (MBG); The Kalahari Typing School for Men (KTM); The Full Cupboard of Life (FCL); In the Company of Cheerful Ladies (CCL).*

2 See, for example, three recent conferences or conference sections on the topic; 'Postcolonial Postmortems: Crime Fiction in the New Literatures in English' at the international conference 'Transcultural English Studies' at Frankfurt/Main, ASNEL Conference, May 2004, 'Anomalous Eyes: Postcoloniality and the Detective' at the MLA in Philadelphia, December 2004, and 'Detective Fiction and Postcolonial Studies' at 'Le Roman policier: thèmes et perspectives/The Detective Novel: themes and perspective' in Paris, May 2005.

3 The 'writing-back paradigm' was initially presented by Bill Ashcroft, Gareth Griffiths, and Helen Tiffin, in *The Empire Writes Back*. Though widely criticised since then, it has remained influential on postcolonial literary studies until today.

4 For an essentially conservative view on crime fiction see Dennis Porter, *The Pursuit of Crime*; and John G Cawelti, *Adventure, Mystery, and Romance*; cf Andrew Pepper, 'Black Crime Fiction' (211). For an overview see Stephen Knight, *Crime Fiction, 1800–2000*.

5 Bryan S Turner, 'A Note on Nostalgia' (148); Dennis Walder, 'Remembering Rousseau' (424). For a detailed history of nostalgia see Svetlana Boym, especially Part I 'Hypochondria of the Heart: Nostalgia, History and Memory'.

6 For examples see McCall Smith (*LDA* 133; *KTM* 15–16; *CCL* 12–13). Cf Bettinger (np).

7 According to Suzanne Bray, Université Catholique de Lille, the books have also been well received in Botswana for projecting a widely popular image of the country (personal conversation, Paris, May 2005). Bettinger moreover notes that the series has deflected tourist interest from the Okavango Delta to Mochudi and Gaborone (np). See also Anon (np).

8 See also Dennis Walder, 'Writing, Representation and Postcolonial Nostalgia' (5).

9 For a detailed analysis of cultural nationalism see Frank Schulze-Engler, *Intellektuelle wider Willen*; for an introduction to the *négritude* movement see (F) Abiola

Irele, 'What is Négritude' and 'The Harlem Renaissance and the Negritude Movement'. Cf Simon Simonse, 'African Literature Between Nostalgia and Utopia'. Interestingly, one of the most celebrated poetic texts of the *négritude* by Aimé Césaire echoes ideas of *nostos* and *algia* in its title: *Cahier d'un retour au pays natal* (*Notebook of a Return to My Native Land*).

10 For examples see: Kathleen McLuskie, and Lyn Innes; Mineke Schipper, 'Mother Africa on a Pedestal'; Abena P A Busia, 'Silencing Sycorax'; Rebecca Stott, 'The Dark Continent'; Florence Stratton, *Contemporary African Literature and the Politics of Gender*.

11 Note how the 'pot' of the 'pot of culture strand' beautifully matches the 'pumpkin'.

12 'things that appeared to be mysteries were usually no such thing. The unexplained was unexplained not because there was anything beyond explanation, but simply because the ordinary, day-to-day explanation had not made itself apparent' (*CCL* 15).

13 Incidentally, or maybe not quite, the intruder leaves a most luscious pumpkin in exchange for the trousers he had lost trying to escape and which Mma Ramotswe then draped over her veranda. The mysterious pumpkin and its unknown donor become the overarching 'case' in the final novel.

14 Cf Justin Cartwright's novel *White Lightning* (2002): '"memory is a reordering of the present: it can cast a shadow forwards"', quoted in Walder ('Remembering Rousseau' 429); Boym (xvi). See, for example, father's (1) and daughter's (2) understanding of race: (1) 'there is no difference between white men and black men; we are all the same; we are just people' (*LDA* 19); (2) 'Black people, white people: same air' (*CCL* 171).

15 See also McCall Smith (*FCL* 6).

16 Bettinger moreover cautions against an 'undeconstructed notion of simplicity [that] signifies the kind of "Africanness" which is intelligible to Western readers since the modernist cult of "primitivism"' (np).

Works Cited

Anon. 'Bookreporter.com – Author Profile: Alexander McCall Smith' (Author Talk Apr. 2004). <http://bookreporter.com/authors/au-smith-alexander-mccall.asp>. Accessed 10 Nov. 2004.

Ashcroft, Bill, Gareth Griffiths and Helen Tiffin. *The Empire Writes Back: Theory and Practice in Post-Colonial Literatures.* London: Routledge, 1989.

Berlins, Marcel. 'Precious Little Happenings'. *Guardian* Saturday 19 July 2003. <http://books.guardian.co.uk/reviews/generalfiction/0,6121,1001171,00.html>. Accessed 10 Nov. 2004.

Bettinger, Elfi. 'Riddles in the Sands of the Kalahari: Detectives at Work in Botswana'. *Postcolonial Postmortems: Crime Fiction in a Transcultural Perspective.* Ed. Christine Matzke, and Susanne Mühleisen. Amsterdam: Rodopi, forthcoming.

Boehmer, Elleke. 'Motherlands, Mothers and Nationalist Sons: Representations of Nationalism and Women in African Literature'. *"From Commonwealth to Post-Colonial"*. Ed. Anna Rutherford. Mundelstrup: Dangaroo Press, 1992. 229–47.

Boym, Svetlana. *The Future of Nostalgia.* New York: Basic Books, 2001.

Busia, Abena P. A. 'Silencing Sycorax: On African Colonial Discourse and the Unvoiced Female'. *Cultural Critique* Winter (1989–90): 81–104.

Cartwright, Justin. *White Lighting.* London: Sceptre, 2002.

Cawelti, John G. *Adventure, Mystery, and Romance: Formula Stories as Art and Popular Culture.* Chicago: U of Chicago P, 1976.

Césaire, Aimé. *Notebook of a Return to My Native Land/Cahier d'un retour au pays natal.* 1939. Trans. Mireille Rosello with Annie Pritchard. 1956. London: Bloodaxe, 1995.

Christian, Ed, ed. *The Post-Colonial Detective.* Houndmills: Palgrave, 2001.

Davis, Fred. *Yearning for Yesterday: A Sociology of Nostalgia.* New York: The Free Press, 1979.

Fischer-Hornung, Dorothea, and Monika Mueller, eds. *Sleuthing Ethnicity: The Detective in Multiethnic Crime Fiction.* Madison, NJ: Fairleigh Dickinson UP, 2003.

Frost, Caroline. 'Alexander McCall Smith: Profile' (Saturday 14 Feb. 2004 11.15pm–11.45pm). <http://www.bbc.co/bbcfour/documentaries/profile/mccall-smith.shtml>. Accessed 10 Nov. 2004.

Hutcheon, Linda. 'Irony, Nostalgia, and the Postmodern' (1–14). <http://www.library.utoronto.ca/utel/criticism/hutchinp.html>. Accessed 19 Mar. 2005.

Irele, (F) Abiola. 'The Harlem Renaissance and the Negritude Movement'. *The Cambridge History of African and Caribbean Literature.* Vol. 2. Ed. F Abiola Irele and Simon Gikandi. Cambridge: Cambridge UP, 2004. 759–84.

——. 'What is Négritude'. *The African Experience in Literature and Ideology.* London: Heinemann, 1981. 67–88.

Knight, Stephen. *Crime Fiction, 1800–2000: Detection, Death, Diversity.* Houndmills: Palgrave Macmillan, 2004.

Matzke, Christine. 'Musical Passages: Colonial and Post-Colonial Readings of West African Music'. *Zeitschrift für Anglistik und Amerikanistik* 49.3 (2001): 244–55.

McCall Smith, Alexander. *The Full Cupboard of Life.* Edinburgh: Polygon, 2003.

——. *In the Company of Cheerful Ladies.* Edinburgh: Polygon, 2004.

——. *The Girl Who Married a Lion.* Edinburgh: Canongate, 2004.

——. *The Kalahari Typing School for Men.* 2002. Edinburgh: Polygon, 2003.

——. *Morality for Beautiful Girls.* 2001. New York: Anchor Books, 2002.

——. *The No. 1 Ladies' Detective Agency.* 1998. New York: Anchor Books, 2002.

——. *Tears of the Giraffe.* 2000. London: Abacus, 2003.

McLuskie, Kathleen, and Lyn Innes. 'Women and African Literature'. *Wasafiri* 8 (1988): 3–7.

p'Bitek, Okot. 'Pop Music, Bishops and Judges'. *Africa's Cultural Revolution.* Nairobi: Macmillan Books for Africa, 1973. 1–5.

——. *Song of Lawino*. Nairobi: East African Publishing House, 1966.

Pearson, Nels C., and Marc Singer. 'CFP: Postcoloniality and the Detective'. Email from Mark Singer. 9 Dec. 2004.

Pepper, Andrew. 'Black Crime Fiction'. *The Cambridge Companion to Crime Fiction*. Ed. Martin Priestman. Cambridge: Cambridge UP, 2003. 209–26.

Porter, Dennis. *The Pursuit of Crime: Art and Ideology in Detective Fiction*. New Haven: Yale UP, 1981.

Radway, Janice A. *Reading the Romance: Women, Patriarchy, and Popular Literature*. 1984. Chapel Hill: U of North Carolina P, 1991.

Random House website. <http://www.randomhouse.com/features/mccallsmith/ask.html>. Accessed 10 May 2005.

Robertson, Roland. *Globalization: Social Theory and Global Culture*. 1992. London: Sage, 1996.

Schipper, Mineke. 'Mother Africa on a Pedestal: The Male Heritage in African Literature and Criticism'. *Women in African Literature Today*. ALT 15. London: James Currey, 1987. 35–54.

Schulze-Engler, Frank. *Intellektuelle wider Willen: Schriftsteller, Literatur und Gesellschaft in Ostafrika 1960–1980*. Essen: Die Blaue Eule, 1992.

Simonse, Simon. 'African Literature Between Nostalgia and Utopia: African Novels since 1953 in the Light of the Modes-of-Production Approach'. *Research in African Literatures* 13.4 Winter (1982): 451–87.

Stott, Rebecca. 'The Dark Continent: Africa as Female Body in Haggard's Adventure Fiction'. *Feminist Review* 32 Summer (1989): 69–89.

Stratton, Florence. *Contemporary African Literature and the Politics of Gender*. London: Routledge, 1994.

Turner, Bryan S. 'A Note on Nostalgia'. *Theory, Culture & Society* 4 (1987): 147–56.

Walder, Dennis. 'Remembering Rousseau: Nostalgia and the Responsibilities of the Self'. *Third World Quarterly* 26.3 (2005): 423–30.

——. 'Writing, Representation and Postcolonial Nostalgia' (1–10). The Blackwell Lecture 2004. Centre for the History of the Book, Institute for Advanced Studies in the Humanities. The University of Edinburgh. <http://www.arts.ed.ac.uk/chb/blackwell-lecture04.htm>. Accessed 30 May 2005.

Reviews

The Purposeful Silence of the Artist in Full Flight

Anthony Ilona

A Distant Shore
Caryl Phillips
Vintage, London, 2004, pb
312pp ISBN 0 0994 2888 1 £6.99
www.randomhouse.co.uk

Dancing in the Dark
Caryl Phillips
Secker & Warburg, London, 2005, hb
224pp ISBN 0 436 205831 £12.99
www.randomhouse.co.uk

Few novelists have made more of uncertainty and irresolution in human interaction than Caryl Phillips. These concerns are embedded within the very structural composition of his work. They can be said to be definitive themes of the work of any one of a number of modern and contemporary writers but in Phillips' fiction they are so insistent that there is now, with the publication of his eighth novel, a compelling philosophical intensity to their recurrence.

Uncertainty and irresolution percolate through Phillips' fiction. They precede the revelation of a connection between characters and they constitute the fabric of these characters' inner lives. They surface in Phillips' formal aesthetic as a counterpoint to the clear-cut classifications, continuities and foreclosures associated with the progressive logic of enlightened reasoning. Such logic is deemed by Phillips – most notably stated in the final chapter of his 1987 travelogue, *The European Tribe* – to fall short in its advancement of humankind's capacity for empathy, tolerance and change. Neither the representation of human intercourse nor internal reflection are allowed to develop for too long in Phillips' stories without a corresponding sense of hesitation or detachment. The abiding impression of something no longer there but something that intrudes upon the effort to make sense of people and place remains the metaphysical motif in his work. For this reason Phillips might be accused of having a bleak vision — in the style of, say, a Conrad or a Naipaul. However, uncertainty and irresolution define Phillips' characters' lives only in so far as they are key signs of a vulnerability that allows people to recognise and connect with each other as human beings. 'I wander in the darkness that makes human beings of us all', says the conflicted protagonist of his latest novel.

In Phillips' fiction, the modern world is populated with uprooted individuals of diverse backgrounds. These individuals invariably find themselves in a new place and amongst strangers as a result of some past experience – recent or remote – of social upheaval, and they do so without the necessary psychic preparation and aftercare to fully integrate into their new circumstance. Religious persecution, the Atlantic slave trade, the Holocaust, World War, mass migration and more become the pre-text (sic) in Phillips' stories for the invention of characters whose lives coincide, overlap, become entangled and are eventually pulled apart. As such, there is no straightforward comprehension or sense of security within and between characters who – even after they meet, console and affirm each other – continue to vibrate with the pain of separation from community, culture and kin.

This much is also evident in Phillips' two most recently published novels, *A Distant Shore* and *Dancing in the Dark*. Both are concerned with the disorienting effects on the psyche of a personal

Wasafiri Vol. 21, No. 1 March 2006, pp. 72–91
ISSN 0269-0055 print/ISSN 1747-1508 online © 2006 Wasafiri
http://www.tandf.co.uk/journals DOI: 10.1080/02690050500475955
Routledge Taylor & Francis Group

history of separation and loss and with the transformative potential such effects can have on the nature of human interaction.

A Distant Shore is set in the near-contemporary and tells the tale of two protagonists, Dorothy Jones and Solomon Bartholomew. Dorothy is a newly retired, former schoolteacher and Solomon is the Caretaker of a regenerated cul-de-sac in the fictional northern English town of Stoneleigh — the same location Dorothy has chosen as her retreat. In the scheme of their overwrought lives, Dorothy, aged 55, and Solomon, aged 30, encounter each other on only a handful of occasions. Indeed, they barely get to know each other beyond a mutually cautious introduction before Dorothy learns – second-hand – of Solomon's untimely death. Though their encounters are brief, the impression Dorothy and Solomon make on each other provides the only relief in a 'coarse' and 'bracken-strewn' environment devoid of much human sustenance.

This relationship between Dorothy and Solomon is the latest manifestation in Phillips' work of what he describes as, 'th[at] most explosive of all relationships, seldom written about, seldom explained' but most often 'feared, observed, hated' (*Shelter* 10–11). It is the *black man–white woman* relationship that has been a key dimension of Phillips' literary output since the production of his 1984 playscript, *The Shelter*. Though their encounters are chaste, the mere sight of Dorothy visiting Solomon for the proverbial cup of tea or alighting at her doorstep from his car is enough to provoke 'the greatest conflict, the most fear, [and] the most loathing' (10) within the provincial English enclave of Stoneleigh. This much is implied in *A Distant Shore* as the motive for Solomon being discovered face down in Stoneleigh's local canal little more than a year after his own settlement there.

The premature death of Solomon becomes the final straw for an individual who has struggled to maintain her normal frame of reference after a series of let-downs and failures in her own life that include separation and divorce from a thirty-year marriage to an adulterous husband, the death of both her parents in close succession, the loss of her sister to cancer and forced early retirement. '[T]here is something comforting about hearing that they are finished', Dorothy reflects in denial of the end of one of her post-marital affairs, 'implying as it does that they were actually started' (*Distant* 235). Henceforth a combination of suppressed grief and an acute sense of detachment turns Dorothy into an unreliable narrator of her own memories and of her impact on the lives of others. Most impressive here is Phillips' inflection of Dorothy's reflexive first person voice. He evenly sustains the refined, limpid and sometimes girlishly naïve register of his West Midlands-derived protagonist.

Solomon's story is as fulsome as Dorothy's and rendered in interchanging sections of the novel. Dorothy's perception of his unassuming and routine presence in Stoneleigh belies a background more riven with incident and adventure than her own. Solomon, the reader learns, is a legally classified asylum seeker from an unnamed West African country in the throes of inter-tribal civil war. This country could quite easily be imagined as Sierra Leone or Liberia given the novel's contemporary setting. Phillips recounts Solomon's harrowing tale of service in the brutal rebel army and his flight to England across multiple African and European borders in such a protracted, linear way that this section of the novel seems much heavy-going — in juxtaposition with Dorothy's own relentless tale of woe. Its most stirring passages are contained in Solomon's witnessing of the vengeful execution and rape of his mother, father and two sisters by government troops. It is a scene that continues to haunt Solomon long after the event and it is only through the kindness of strangers that Dorothy encounters Solomon in the comparatively thriving condition he appears to be in when they first meet — albeit suffering the harassment of persistent racist hate-mail.

Once their stories are told, the affinity between Dorothy and Solomon, different as they are, remains clear to the reader. They intuit from each other the mutual need for shelter from worlds struck by disaster. 'I had a feeling that Solomon understood me', Dorothy says towards the end of the novel. Their tolerance, discretion and courtesy towards each other are in direct contrast to the complacency of almost everyone else they encounter. This, as the implied logic of Phillips' fiction would have it, is the gift of good grace endowed upon personalities tempered by experiences of bereavement and abandonment. Each demonstrates an open-minded accommodation of the other's vulnerability. This open-mindedness is, in Phillips' work, the humanising upshot of egos/identities held in check by uncertainty and irresolution. It is the acknowledgment of intervening forces of dispossession and possession at work in the modern universe that are not subject to timetables or borders. In this sense, *A Distant Shore* is a natural extension of the mid-nineteenth-century tale of the plantation master's daughter, Emily Cartwright, and the eponymous slave in Phillips' fourth published novel, *Cambridge* (1991); or of the wartime story of Joyce and Travis in his subsequent novel, *Crossing the River* (1993). As in *A Distant Shore*, those earlier stories render brief and affective encounters that are tragically cut short by the divisive ideals at large in supposedly rational and progressive social contexts.

By contrast, Phillips' latest novel contemplates what happens when the very thing that is pulled apart is identity itself and the effect – creative as well as reductive – this can have on the individual's ability to connect with others. *Dancing in the Dark* is a novel based on the life of the distinguished Broadway entertainer, Egbert Austin ('Bert') Williams. Williams remains renowned for his performances in the early twentieth-century New York theatres and music halls alongside his life-long stage partner and friend, George Walker. Williams and Walker developed a Vaudeville-style double act that brought them widespread recognition and international acclaim. It also contributed, after Walker's death in 1911, to Williams' eventual status as the highest-paid entertainer in the US — with the likes of Buster Keaton, Maurice Barrymore, Fanny Brice and Florenz Ziegfield among his friends and admirers. *Dancing in the Dark* is a lyrical, impressionistic and, for the most part, faithful invocation in fiction of the almost forgotten biographical details of Bert Williams' life and career. Narrated in three acts spanning the early, middle and late periods of Williams' life, this novel contemplates the fractured identity and increasing isolation of this sensitive, cerebral and misunderstood performer.

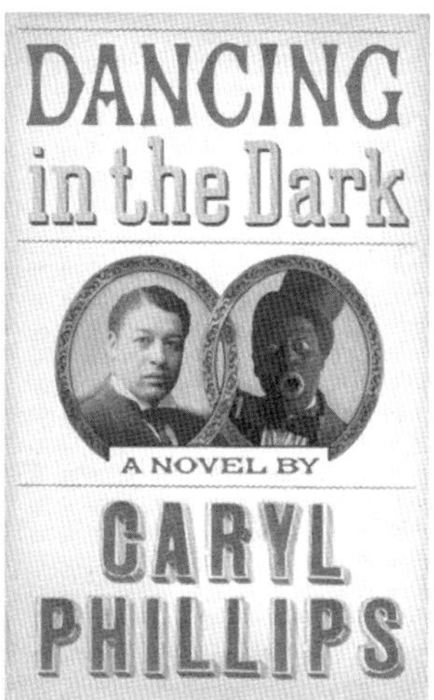

Born in the Caribbean in the mid-1870s (conflicting accounts record his birth date between the years 1874 to 1876), it was on a street corner in San Francisco that Bert Williams, in his late teens, met his match for talent and ambition in the banjo-player, George Walker. Williams and Walker created and refined an on-stage dynamic that soon brought them prosperity. Their act consisted of the larger of the two, Williams, playing the unadventurous, unlucky and naïve foil to the get-rich-quick scams of Walker's self-regarding dandy. Their costumes comprised of ill-fitted formal attire (usually second-hand top-hat and tails) and 'black-face' make-up fashioned from a purée of burnt cork mixed with water or from greasepaint. This mask is a key component of the traditional costume derived from the minstrel show, a theatrical genre pioneered by white working-class entertainers in 1830s America. In its earliest days, black entertainers were prohibited from performing in minstrel shows and later performers chose to steer clear of what they generally saw as a dehumanising genre. By the time Williams and Walker performed in its costumes at the turn of the new century, the genre had reached a definitive peak. In billing their own performances under such titles as 'A Lucky Coon', 'Sons of Ham' and 'The Two Real Coons', Williams and Walker were initially considered to be the pioneering, ironic appropriators of this genre away from its hitherto exclusive status as the domain of white entertainers. It is the most popular of these three shows, 'The Two Real Coons', that the US film-maker Spike Lee adapts as homage to Williams and Walker in his cinematic critique of the representation of African Americans in the US popular entertainment industry, *Bamboozled* (2000).

Phillips' concern in *Dancing in the Dark* is with the psychological complexes and social withdrawal that took its toll on the life of Bert Williams as a result of his visible public profile as an entertainer known for performing in 'black-face'. Phillips renders well the mental distinction and courage required by a young Williams to overcome the deep sense of shame felt on his first dressing room experience of applying the minstrel mask: '[A]s I smear the black into my already sable skin, as I put on my lips, I am leaving behind Egbert Austin Williams. However, I can, at any time, reclaim this man with soap and water and the rugged application of a coarse towel' (57). This habit of detachment would later result in his emotional guardedness and in his unease in communicating with others. Indeed, it is a more mature Bert Williams that, later in the novel, lapses into virtual silence in his relations with his long-suffering wife, Lottie. Phillips represents his condition in similar terms as the above:

> [A]s she set down the newspaper she looked through her husband as though he was not present. He wanted to talk to her, but he understands that in order to do so he will have to travel [. . .] back to a place and to a time when he was not yet two people. The one pitying the other. (127)

Williams' hesitance in communicating with the one person closest to him in life is the measure of just how severely conflicted his own personality has become by the bothersome clown-mask. This silence and unease is less some kind of psychic paralysis than an extension of his earlier act of compartmentalisation. It is a deliberate refusal to perform in private for fear that his actions may fulfil and reinforce the stereotype that he commits to reproducing in the public arena. 'Bert behaves', his partner George Walker observes, 'as though his make up is an extra layer of skin that he cannot rub away' (110).

However, Phillips' mellifluent – and, frankly, a little too audibly musical – prose offers no balm to the intensifying image of social alienation and internal division that is his subject. Bert Williams' conflicted mind remains further compounded by his intellectual dissatisfaction with the alternative sources of identification available to him beyond the fading irony of his appropriated stage mask. There is no satisfaction with the *en vogue* African revivalism signalled by the domestic and international success of their 1903 musical, 'In Dahomey' — a show with a 'back-to-Africa theme' developed by and starring Williams and Walker themselves and featuring an unprecedented fifty-strong all-black cast. Nor does Williams find satisfaction in the burgeoning radicalism and confrontational 'fighting-talk' of his partner George Walker who, having altogether dispensed with the minstrel mask, admonishes his partner with the words, '[W]e coloured Americans no longer recognize you for we are trying to move on' (100). There are also the cosmetic privileges of bodily and economic assimilation — each respectively demonstrated in the effects of the 'hair-straightening and skin-bleaching creams' popular among the female cast members of 'In Dahomey' and in Williams' reluctant acceptance of the invitation to see out his stage career as the only black, and 'black face', performer in Florenz Ziegfield's long-running musical variety show, the 'Follies'.

For Williams, these various responses to the social disadvantages of his status as an African American performer in the early twentieth century seem in their reactionary zeal to be in danger of repeating the same racist myths that gave rise to minstrelsy. They are inconsistent with the creative approach to self-determination and self-reconstruction gleaned from his own private reading of the works of Booker T Washington and W E B Dubois. Instead, Phillips presents Williams' social withdrawal as a commitment to remain, 'as purposefully silent as a bird's flight' (17). This phrase is important to Phillips as it also appears in the final paragraph of *A Distant Shore*. It encapsulates what Bénédict Ledent, in her pioneering study of Phillips' work, describes in reference to the author himself as 'the odyssey of the artist' (11). This odyssey and its observed 'silence' necessarily leaves Williams disavowed of ideological bias and ever open to the possibility of change. Uncertainty and irresolution therefore become the hallmark of the performer in motion, loyal only to the transformative potential of his art: 'Mr. Bert Williams has developed his timing to the point where he knows how to delay and hold back. The audience may think they are watching a powerless man but they are, in fact, watching art' (121).

To a large extent this ethos is mirrored in *Dancing in the Dark*'s fragmented, episodic structure and chronological interweaving of the biographical details of Bert Williams' life. Phillips presents Williams' life story in such a way as to make the reader participate in the interpretive work of narrative re-construction. The novel form is so imbued with the idea of continuity and closure that Phillips makes it the reader's task to imaginatively fill the breaks and splinters of absent information that perforate the archive of a life lost to time and history. Ledent herself confirms this much in terms not dissimilar to those quoted above in mitigation of Williams' 'art': '[T]he gaps and silences punctuating the text are not artistic failures but evidence of a complex fictional strategy that requires concentration and imagination on the readers part' (115). This is a common formal trait in Phillips' work that, like Williams' stagecraft, defines the order of his fictional odyssey. It signals Phillips' dispensation with the ideological intrusion of the prescriptive author who would impose continuity and conclusion when expressing facts about the past where none may actually exist. Elsewhere Phillips has been criticised for 'abandoning straightforward linear narration' and for having 'yet to essay a truly large fiction' (Stranger 198). The problem with *Dancing in the Dark*, however, lies less in its deferral of continuity and definition in the construction of its narrative than in the heavy-handedness of its ending. Here, in his epilogue, Phillips lurches toward closure by speculating on a happy-ever-after scenario of reconciliation between Williams and his pre-mask childhood in The Bahamas. This un-ironic return to an imagined condition of wholeness contradicts all that has gone before in the form of Williams' fractured but creative personality. It is reminiscent of the much-disputed ending of Jean Rhys' novel *Wide Sargasso Sea* (1966) in its exploitation of the perspicacity of the novel form. That is, its use of the novel's capacity to express the inner as well as outer lives of its fictional characters; its ability to make human desire and intention visible beyond their outward concealment.[1] As with the childhood reunion hallucinated by Rhys' self-immolating protagonist – doubly named Antoinette Cosway/Bertha Mason – the integrity of Bert Williams' own life-long restraint and endurance in the face of social degradation seems compromised by the all-too easily satisfying leap back in time signalled by the image of reunion in the final paragraph of *Dancing in the Dark*.

Note

1 See E M Forster's discussion of the novel's annealing facility to simulate intimate knowledge as antidote to the 'spectre' of 'dim and makeshift' understanding that haunts the reality of human intercourse in his *Aspects of the Novel* (69–70).

Works Cited

Coetzee, J. M. *Stranger Shores: Essays 1986–1999*. London: Secker & Warburg, 2001.
Forster, E. M. *Aspects of the Novel*. 1927. London: Penguin, 1990.
Ledent, Bénédicte. *Contemporary World Writers: Caryl Phillips*. Manchester: Manchester UP, 2002.
Phillips, Caryl. Introduction. *The Shelter*. Oxford: Amber Lane Press, 1984.
—. *Cambridge*. London: Bloomsbury, 1991.
—. *Crossing the River*. London: Bloomsbury, 1993.
Rhys, Jean. *Wide Sargasso Sea*. 1966. London: Harmondsworth, Penguin, 1968.

Suman Gupta

The Ethics of Identity

Kwame Anthony Appiah

Princeton University Press, Princeton, 2004, hb
384pp ISBN 0 6911 2036 6 £18.95
www.pupress.princeton.edu

Appiah's most recent book is an attempt to reconcile identity politics with liberal political philosophy. This is concerned with identity politics in that Appiah addresses the kinds of social commitments and responsibilities, or ethics, that arise for individuals and states from the identification of (and with) social groups. Social groups are broadly understood as social attributions, alignments and allegiances in terms of race, gender, sexual orientation, nationality, class, religion, ethnicity, etc. Appiah doesn't engage with identity politics in the sense of delving into the particularities of a specific identity-based position, but in a panoptic fashion with regard to a wide variety of notions of belonging to social groups. This is identity politics in the contemporary social constructionist sense, associated with ongoing discussions of pluralism, diversity, and multiculturalism. In fact, Appiah does not use the phrase 'identity politics' himself, probably to avoid confusion with its older essentialist and particularist nuances, but it is pretty clear that identity politics in the wider sense is what he has in mind.

An attempt to bring together identity politics, thus understood, and liberal political philosophy is not new; pluralism, diversity, multiculturalism have been pondered and agonised over constantly by liberal philosophers, particularly since the 1970s, and are recognised as key concepts in liberal philosophy. What is new in Appiah's book is the strength of the desire for reconciliation with which this task is undertaken. Despite sympathies and convergences, liberal political philosophy and identity politics have had a resistant relationship, fraught with tensions and contradictions. Peter du Preez's comparatively early approach to this area, for instance, presented identity politics as a con which undermines liberal aspirations. John Rawls's attempts, in the course of the 1980s, to theorise pluralism in a well-ordered liberal society was largely undermined by his conceptual need to regard that society as closed. Charles Taylor's influential essay on multiculturalism in 1992, though sceptical of deep individualism, could give only qualified and limited approval to multiculturalist policies. In general, a liberal desire to recognise and empower social groups in their own terms and simultaneously maintain the rational freedoms of individuals (and majorities) in a liberal state has led to inconclusive weighing of prerogatives, overstatement of one position or the other, and been conducted with an air of unease and concern. Jürgen Habermas, Gerald Dworkin, Thomas Nagel, Amy Gutmann, Joseph Raz, John Gray, Michael Walzer, Will Kymlicka and others have criss-crossed this area, defiantly prescriptive and cautiously tentative at the same time, always optimistic and always on the verge of defeat. Appiah brings to this area a breezy confidence in reconciliatory possibilities, and engages in a kind of conversation with all the above-named — sorting out their problems along the way. To situate himself *vis-à-vis* these discordant liberal voices, and maintain a suitable distance from them at the same time, Appiah decides to read John Stuart Mill's works with approval, making Mill his *locus standi*. This is a useful methodological ploy since Mill can be regarded as both contextually anterior to much contemporary liberal thinking, and can be conveniently rediscovered and selectively appropriated as an authoritative vehicle for Appiah's ideas in the current context.

Appiah adopts two familiar strategies in the liberal philosophical tradition: one, he places an obvious-sounding and therefore ostensibly unquestionable characterisation of the individual-in-society at the heart of his argument; and two, with that in mind, his argument develops through the discernment of reasonable compromise between apparently opposed positions. In this instance, the characterisation of the individual in society, which is the substance of Chapter 1, is understood in terms of 'tell[ing] a story of one's life that hangs together', which entails ethically effective 'soul making' with reference to extant models of social identity but without losing sight of the distinctiveness of individual identity. For Appiah the models of social identity that are available are precisely collective identities like race, gender, nationality, class, religion, etc. The notion that individual identity and social identity are inextricably mutually defined and intermeshed has been the mainstay of liberal philosophy, but the *social* in 'social identity' has generally been conceptualised in as abstract and fluid a fashion as the *individual* in 'individual identity'. By giving the very idea of the *social* more definition, by presenting the *social* as constituted along the lines of existing collective identities, Appiah circumvents much of the resistance that liberal thinking feels with regard to identity politics. It is no longer necessary to ask 'what sort of society' or 'society in what context' or 'what kinds of social relations'; society is here already prefigured by collective identities. In brief, identity politics thereby becomes pre-legitimised as deriving from the inescapable constitution of the social, and therefore the unavoidable canvas against which negotiations between individual autonomy and state engineering have to be figured. This description of the individual in society also has the effect of rendering individuality more tractable, more like concretised and distinct overlappings of existing models of collective identity. Defences are thus also erected early against the neo-liberal politics that accepts an uncompromising inviolability of individuals.

The reasonable compromises follow with this central apprehension of the individual-in-society in place. In Chapter

2, conflicting subject-centred and social-centred accounts of autonomy are considered, and a way out is offered through, simplistically put, conceptual acceptance of both but with emphasis placed on one or the other according to need and existing practice. In Chapter 3 Appiah mediates the contradictions that arise between individual rights and collective rights. He rejects both hard individualism and hard pluralism, where 'hard' is understood as intransigent assertion; demonstrates the difficulties of adhering to absolute neutrality with respect to collective rights; and recommends, with numerous legalistic qualifications, a pragmatic disposition to 'neutrality as equal respect' on the part of a liberal state. Chapter 4 surveys different liberal attitudes to culture: as a primary good and as a social good; as something that has to be preserved at all costs or something that should be negotiated for progressive ends and harmonious coexistence; as expressed in different perceptions of diversity; in terms of whether diversity is desirable or whether universality should be championed. Unsurprisingly, in relation to the happening world Appiah finds that these oppositions are often not particularly debilitating, and decides that seeing anything as an ultimate or absolute good is undesirable. Somewhat paradoxical accommodative principles usually resolve apparent conceptual oppositions, he suggests, such as: 'upholding differences among groups may entail imposing uniformity within them' (151). To what degree a state should engineer the lives of individuals for their good and to what degree individuals should construct their own lives in a rational fashion is the question that is taken up in Chapter 5. That these are mutually determined is the reasonable answer that emerges here, with interesting discussions on the impediments that arise in, and some of the key factors that mediate, the relationship between individual and state (like the role of education and information provision). Finally, in Chapter 6 Appiah argues for the development of a cosmopolitanism which allows for reasonable, indeed inevitable and natural, biases and partialities. The apparent tautology is shown not to be one in actuality, and it is argued that such 'rooted cosmopolitanism' allows for meaningful dialogue across cultures and identities. This section is approached through the example of his father's patriotic cosmopolitanism — a personal touch that turns this book into a vindication of the author's own 'soul making'. That the rational self of liberal philosophy and the embodied authorial voice thereby become one may be received as a gesture of conviction, or be regarded as an inconvenient rhetorical stance that discourages dissent because dissent might be impolite if not unreasonable.

A great many issues and arguments are revolved in these chapters. One may quibble with specific formulations and inferences here, but on the whole these are all thought-provoking and useful and will, no doubt, interest philosophers working on these issues of our time. This is where I have a complaint of a general nature – not one that is confined to this study alone – addressed to the language and methodology of liberal philosophy at large, of which Appiah's book is a good example. This study revolves around abstractions which, despite relevant historical illustrations and references, ultimately fail to convey a sufficient awareness of our time. Illustrations surface like ripples only to get submerged again before their import can be grasped; the complexity of economic and political and ethical interrelationships is muted in favour of a wide range of references to prove or support abstractions that have, apparently, an autonomous self-contained flow. Fredric Jameson's dictum, 'Only historicize!', has little impact on Appiah's thinking. Amenable events are plucked *out* of history randomly, from different parts of the world, shorn off their material particularities, to cohere arbitrarily within the flow of abstractions, like so much flotsam and jetsam. And yet, this sort of opportunistic appeal to historical and social events doesn't render the abstractions about identity, society, self, etc convincingly all-embracing or (in a practical way) universally applicable — though the liberal register employed, and the tradition it derives from, seems to reach in that direction. Appiah's voice appears to speak for and on behalf of all humanity. I don't mean to say this is an impossible intellectual endeavour; I simply mean that in using the liberal methodology and register, Appiah, like many of his liberal forebears, defeats that ambition. At no point does he wonder, as Charles Taylor did, whether this liberal voice itself is necessarily constructed by the standards of 'North Atlantic civilization' (71). Following an interest in jurisprudence which is now firmly associated with the liberal tradition, Appiah often cites particular US civil law cases to anchor his general arguments to, but continues to treat his inferences as generalities rather than juridical particularities. He doesn't turn his thinking in upon its own historical contingencies and anchoring. A universal reach, I suspect, may be better attempted by dwelling more carefully on contextual and material details, or better anchored to a stronger sense of history and social and political materiality.

Works Cited

du Preez, Peter. *The Politics of Identity: Ideology and the Human Image*. Oxford: Basil Blackwell, 1980.
Nozick, Robert. *Anarchy, State and Utopia*. Oxford: Basil Blackwell, 1974.
Rawls, John. *Political Liberalism*. New York: Columbia UP, 1993.
——. *The Law of Peoples with 'The Idea of Public Reason Revisited'*. Cambridge, MA: Harvard UP, 1999.
Taylor, Charles. 'The Politics of Recognition'. *Multiculturalism: Examining the Politics of Recognition*. Ed. Amy Gutmann. Princeton: Princeton UP, 1994.

Hena Maes-Jelinek

Revisiting Slave Narratives

Judith Misrahi-Barak

Collection 'Les Carnets du Cerpac' n°2, Université Paul Valéry, Université Montpellier III, 2005
574pp ISBN 2 8426 9648 4 €20
http://publications.univ-montp3.fr/

In *The World, the Text, and the Critic* Edward Said writes that 'the critic is responsible to a degree for articulating those voices dominated, displaced or silenced by the textuality of texts' (53). At that stage in his career Said was still under Foucault's influence and gave the critic credit for bringing to life a reality abstracted in 'the textuality of the text'. But such an emergence from invisibility was first of all the achievement of the slave narratives, and only *then* of the critical studies that brought them to light mostly from the 1980s onwards in spite of a few earlier exceptions.

The narratives are an essential element of the foundation of African-American literature. They emerged from the abolitionist cause, whose aim was to make the public aware of the conditions of slavery, and they also served that cause. Originally, African-American literature was essentially oral and the narratives were first told then transcribed, thus creating a link between the oral and the written traditions. Apart from poems written by female slaves such as Phyllis Wheatley, they are the first trace of African-American writing. They finally came to attention at the time of the civil rights movement, and there is an obvious parallel between the political action of African Americans to assert their position in American society and the recognition of their ancestors' evocation, in literary texts, of their condition as slaves

If anything, the impressive volume collected and edited by Judith Misrahi-Barak brings to light the prolific creativity inspired by the subject of slavery. The essays were read at a conference organised by the editor at Paul Valéry University in Montpellier in 2003. They are divided into several sections including 'Thresholds', 'The Americas', 'The Anglophone Caribbean', and 'Africa and the Francophone Caribbean'. As Misrahi-Barak points out in her introduction, it was probably the first time that 'The American neo-slave narrative, which is generally granted pride of place, was considered side by side with the new generation of Caribbean neo-slave narratives, be they Francophone or Anglophone' (12–13). Indeed, apart from Equiano's *Interesting Narrative*, the writings of British slaves were not as well known as the literature of their American counterparts. However, the focus on similar experiences in various areas of the Americas is the more significant as the slave narratives written in America before the civil war as well as the neo-slave narratives written after it, including the twentieth-century novels pioneered by Margaret Walker's *Jubilee* in 1966, are generally about slavery in America only. On the contrary, novels by West Indian writers, especially Fred D'Aguiar and Caryl Phillips, recreate the experience of slavery and its contemporary consequences in both America and the Caribbean. The first and last chapters are by these two creative writers.

In his keynote address Fred D'Aguiar develops the original argument that Wilson Harris's intuitive fiction, especially *The Mask of the Beggar* (2003), which he analyses, and novels about slavery evince similar approaches to their subject: both are the fruit of a collective memory which counteracts Toni Morrison's statement 'we live in a land where the past is always erased' (quoted in this volume); they operate 'at the expense of fixed dualisms' (a feature emphasised in the essays on Caryl Phillips's novels); the characters leap back into history and forward from history into the present day; the artist's studio in Harris's novel creates 'a world for generating people and ideas', and 'becomes a living space for dead presences', and also, like the novel, slave narratives combine history with 'a mythical quest for freedom'.

Most of these points are discussed as major arguments in individual essays. Among the recurring subjects of reflection, in both narratives and essays, is the fact that learning to read and write was a way to emancipation (which we see tragically fictionalised in some of D'Aguiar's and Phillips's novels, but less appallingly so in David Dabydeen's *A Harlot's Progress*); also the assertion that 'studying *form* means hearing a black voice exclusively'.

The majority of the essays naturally emphasise the mnemonic role of the narratives. Interestingly, they illustrate different kinds of critical approaches, whether textual analysis, historiography, theory, and underline the importance of rewritings. The last section on 'Africa and the Francophone Caribbean' is written in French, as the papers were probably delivered at the conference. The essays discuss writers and works absent from the major corpus in English, namely Alex Haley's *Roots* and Patrick Chamoiseau's novels. There is also a comparative essay on Toni Morrison and Maryse Condé which emphasises their revisionary characters.

An apt conclusion to this collection is an extract from Caryl Phillips's novel, *A Distant Shore* (2003), which the writer read at the conference. It is preceded by comments he made on 'Our Modern World', in which he states that 'the make-up of our modern, increasingly globalized, world has been to a large extent determined by the events which surrounded the Atlantic Slave Trade.' He then points out the increasing pre-eminence of the subject of slavery in contemporary literature by writers of different origins, African, American, European, black and white. Most importantly, he refers to the 'inescapable legacy' of slavery and its concomitant racism in the modern world. This is substantiated in *A Distant Shore*, in which, in spite of the kindness his African protagonist, a refugee from a war-torn Africa, meets with, he finally falls prey to racist thugs. Phillips's conclusion is followed by a useful bibliography and by abstracts of each critique.

A few essays analyse similar aspects of the African and the Jewish diasporas as dealt with in some novels, which reminds us of Fanon's early comparison in *Peau noire, masque blanc* and of Phillips's frequent association of the two in his fiction and in West Indian culture generally with its frequent allusions to 'Babylon'.

Altogether, the volume throws light on the widespread and complex consequences of the slave trade. It is a must for anyone interested in the literary interpretation of slavery and its influence in our diasporic world.

Work Cited

Said, Edward. *The World, the Text and the Critic*. London: Faber & Faber, 1983.

Ursula Kluwick

The Great Art of Making Real: Salman Rushdie's *The Ground Beneath Her Feet*

Elsa Linguanti and Viktoria Tchernichova, eds

Edizioni ETS, Pisa, 2003
262pp ISBN 8 8467 0906 3 €15
www.edizioniets.com

Magic(al) Realism

Maggie Bowers

Routledge, London and New York, 2004
160pp ISBN 0 4152 6854 0 £10.99
www.routledge.com

Magic realism is a phenomenon that has received regular waves of attention throughout this century. Coined in the early 1920s in Germany in connection with a newly emergent style of painting, the term 'magic realism' has since travelled across countries, continents and cultures, and come to be applied to various artistic genres. Ironically, however, given the international and interdisciplinary success story of the term, 'magic realism' is no longer used for the style of painting for which it was coined. In fact, the term was never successful as a description of this artistic school, and it was even, eventually, discarded by Franz Roh, the man generally thought to be its originator, who adopted the by then more accepted term Neue Sachlichkeit (New Objectivity). Despite Roh's decision to abandon the expression 'magic realism', however, his book *Nach-Expressionismus, Magischer Realismus: Probleme der neuesten europäischen Malerei* (1925), which represents one of the first instances in which the term was used, was paramount in making the term 'magic realism' popular. It was through the translation of Roh's book that the term was circulated in both Europe and Latin America, where it was adopted and turned into an influential literary and cultural concept in the 1940s, before finally achieving international acclaim in the wake of the Latin American Boom. It is largely due to the impact of the Boom that magic realism is nowadays first and foremost associated with literature, and it is within this field that it has received most critical attention. Yet while the prominence of Latin American magic realist novels has led many critics to regard magic realism as a Latin American style of writing, magic realism has in the last few decades evolved into a fully global phenomenon.

It is one of the major assets of Maggie Ann Bowers's *Magic(al) Realism* that it does credit to the international character of magic realism. Though she stresses that magic realism can never be tied to geographical locations, Bowers devotes separate sections to variants of magic realism as they appear in Latin America, the English-speaking world and mainland Europe, thus both stressing the international appeal of magic realism and contesting the prominence of Latin American fiction in this field. Simultaneously, Bowers also highlights the fact that even within one location, magic realism is never 'one uncomplicated category', but that it surfaces in highly individual rather than homogeneous forms. In addition, Bowers stresses the international aspect as well as the diversity of magic realism by continuously drawing on an impressively wide range of magic realist works from across the literary world in order to illustrate her theory. Thus Bowers proposes an emphatically open and inclusive model of magic realism which leaves ample room for a writer's idiosyncrasies, and rejects restrictive definitions of the mode which are mainly concerned with establishing clear-cut definitions whose narrowness excludes much arguably magic realist writing.

One of the few facts that critics of magic realism agree on is, in Bowers's words, that magic realism is 'notoriously difficult to define'. Bowers's definition of magic realism seeks to resolve the current confusion surrounding the term by delineating three different forms of magic realism, which she regards as separate due to their derivation, as well as to their underlying concepts of magic. Thus Bowers differentiates between magic realism, which is based on an understanding of magic as 'the mystery of life' and which she defines as a 'term introduced in 1925 referring to art that attempts to produce a clear depiction of reality that includes a presentation of the mysterious elements of everyday life'; magical realism, which relies on a view of magic as 'anything spiritual or unaccountable by rational science', and which she describes as a 'term introduced in the 1940s referring to narrative art that presents extraordinary occurrences as an ordinary part of everyday reality', and marvellous realism, a term used in a Latin American context and coined in the 1940s 'to refer to narrative art that presents the mystical and magical elements as an integral part of everyday reality in Latin America'. 'Magic(al) realism', finally, is Bowers's umbrella term for forms that encompass aspects of both magic and magical realism.

Bowers's attempt to elucidate the unfortunate terminological chaos of magic realist criticism is decidedly innovative. It is doubtful, however, whether Bowers's proposal really corresponds to the contemporary state of affairs. Critics seem to use the terms magic and magical realism indiscriminately, with the choice between the two depending more on personal taste than on underlying theoretical concepts. Thus Bowers's differentiation between the two terms appears to be more a superimposition of an unusual concept than a description of current usage, the more so since her own employment of these terms is not always completely lucid or consistent.

If in the 1980s magic(al) realism was celebrated as a new and powerful form of expression for marginalised groups and cultures, the mode has since come under suspicion. Bowers acknowledges the ways in which magic realism has come to be exploited as a 'marketing tool' by publishing companies, and she draws attention to the fact that due to the hype of magic realism as a mode of writing particularly well-suited to non-Western cultural production, many cross-cultural writers have since rejected the term magic realism for their own writing. In an extremely well-balanced discussion, in which she cites many severe critics of magic realism, Bowers herself convincingly argues for the undiminished political possibilities of magic realism, suggesting that its adoption by so many writers from marginalised contexts indicates its potential 'as a liberating and transformative narrative mode'.

What renders Bowers's *Magic(al) Realism* such a valuable and comprehensive introduction is that in addition to literature, she also considers artefacts from other fields of cultural production. Though brief, her discussion of magic realist children's culture, film and painting is highly illuminating, and it alerts the reader to the impact of magic realism not only as a literary but a fully-fledged cultural phenomenon. In this context, Bowers's analysis of magic realism also proves exceptional in that she repeatedly draws attention to the importance of the cultural location of the audience in receiving a work as magic realist. It is one of the best aspects of her book that she concedes the possibility of non-magic realist readings of books which she regards as magic realist.

One of the most famous representatives of magic realism is Salman Rushdie, and it is with his work that Elsa Linguanti and Viktoria Tchernichova's collection *The Great Work of Making Real: Salman Rushdie's The Ground Beneath Her Feet* concerns itself. Linguanti and Tchernichova are the first to have undertaken the task of compiling a collection of essays devoted to one of Rushdie's less frequently discussed novels. Their purpose is to elucidate and explain the plethora of inter- and extra-textual references in Rushdie's novel, and this purpose is met admirably. Focussing on various different aspects of the novel's typically Rushdiean profusion of cultural resonances, the contributors illuminate Rushdie's indebtedness to Greek, Roman and Hindu mythology, the Bible, music, Rilke, colonial narrative, travel writing, the topography of Bombay, cultural history, and popular culture.

As a sourcebook which reveals Rushdie's mythological and other allusions and explains his cultural references, *The Great Work of Making Real* is very useful and informative. What most of the contributors to this collection fail to do, however, is to suggest any new readings of the novel based on their findings. Yet this seems to be based on a conscious decision by editor Elsa Linguanti, who reveals in her introduction that she prefers readings which focus on intertextual and textual features of literature to critical discussions which, by exceeding a mere text-centred analysis, 'end up dominating the book and eventually, acting from the outside'. It therefore remains left to others to use the valuable findings that *The Great Work of Making Real* offers in exciting and original interpretations of Rushdie's novel.

The editors Elsa Linguanti and Viktoria Tchernichova repeatedly stress their concern with textual accuracy, and Tchernichova, especially, deplores the textual inaccuracies that she has discovered in critical discussions of Rushdie's *The Ground Beneath Her Feet*. It is all the more unfortunate that a few essays in *The Great Work of Making Real* contain a number of mistakes that betray inaccurate reading. Homi Catrack, for example, is called 'a builder' (135) when he is really involved in the film industry, and the author mistakes Homi Catrack for Narlikar when she claims that he is engaged in a project with tripods as part of a Bombay land reclamation scheme (132). Silvia Abertazzi mistakenly attributes the last sentence of the novel to its narrator Rai (97), and Elsa Linguanti refers to Ormus's mother as 'Lady Standish', when she is really Lady Methwold (205).

Despite these shortcomings, however, *The Great Work of Making Real* will certainly prove valuable and informative to anybody interested in tracing the richness of Rushdie's mythological references.

Work cited

Roh, Franz. *Nach – Expressionismus, Magischer Realismus: Probleme der nevesten europäischen malerei*. Leipzig: Klinkhardt & Biermann, 1925.

Florian Stadtler

Shalimar the Clown

Salman Rushdie

Jonathan Cape, London, 2005, hb
416pp ISBN 0 2240 6161 5 £17.99
www.randomhouse.co.uk

In his latest novel, Salman Rushdie returns to India and takes his readers to one of the globe's most fiercely fought over territories — Kashmir. In a story that spans the globe, bringing together three different localities – Los Angeles, 1930s/40s France and Kashmir – he writes a seemingly political tale and shows how the conflict in a small north Indian valley affects people living in disparate localities and has a bearing on world politics. The novel has the mythic grandeur of Rushdie's previous work and is global not only in the geographical sense, but also in the subjects it is tackling.

Rushdie has always had a great interest in Kashmir, being of Kashmiri ancestry himself, and spending many summer holidays during his childhood there. He has written about the Kashmir conflict in his non-fiction, but in his fiction Kashmir has only appeared twice before. *Midnight's Children* begins in Kashmir and his short story 'A Prophet's Hair' is also set in the valley surrounded by the peaks of the Himalayas. In his 1987 documentary 'The Riddle of Midnight' Rushdie visits a village of travelling players much like Pachigam where part of the novel is set. His children's novel *Haroun and the Sea of Stories* is set in a fictionalised Kashmir, the valley of K, where the sign leading into the valley has been dubbed 'welcome to Koch-mar'. While *Haroun* hints at the political conflicts of the valley, in *Midnight's Children* the reader encounters its Edenic, mythic quality, still unspoilt by the wranglings of India and Pakistan. In *Shalimar the Clown*, Rushdie revisits this troubled territory, investigating why and how the paradise of Kashmir is living its own *cauchemar*. The novel begins in Los Angeles with the murder of Max Ophuls, Résistance fighter and former American ambassador to India, on the doorstep of his illegitimate stepdaughter, slaughtered like a halal chicken by his Kashmiri chauffeur, the enigmatic Shalimar the Clown, in an assassination that at first sight looks like a political murder. The identity of the murderer is revealed in the first pages, so rather than a 'who-done-it' Rushdie's tale is a 'why-done-it', but out of this 'why' (crime of passion or politically motivated assassination?) Rushdie spins an intriguing, thrilling tale, a page-turner for our troubled times.

The emotional core of the novel gravitates around the love triangle of Max, Shalimar and the woman they both love, Boonyi. After their first lovemaking Shalimar says to Boonyi: 'Don't you leave me now, or I'll never forgive you, and I'll have my revenge, I'll kill you and if you have any children by another man I'll kill the children also.' To which she replies carelessly 'What a romantic you are [. . .] you say the sweetest things.' This oath, uttered by Shalimar in all seriousness and brushed aside by his lover, is Shalimar's driving motivation and links the wider politics of the novel with the intensely personal. Rushdie investigates, against the backdrop of the destruction of Kashmir, several kinds of love: the passionate first flush of love, the mature love of old age, unrequited love, obsessive love, unconditional love and betrayed love. Boonyi's and Shalimar's beautiful love story turns sour, unleashing the destructive potential of their consummated love: 'the immense crater left behind by the destruction of that love had at once been filled by a sea of bile-yellow hatred'. The mad passions that the betrayal stirs up lead Shalimar to train as a terrorist and to commit murder. Rushdie deliberately blurs the boundaries of the political and the personal worlds his characters inhabit. Thus their dying love is paralleled with the decline of the pluralistic community of Kashmir, represented in Srinagar's Mughali Shalimar Gardens as well as the village of Pachigam. Rushdie's story is an elegy for a society where Hindus, Sikhs and Muslims coexisted side-by-side in relative harmony. 'The words *Hindu* and *Muslim* had no place in their story [. . .] In the valley these words were merely descriptions, not divisions.' This eclecticism becomes concrete in the Hindu–Muslim marriage of Shalimar to Boonyi, supported by the whole village in defiance of the iron mullahs who have started to stir up communalist hatred in the valley. However, not satisfied with what she has, Boonyi falls for the American Ambassador to India, Max Ophuls, at one of the village's *bhand pather* clown story performances. Ironically, frustratingly and tragically, Boonyi does not make anything of her opportunity to escape, but instead is imprisoned in a golden cage, loses Max's affection and becomes a gluttonous drug addict burdened with his child. As she betrays her love for Shalimar, the political situation in the valley worsens and the Kashmiris find themselves trapped between opposing political forces.

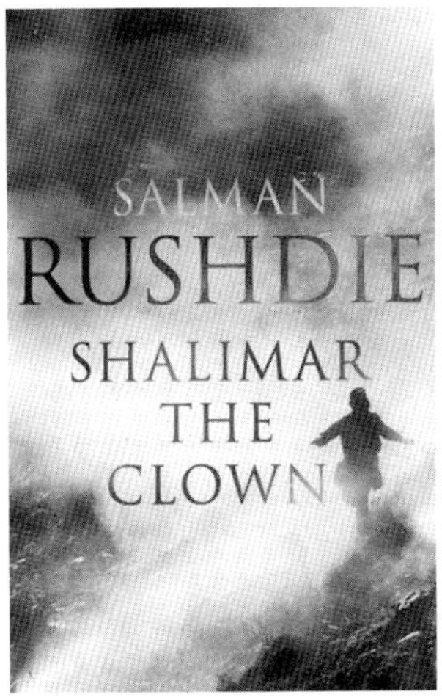

Shalimar the Clown is a dazzling novel with a clear political theme investigating terrorism in a world that is becoming more and more interconnected. Rushdie debates the nature of terrorism in different settings and timeframes, contrasting the resistance movement in France during World War II with the Mujaheddin in Afghanistan, the insurgents in Kashmir and the rise of Islamic fundamentalists, showing how in the wake of economic and political globalisation, terror, too, is globalised. Rushdie probes into the mind-set of a would-be terrorist like Shalimar and the brainwashing he undergoes at the hand of the iron mullah Bulbul Fakh, who seems like a sinister version of the Tin Man from *The Wizard of Oz*. Rushdie asks hard-hitting questions about the nature of terror as the boundaries between insurgent, freedom fighter and terrorist are increasingly blurred or the definition is applied at random, according to political and national allegiances. Rushdie, however, does not provide any answers. How believable a choice it is for the jilted lover Shalimar to enter the terror training camps may be questionable, but it is a reminder how close the boundary between love and hate is.

So far, Rushdie's novels have mostly been set in urban spaces – Bombay, London, New York – and Rushdie's attempt to break the mould he has created for himself is admirable. The novel works best when set in Kashmir. The section set in 1940s France reads too much like journalism and is reminiscent of the many documentaries on the subject that clutter up our TV screens. And the characters of that section read like caricatures. While Rushdie attempts to write a grand, many-faceted life for Max, it seems he too cannot wait to get back to Kashmir and the novel takes flight whenever it returns to the valley. In this village setting, the magical realist tradition of Garcia Marquez, with which Rushdie is often compared, seems to ring through more than ever. Pachigam and Shermal have a resemblance to the mythic remote South American village of Macondo in *One Hundred Years of Solitude*. Pachigam is set up as primordial, mythic and tolerant, increasingly under threat from its neighbours as well as the rivals India and Pakistan. The villagers of Pachigam are written with humour, sensitivity and passion and Rushdie has created some of his most memorable characters there. They grow close to the reader's heart, making the destruction of the village by the juggernaut of the Indian Army almost unbearable to read.

Now characterised by lucid clarity, Rushdie's prose has mellowed over the years but he still paints his fictional landscape in vivid colours, giving each setting its distinctive tone. The novel is an all-encapsulating tale that like *Midnight's Children*, *The Satanic Verses* or *The Moor's Last Sigh* blends comedy, romance, melodrama, and thriller like a Shakespeare play or a Bombay film. Rushdie has a knack for dramatic timing and this makes the novel not only another *tour de force*, but a veritable page-turner, lamenting the loss of an Edenic paradise equated with its pluralism, similar to the elegy for Bombay's pluralistic culture in *The Moor's Last Sigh*. The loss of paradise is man-made as Kashmir is smashed up, squeezed between the two nuclear powers India and Pakistan. While the natural beauty remains, the pluralist and tolerant society that Kashmir was is forever lost, much like the love of Boonyi and Shalimar. At the end, Max and Boonyi's daughter India/Kashmira, and the reader, are left with the broken pieces of their love and Rushdie's fictional Kashmir. Both have to accept that 'our human tragedy is that we are unable to comprehend our experience'. In *Shalimar the Clown*, Rushdie powerfully demonstrates that the novel, because of its immediacy, elasticity and ability to bring together vastly different experiences, can help us to comprehend our experience. *Shalimar the Clown* reveals how important India is for Rushdie's imaginary realm; it is his Sea of Stories. Let's hope he will continue to tap into it.

Tabish Khair

A Red Death

Walter Mosley

Serpent's Tail, London, 2004 (reprint), pb
284pp ISBN 1 8524 2769 8 £7.99

The Man in my Basement

Walter Mosley

Serpent's Tail, London, 2004, pb
249pp ISBN 1 8524 2790 6 £10.99
www.serpentstail.com

A novel by Walter Mosley is always good news and two novels are doubly so — even if one of them is a reprint.

A Red Death was first published in 1991 – the edition under review is a 2004 reprint – and *The Man in my Basement* in 2004. The latter is informed by the American presence in Iraq, while the former was obviously written before any such blatant turn in the course of imperialism, with its 'democratic' reframing (and, to be honest, problematising) of the old colonial-Christian discourse of the civilising mission. But there are passages in *A Red Death* that hold a chilling contemporary significance. As an FBI agent tells Easy Rawlins, the protagonist-narrator, 'We've got enemies all over the world; in Europe, in Asia, everywhere. But the real enemies, the ones we really have to watch out for, are people right here at home. People who aren't Americans on the inside.' Either you are with us or you are against us. Real Americans wave the flag, no matter what.

One of the most important crime writers of his generation, Walter Mosley is a genius at expanding the borders of the genre without breaking out of its bounds. Of the two novels under review, *A Red Death* conforms more to the generic expectations of Crime Fiction: it features Easy Rawlins, a black man who operates in a zone between legality and illegality, partly given the fact that these are terms defined by whites. He is part philosopher (Easy is short for Ezekiel) and historian of his community and part criminal and detective rolled into one. In short, he serves as the fulcrum around which Mosley revolves his exploration of human evil and good, subtly informed by the double-consciousness and historical experience of Africans in America.

When Rawlins is called up by the tax department to account for taxes that he has not paid and offered by the FBI, as a way out, the 'job' of spying on a black church in his neighbourhood, he finds himself embroiled in a series of murders whose only connecting link appears to be his presence at the site. Easy Rawlins comes across – his popularity as a series figure who also appears in eight other Mosley novels (*A Little Yellow Dog* and *Devil in a Blue Dress*, for instance) attests to this – as a fascinating character, a post-World War II and specifically-located (in terms of class, colour and neighbourhood) version of what Slavoj Zizek has described as 'the hard-boiled detective', the (usually, like Rawlins, hard-drinking and oft-bedding) detective who gets personally involved in cases and clients. In other novels, Mosley has taken Rawlins to the late 1950s and the 1960s, but Rawlins has remained identifiable as a contradictory character and a figure of transgression whose very position between the structures of middle-class (white) society and the black ghetto serves to raise questions and doubts on both sides.

Set in recent times, *The Man in my Basement* comes close to escaping the generic confines of Crime Fiction — to simply call it Crime Fiction would be a bit like calling Ernest Hemingway's *The Old Man and the Sea* a fishing book. Like Hemingway's book, *The Man in my Basement* is partly allegorical, without ever becoming simply symbolic or losing its tight grip on a spare realistic style. Unlike Easy Rawlins, the protagonist-narrator of *The Man in my Basement* is not a man of action: Charles Blakey has inherited a large house from ancestors (some of whom were the first to settle in the area as indentured labourers or African sailors, a fact that is lost on a white 'pioneer'-descendant in the novel) and has largely spent his small fortune on drink. With mortgage arrears forcing him into reluctant action, he is offered a small fortune by a white man who wants to rent out the spacious cellar of his house. Blakey finally lets out the cellar to the man, who – it turns out – wants to be imprisoned in the cellar, with Blakey as his guard, to atone for 'crimes' that he has committed. In some ways, his new tenant, the white man, is Blakey's opposite: he is a man of action and cold calculation who has accumulated an immense fortune by immoral and brutal means. As the relationship between the prisoner and the guard assumes the shades of a psychological thriller, the novel also poses its main question to Blakey and, hence, to the reader: 'You think that you can have the easy life of TV and gasoline without someone suffering and dying somewhere?'

Appearances are deceptive in both the novels. Charles Blakey, in spite of all his inertia, is not as innocent as he appears to be. The white man who rents his cellar is not really white. The worst villain in *A Red Death* is not the black man who likes to kill other men because it establishes his physical dominance but the man who is driven by a cerebral hate and an almost impersonal greed, all of it whitewashed into respectability. To say more would be to spoil the suspense – an unforgivable crime on the part of the reviewer when writing about good thrillers – but it needs to be added that in both the novels the tension, though very different in each case, is finely and acutely maintained until the end.

Mosley belongs to a tradition more evident in American fiction than anywhere else (except as replica, as is the case of some Danish writing). It is a line that runs, in different ways, from Hemingway to Raymond Chandler: a spare, hard-fisted yet poetic style, with an ear for the spoken word, that is actually social realist without being moralising or sentimental.

In some ways, actually, both Charles Blakey and Easy Rawlins are, to some extent, morally stunted. In that they are ordinary citizens of a particular kind of society. However, unlike the real villains in both the novels, they are not morally and emotionally dead. They are people who deceive at times, but they are not complete hypocrites. They are people who do not always understand or see suffering, but they still tend to get involved. Through their moral (and other) limitations, Mosley aims an implicit critique not at the characters but at the society around them. Partly because of the dictates of the genre (morality and Crime Fiction do not mix) and partly because of the hard realities that he wants to portray, Mosley's novels avoid a moralising stance in the conventional sense. But they remain intimately and intricately concerned with matters of evil, race, guilt, betrayal and power. In that sense, they remain concerned with issues of morality and it is this, above all, that makes Mosley much more than just a great genre writer.

No account of current genre, crime or pulp fiction can afford to ignore Walter Mosley. Both Stephen Knight (*Crime Fiction 1800–2000*) and Scott McCracken (*Pulp: Reading Popular Fiction*) devote considerable space to his work. But in the longer run, Mosley's novels – including the strongly generic Easy Rawlins series – will survive simply as excellent novels that used and went beyond generic features.

Michael Niblett

It Falls Into Place

Phyllis Shand Allfrey

Papillote Press, London, 2004, pb
144pp ISBN 0 9532 2241 1 £7.99
www.papillotegardens.org

Julie Mango

N D Williams

Peepal Tree Press, Leeds, 2004, pb
300pp ISBN 1 9007 1577 5 £9.99
www.peepaltreepress.com

'Life has come down to this: a place in the world where someone knocks and asks to borrow sugar, or *What time is it?* or *Please take my life, I am weary.*' So says the narrator of N D Williams's short story 'Light of the World', a dream-like tale of the need to belong, of what it means to be 'here' rather than 'there'. The poetics and politics of place – persistent themes in Caribbean literature – resurface time and again in these short story collections by the Dominican Phyllis Shand Allfrey and the Guyanese Williams. Though written at very different times, and against very different backgrounds, they display a common sensitivity towards the tension between movement and stasis, towards the personal epiphanies that arise from the encounter between diverse peoples. Even as they move out across the wider West Indian diaspora, however, the stories never let their characters – or the reader – forget the voices and landscape of the Caribbean.

Allfrey was born in Dominica in 1908 into an elite white family. Her father was Crown Attorney and she led a privileged early life. Through the patronage of the American millionaire banker J P Morgan she was able to travel as a teenager to New York and London. Ironically, these same travels awakened her political radicalism. The depression in America and the emergence of the Labour party in 1930s Britain fired Allfrey's enthusiasm for the socialist struggle, leading her to participate in grassroots and welfare work. She also began writing intensely, seeking to evoke the Dominican creole world from which her protected upbringing had separated her.

In 1953 her first novel, *The Orchid House*, was published. A successful literary career beckoned, only for Allfrey to confound expectations and return to the Caribbean to found the Dominica Labour Party in 1954. Working tirelessly to ensure the voices of the black peasantry were heard, she was ultimately expelled from the Party and excluded from island politics once the very nationalism she had fought so hard to foster made it expedient. Shunned primarily because of her whiteness, Allfrey refused to be silenced, establishing a newspaper and becoming spokesperson for the political opposition. She continued to campaign for social causes and dedicated much of her money to fighting injustice until she died, in poverty, in 1986.

The fourteen stories collected in *It Falls Into Place* reveal a literary voice whose political career prevented her from achieving the acclaim within West Indian literature that her talent deserved. Unlike her compatriot Jean Rhys, Allfrey has been largely ignored as a writer; her poems remain out of print and some of her stories unpublished. Nevertheless, the work showcased here substantiates calls for her to be more widely recognised. Her writing combines a delicate yet assured touch with a subtly ironic edge, celebrating the complexities of cultural interaction while satirising the pretensions and prejudices it can bring. 'Uncle Rufus', for example, tells of a white family's chagrin when the eponymous uncle marries a coloured woman; the story gently mocks the lengths the family go to in order that the relationship be hushed up, before revealing their humorously begrudging acceptance of Rufus's wife and mixed race children:

> We found her as ugly close-to as she was at a distance, but very kind and quite modest (strange to say). I must say that they were very happy children and quite respectful, for they called us Miss all the time. (62–63)

Allfrey's stories are full of moments when characters crack the shell of habit to reach a new self-awareness; when the collision of perspectives enables the sudden hatching of a new understanding of the world. In perhaps the best story in the volume, 'A Real Person', which packs into its few pages the travails of a white West Indian teenager, a black watchman, two possessed cats, a Buddhist, and a goat-girl, the central character comes to recognise the potential for hope to transcend violence:

> Walter might never resolve the doubt, but at least he was certain that he was blissfully alive, that he was capable of practically anything, and that in spite of the mysterious and inexplicable conflict of faiths and races in the world, it was still a world in which miracles happened. (107–08)

Alongside such awakenings of consciousness, Allfrey offers a similar awakening to the Caribbean landscape. Her prose is laden with references to its sights, smells, and textures. 'Politics ruined me for writing', she once remarked of her truncated literary career; yet those politics are conveyed just as forcibly by her celebration of the distinctiveness of the West Indian environment.

For Williams, a winner of the Casa de las Americas Prize in 1976, the landscape is an equally potent presence. Often, however, it appears in an oppressive guise. In 'Monkey Wrenching Snaps', for instance, the mud encountered on the road by the protagonist, returning to his island home having migrated to New York, is a reminder of why he left. Indeed, his anxiety that the mud 'would form a cake on his soles; he'd have to clean it off; it could ruin his patent leathers' (140) highlights his fear of being sucked back into island life.

The desire to free oneself from a claustrophobic milieu recurs elsewhere in more explicitly political terms. Though never named, 'The Republic' that features in a number of Williams's stories clearly alludes to his native Guyana in its most totalitarian avatar. Julienne in 'Your Slip is Showing, Comrade!' feels bound to leave this overbearing body politic the way 'most people left it, wrenching themselves from its pincer-like grip of low wages and unending misery; leaving relatives behind like bits and pieces of wailing flesh trapped in the pincers' (59).

Like many of Williams's protagonists, Julienne experiences the temptation of movement as a means to escape the limiting postures society would impose upon her. While she seeks to flee the burden of playing the dutiful daughter of a prominent member of 'the Party', the roles adopted by, or forced upon, other characters gesture towards the legacy of colonialism. Nowhere is this made more manifest than in 'Trinculo Walks the Dog'. Here the main character becomes trapped in the persona of the character from *The Tempest* he once played as a schoolboy, an inescapable mask that points to the other roles he is condemned to act out, most notably that of the virile black male who services the sexual needs of the frustrated white wife of the English schoolmaster.

Just as an undercurrent of sexual tension – the erotic atmosphere charged by Williams's tangy prose – snakes through all these pieces, so the intertwining of sex with issues of race and politics becomes a repeated theme too. It is best exemplified by 'The Wall', in which a complex narrative structure weaves together an affair between a West Indian *au pair* and her white employer with allusions to the fate of Maurice Bishop's New Jewel Revolution in Grenada in 1983. This entangled structure is typical of many of the stories in the collection as they shift between geographical locations, between past and present, personal memory and political history. Though sometimes lacking the startling piquancy of Allfrey's works, their admixture of narrative strands does capture the complexities of the migrant's history — that sense of instability, of not quite belonging in one place or the other that haunts Williams's protagonists.

While movement may define these characters, however, what lies beneath each tale is that need to find a space for oneself articulated in the opening quotation. The desire to leave is shown to be less a rejection of a particular place than a rejection of the suffocating confines of its proscribed social moulds. As the narrator in 'Light of the World' shows, when the individual is able to express an identity on his or her own terms, what once was an alienating landscape to be abandoned becomes a source of strength and security: 'Time to take off' (96) becomes 'Time to go home' (117). The same plea for tolerance that animates Allfrey's prose resonates here also then. And if not all the stories offer the resolution achieved by the narrator in 'Light of the World', the generosity of Williams's writing, the way in which he makes space for the viewpoints of so many individuals, from Rastafarians to Government officials, from immigrant tow-truck drivers to university lecturers, reflects the ever-present potential for the reconciliation of diverse voices.

If at times the plots of Williams's stories drift towards the familiar, any sense of cliché is avoided thanks to the roundedness of his characters. Despite the different contexts from which they emerge, both Allfrey and Williams share a will to go beyond polarisation and the easy denunciation of opposed outlooks. Whether through the wry take on the world offered by the former, or the more caustic tone of the latter, both writers seek to puncture the pretensions of absolutist manifestations of power. And in the humour and the acceptance – indeed, celebration – of human fallibility that marks their work exist the promise of an inclusive, redemptive vision for the world.

Shirley Hughes

Minaret

Leila Aboulela

Bloomsbury, London, 2005, hb
276pp ISBN 0 7875 7626 2 £12.99
www.bloomsbury.com

Minaret describes the voyage of a happy Sudanese girl from Khartoum, where she was part of a loving Sudanese family, to a cold and alien London. There she comes down in the world and loses everything: family, money, boyfriend. The sadness and poignant sense of loss is counterbalanced by her quest for Allah. She ultimately finds inner peace in the Muslim religion and the support of a women's community at a Mosque.

The novel is in the first-person, the narrator being Najwa, the daughter of a rich Sudanese politician. In 1984 she and her twin brother Omar attend Khartoum University, where fewer than 30 per cent of the students are girls. There is a political coup, their father is arrested and eventually executed on a charge of corruption. The family then flee to London where Omar is imprisoned for drug-peddling, the mother dies of heartbreak and Najwa is left alone with only a few relatives who are also refugees. The father's fortune is sequestered. Najwa helps her aunt in a familiar Sudanese-style household and then drifts into domestic work, an anathema for someone who was used to having servants herself. She had been friendly with a communist student in Khartoum, Anwar, who also seeks political asylum in London. A sexual relationship develops, but the liaison breaks up when the self-seeking Anwar marries his cousin. In the meantime, Najwa's dormant religious yearnings lead her to take instruction at the Regent's Park Mosque (hence the minaret of the title). Pursuing her livelihood as nanny and servant to a Sudanese family in St John's Wood, she becomes attracted to the younger brother, Tamer, who is a devout Muslim. Despite their age difference, they fall in love and are caught kissing in an unguarded moment.

This book is not autobiographical although, as always, the writer has wisely drawn on her own experience and background for the setting. Aboulela's father was Sudanese and her mother Egyptian, and she was educated at an American school. She came to England from Khartoum in 1987 at the age of twenty-three to study at the London School of Economics, became a British citizen in 1993 and now lives with her English husband and their two boys in Aberdeen, commuting to Dubai. Homesick, she found that writing stories alleviated the alienation and sense of displacement. Although she had at first wanted to write non-fiction and newspaper articles to counter the anti-Arab feeling which followed the first Gulf war, it was fiction that came out of this effort. Her first novel, *The Translator,* was well received in 1999. In 2001, a collection of her short stories appeared in *Coloured Lights*, one of which, 'The Museum', won the inaugural Caine Prize for African Writing. Although *The Translator* was a slightly happier novel than *Minaret*, Leila's Muslim faith and an obvious sense of humour have buoyed her in an exile which has lasted for nearly twenty years and her writing has placed her in demand for interviews at such prestigious venues as the Hay-on-Wye Literary Festival, the Royal Festival Hall in London, and in Edinburgh.

Minaret 'reeks' of alienation and the search for identity. The novel, however, is not about discrimination but about people who happen to be immigrants. Her characters are certainly portrayed differently from immigrants described by Monica Ali or Nadeem Aslam, for example, in *Brick Lane* or *Maps for Lost Lovers* respectively. *Minaret* is about the consequences of Sudanese political unrest as reflected in the lives of its characters. Najwa meets some distasteful racism when, on the top deck of a bus one evening, three young drunks throw Tizer over her, calling her 'Muslim scum'. The author may be expressing in this one overt incident distress at an increased excuse for anti-Muslim feeling after 9/11, for *Minaret* was written after that atrocity (and of course this anti-Arab feeling will be intensified again after the recent London bombings). However, there is little talk about colour – only a reference to Najwa's 'shitty' skin – for it is not skin colour which labels her before she speaks to an observer, but the hijab or headscarf. The publishers deserve praise for their dust jacket which depicts a beautiful woman wearing a hijab — a word which in the Qur'an or Muslim scriptures, denotes 'cover' or 'protection'. Along with its title, *Minaret*, this makes no compromise in view of possible prejudice.

The politics affecting Sudan are skilfully woven into the narrative, unfolding in the memories of characters as the reader follows their story. Sudan celebrated Independence in 1956. This was followed by a series of military coups and internal unrest, until the military government of Nimeira seized power in 1969. By 1984, the year when Najwa's family fled to London, it had deteriorated into a reign of terror marked by a series of strikes, which eventually led to Nimeira's overthrow. Corruption was rife and this is revealed through Najwa's friend Anwar, who is a member of the students' communist band, the Democratic Front and who, as a victim of torture where his leg was held in a bucket of ice for days, ends up in London after another coup in 1989. His frequent digs at her father, who was in charge of the President's office, and called 'Mr 10 per cent' because he took commissions on every deal the government made with a foreign company, is a constant source of quarrel between them in Khartoum.. Your family has six servants for four people, he states, 'Does it not strike you that it is wrong for such wide discrepancies to exist between people? There's famine in the west. This country is one of the poorest in the world' (33). Anwar blames the troubles on the land-owning families, the capitalists and the aristocracy in defiance of the textbooks which suggest that colonialism is the cause of underdevelopment. While Najwa wonders what is the point of it all: coup after coup like musical chairs.

Whereas Najwa grew up in a household where only the servants prayed, and always felt a hollow and numb space when she watched Muslims praying at university, it is ironic that she finds refuge in the Mosque when she too becomes a servant. This obviously changes her outlook on things, and sex with Anwar, which is delicately expressed in the novel, makes her feel guilty. She hankers after a Muslim wedding in Khartoum and imagines her mother and father arguing over whom to invite. The turning point comes when her friendship with Anwar leads her to forget the great religious festival of Ramadan which they had always marked at home.

The tone of the novel is one of gentleness and love. Najwa's gradual awakening to the Muslim faith, which teaches prayer, charity, truth and goodness, is beautifully depicted and it is the love of Allah which gives her back her self-respect. Yet this is mixed with an atmosphere of regret set out at the beginning: 'I had come down in the world', words which today may have a quaintly archaic tone. However, the novel is superbly crafted, with clear prose, drama and a relaxed dialogue. The plot is told in a series of chapters which travel backwards and forwards in time, although predominant use of the present tense gives the plot immediacy, and each part is dated so that there is no confusion. It starts with a short, prefatory chapter entitled '*Bism Allahi,*

Ar-rahman, Ar-raheem', meaning 'In the name of Allah, the Merciful, the compassionate', which precedes chapters of the Qur'an and is used to introduce many Muslim activities. There are hints of the story to come, for Najwa meets, fleetingly, the young lad Tamer with whom she will fall in love. Aboulela's prose is highly metaphorical, the autumn trees in the park across the road, for example, are described as scrubbed with silver and brass. But this is balanced by matter-of-fact details, such as a door which, when opened, rubs on the carpet in the opulent flat of her employer, which often go unnoticed but bring a scene back, very much, to reality. Aboulela's venture into first-person narrative is successful and she overcomes the difficulty of gaps opening in the narrative which this can produce. The description of Najwa herself, for instance, is given partly by her reflection in a mirror, covered in a white headscarf, when she is a devout Muslim, her curls repressed under the fabric. The text cannot be labelled postmodern, although there are many dreams. In fact the final chapter ends with a dream in which Najwa visits her family home in Khartoum and finds the walls crumbling and smeared with guilt. It is a sadly conclusive ending although there is hope, because Najwa is going on Hajj to Mecca — her lifelong ambition. A glossary of Arabic terms would have been useful in this novel, although this is not the done thing today.

In an interview with Caryl Phillips, George Lamming describes books as 'unique window[s] on the world' (Nasta 185). The writings of new neighbours who come from diverse backgrounds are particularly valuable in our multicultural society today. The BBC last year interviewed a number of Muslims in England to find out how attitudes towards them altered after 9/11. The title of the programme was, regrettably, 'Don't Panic, I'm Islamic'. If Aboulela's novel is intended to show that the hijab, the most visible outward sign of a Muslim woman, hides a friendly and peace-loving personality, it certainly succeeds.

Work Cited

Nasta, Susheila, ed. *Writing Across Worlds: Contemporary Writers Talk.* London: Routledge, 2004.

Devon Campbell-Hall

Looking In, Looking Out

Shanta Acharya

Headland Publications, Wirral, 2005, pb
ISBN 1 9020 9689 4 £7.50

Wish-granting Words

Smita Agarwal

Ravi Dayal, Delhi, 2002, hb
53pp ISBN 8 1753 0046 9 Rs70
www.orientlongman.com

Tartan & Turban

Bashabi Fraser

Luath Press, Edinburgh, 2004, pb
107pp ISBN 1 8428 2044 3 £8.99
www.luath.co.uk

The first thing that occurs to me as I stand back to consider these three recent volumes is how commendable it is to see small presses defying convention by taking the risk to publish poetry in this market-driven climate. The second is how neatly these collections seem to fit into the categories of youth, adulthood and maturity. Bashabi Fraser's third collection of poetry, *Tartan & Turban*, pulses with a youthful vitality that invites readers to partake of her hospitality, as she mischievously pokes fun at language and the vagaries of her Indo-Scot migrant existence within this well-structured collection. Fraser elegantly dances between the first- and second-generation cultural perspectives, as her enthusiastic writing takes us from West Bengal to London to the Highlands of Scotland. In 'The Affirmation', Fraser describes a Scottish christening at which she was asked where she was *actually* from.

> I heard the pride
> In my voice as I said 'from India'
> Which reassured her; but sparks appeared
> In my daughter's eyes — dark and protesting
> Drowning my explanation, as they explicitly affirmed
> That she was from *here* and not just there. (92)

With a language both playful and substantial, Fraser manages to contend with themes as diverse as war, displacement, and urban migrant identity, while successfully weaving in the roles of migrant women in a post-devolution Scotland still coming to terms with its emerging multiculturalism.

A delightful, coherent collection in its own right, *Tartan & Turban* notably brings to light the complex historical links between Scotland and India, particularly Bengal. Whilst this volume cogently argues for the recognition of Scotland's new multiculturalism, it maintains an idiosyncratic precision. Fraser describes in 'The Moving Image' how

> A city is your city when it
> Leaves a space for you
> In its moving image and
> Invites you to step in line
> With its unfolding storyline
> (103)

The personal becomes political within this collection. That Fraser provides a footnoted glossary to explain the Bengali cultural references within her poems indicates that these pieces are not intended to distance readers, but to *welcome* them into her lyrical world. *Tartan & Turban* will no doubt become a valuable resource for students of contemporary Scottish literature.

Shanta Acharya's recent collection, *Looking In, Looking Out*, radiates a very adult intelligence and an irreverent sense of humour, as she deftly rejects the 'ethnic' classification as a poet who primarily represents British Asian migrant experience. This is elegant writing that reflects not only a highly

educated mind but an extraordinary sensitivity to the absurdity of everyday life. I laughed out loud to read her version of a job interview in which

> After the initial screening
> I was ushered in
> for an aptitude test in
> the boss's limousine. (39)

Acharya's writing is both solidly grounded and satisfyingly complete; her language is never overloaded, but chosen with a meticulousness that perfectly expresses her calm observations. This poet has an innate gift for expression; even the most mundane of everyday experiences, visiting the optician, becomes a platform for Acharya's sense of wonder.

> *Much depends on how much*
> *you want to see,*
> he muttered having explained
> my failure to see the world
> as it is. (43)

Although her poems are thematically concerned with very adult issues, they are in no way staid; on the contrary, these pieces radiate a developed sense of the ironic. Acharya gently leaves her readers in no doubt that they are in the hands of a consummate professional. My favourite piece has to be 'Mrs Kafka's Dilemma', in which readers are treated a different version of 'The Metamorphosis', in which

> She dreaded her husband
> coming to see her
> fearing that sooner or later
> a single strand of her own hair
> would betray her, making
> her a liar
> for confessing her snake-hair
> killed her partner,
> that she herself was quite
> innocent in this matter. (50)

Not only do Acharya's poems interrogate lackadaisical patriarchy, they challenge its illogicality with a serenity devoid of anger. *Looking In, Looking Out* deserves to be taken seriously. Not only is Ms Acharya an accomplished poet, she is also published in the world of business and finance, and now serves as Associate Director of Initiative on Foundation and Endowment Asset Management at London Business School. I must confess that my least favourite of her poems are those reflecting her experiences in the world of professional business and IT. Yet they naturally flow with her other selections, so I must put my personal bias aside to concentrate on the strengths of this volume. There is nothing particularly dynamic about these pieces, yet they do indeed possess a calm maturity that renders them accessible to many levels of audience, from the casual reader to the student of contemporary British verse. I will certainly be on the lookout for more of Shanta Acharya's writing.

Although she has been widely published in India and abroad for more than twenty years, *Wish-granting Words* is Smita Agarwal's first collection of poetry. She simultaneously invites the reader in whilst keeping them safely at bay. Agarwal's poetic insight allows glimpses into her imagination, yet she appears to reveal very little of herself in this diverse collection of thirty-two poems, which veers from the exotic to the defamiliarised. This work is strangely reminiscent of Craig Raine's Martian poetry, especially those pieces with an airborne theme, such as 'The Lie of the Land: A Letter to Chatwin'.

> Upright, I'm uptight; I hardly
> Ever range beyond my nose.
> Avian,
> On my belly, I'd at least see
> The ditches, gullies,
> promontories (9)

This is not to say that Agarwal's poems are overly detached; she does indeed offer glimpses of hopeful optimism in these painfully mature pieces. Yet the sense of an unchangeable fate colours the entire collection with a seriousness that evades the casual reader. For example, in 'The Planetoid', she writes of how it 'wishes to avoid/ Disfigurement. But it cannot/Veer out of a predestined course' (27).

Yet within *Wish-granting Words*' measured lines are moments of sensual chaos. 'Scrubbing with soap and// water, using a mild stain remover,// heightens the colour;//firming up a faith//in the power of bonding' (12). Agarwal's themes flow from male midlife crises and the impossibility of intimacy in a dissolving marriage to a nostalgically remembered childhood. These are introspective pieces that render the reader a near-voyeur while still managing to retain distance from the painful realities the poems illustrate.

I feel the strongest pieces in this collection self-consciously address the act of creating poetry, such as 'The Word-worker'.

> Words scurry down dark lanes
> Or brightly lit streets. I rip
> Off masks, bequeath new skin,
> Dragoon words into
> birthing . . . (28)

There are incisive phrases such as the above within this collection that demonstrate an articulate voice. With so many themes addressed in this loosely-structured volume, many of the pieces are best read individually rather than as a collection. This is a nicely-packaged hardback volume that will appeal to many readers, especially those just beginning their journey into Indo-Anglian poetry.

Overall, these three volumes by three very different poets represent significant contributions to the ever-growing field of contemporary Anglophone poetry. Whether readers are looking for youthful exuberance, adult observations or mature misgivings, there is bound to be something within this trio to appeal.

Sarah Campbell

India Calling

Cornelia Sorabji

Trent Editions, Nottingham, 2004, pb
250pp ISBN 1 8423 3077 2 £9.99
www.ntu.ac.uk/acc/specialist_centres/English/trent_editions/

Dwelling in the Archive: Women Writing House, Home and History in Late Colonial India

Antoinette Burton

Oxford University Press, New York, 2003, pb
240pp ISBN 0 1951 4424 4 £12.99
www.oup.co.uk

This recent reprint of Cornelia Sorabji's memoirs recounts the story of how she trained as a barrister at Oxford in the late 1880s and then managed to find a niche for herself practising law in India as a pleader for the Court of Wards representing *purdahnashin* (secluded women). As 'alternative' archival sources, Burton's *Dwelling in the Archive* considers Sorabji's memoirs alongside Janaki Majumdar's 'Family History' and Attia Hosain's *Sunlight on a Broken Column*, which report a different version of 1930s India, embedded in the perspective of the domestic sphere which was so often signified from without by politicians of this period.

There are two organising motifs which run through Sorabji's text: the first is her construction of the zenana as both an imagined space and a political ideal; the second, which runs in counterpoint to this, is her self-construction as author and subject.

Sorabji's portrayal of the zenana is in many ways contradictory — it is posited as both the unchanging essence of traditional India, and the potential site of reform and salvation for the subcontinent. This tension reflects not only the ambiguous attitude of India's colonisers to their subjects, but also Sorabji's dual role as advocate for and authority over the zenana women. Indeed, her employment by the civil service was dependent on her ability to present herself to the British as both a 'native', and so a source of valuable knowledge about the customs of zenana women, and as somebody who shared British values and a critical distance from her secluded clients. As Burton points out, Sorabji sought to wrest the political capital of knowledge of the zenana from nationalist reformers by claiming superior understanding of both its current state, and, crucially, what form it ought to take in an India rapidly moving towards modernity.

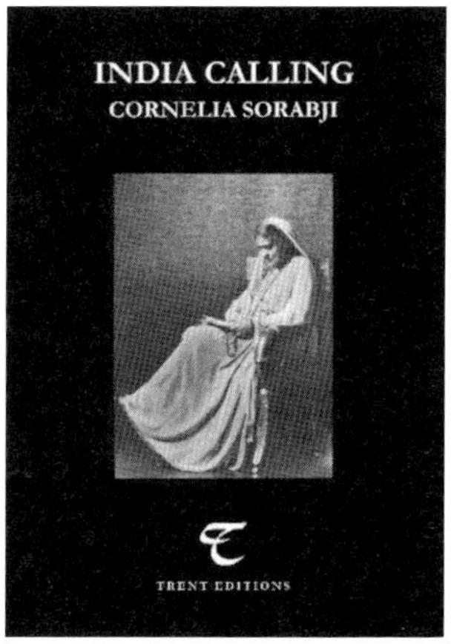

India Calling's first passage on the zenana portrays it as dead, backward and illiterate, with all real life, political and otherwise, residing outside it. An illustrative anecdote is recounted concerning a 'thankurani' who 'had never seen growing things, never seen a garden', and who is amazed by Sorabji's gift of a rose bush. The zenana is repeatedly figured in terms of lack (it is 'bare of furniture'), but also as a site of undisciplined excess and potential disruption, which requires the restraining force of the British administration, and in particular that of Sorabji herself.

The political power struggles which do take place between the women of the zenana, are dismissed by Sorabji as 'shortsighted', often because the goals pursued by the women were primarily concerned with other members of the zenana rather than the maharajah or colonial authorities. Yet while the potential for scholarly and political accomplishment from within the zenana is unacknowledged directly by Sorabji, it peers through in moments such as her sketches of zenana ladies meditating and reading shastras, editing vernacular newspapers, riding and hunting. One particularly telling vignette is Sorabji's depiction the scene in a zenana courtyard immediately before a disputation between two rival factions over the succession:

> To my left, the Rani and her waiting-women. They sat on their haunches; all alike were dressed in dull white *saris* drawn securely over head and face, revealing no single feature even in the case of the Rani, who was smoking a *huqqa*. She smoked her favourite mixture, treacle and tobacco. There was no sound save the gurgle of the *huqqa*. (130)

While the imagery here is decidedly orientalist ('haunches'), one gets a sense of the power the Rani commanded, which appeared to be augmented by the anonymity she shared with her ladies-in-waiting, none of whom 'revealed a single feature' of themselves. These slippages are permitted by the structure of *India Calling*, which consists of short, multifaceted and interlinked narratives, and reveal that the women Sorabji portrays were, in fact, often highly empowered actors in their spheres, strategically using the position afforded by their seclusion to their advantage — as a pretext for refusing to deal with certain male authorities, for example. Some members of the zenana were also key actors in the Indian nationalist movement, and, as Burton points out, convocations such as the All-Muslim

Ladies' conference regularly met under purdah 'thus quite deliberately mobilizing "seclusion in public" for political purposes'.

The question of Sorabji's positioning of herself as author and subject, however, is arguably the more interesting underside of her depiction of 'the Indian woman' but this is disappointingly underplayed by Burton. While Burton recognises Sorabji's adoption of the western, male anthropological gaze, in order to gain scientific authority as the 'ethnographer for the colonial state', she does not explore the vicissitudes within this perspective, or indeed the extent to which Sorabji views herself as the object of surveillance.

Sorabji frequently writes of herself as a surveyor, a privileged onlooker at the edge of both the colonial man's, and purdahnashin's world. She repeatedly figures the zenana as something which she journeys toward, and which is depicted from the outside before its inner quarters are revealed. Burton notes a similar tendency in the journals of Attia Hossain, who 'offers us only images of the zenana from the outside, or from the courtyard's edge'; however, Burton does not explore in detail the reasons for or consequences of this peripheral perspective. Perhaps Hossain, like Sorabji, struggles to find a position from which to narrate her particular subjectivity. Sorabji's identity as author fluctuates as she establishes various relations to her historical setting. For example, when describing the Zoroastrian community, from which her parents were Christian converts, she first uses the impersonal 'they', then 'we', before moving towards a more personalised account of 'my aunt's' religious practice. This anxiety about her place is evident from the opening of her memoirs, in the way she continually seeks to set herself in a historical context — initially in terms of official Raj history, and subsequently through namedropping and mentioning that events she participated in were written up in other published memoirs.

Sorabji's disquietude about her own identity is also revealed in the sense she has of herself as the object of surveillance and misapprehension, both by the British (as a specimen of 'Indianness' or 'new womanhood') and the zenana women. She describes scenes in which she is asked to disrobe by Italian customs officers, curious about her dress, or in which she is associated with African tribal people by English academics. This discomfiture concerning others' apprehension of her is also evident in accounts of how, in the zenana, she was 'spied on by the skylights' of her room, or, on another occasion, taken

> through narrow tunnels, guarded by armed sentries, up stair after stair – into the daylight of a gorgeous portrait gallery. Here I sat for some minutes, during which time I have no doubt that I was being inspected by many eyes. (102)

It is interesting to note that this second type of surveillance is more frequently described in terms of the depersonalised architecture of the zenana, rather than the rationale of the onlookers. Sorabji could perhaps identify more easily with her English adversaries; also, it seems that she was less willing to articulate the motivations of the purdahnashins, who were conscious of themselves as engaged in a potentially adversarial struggle for power with Sorabji as a representative of the British Raj.

Burton's polemic, which posits the domestic as a alternative space in which women could imagine subjectivities beyond those proscribed by colonial authorities or Indian reformers, emphasises Sorabji's liminal position 'between two cultures'. She argues that this necessitates Sorabji's construction of a third space, of the traditional zenana of the past, through which she imagines a utopian future. While Burton's argument concerning Sorabji's ideological use of the zenana seems valid, the motivations she postulates for this move seem less plausible. In terms of her construction of her own identity, political affiliation, and written style, Sorabji seems almost entirely located in British culture and not, as Burton argues, speaking to both an Indian and English audience, thus challenging the notion that 'British civilisation could deliver Indian women form the backwardness of zenana existence'. While Sorabji admires some 'picturesque' zenana customs, she is categorical in stating that 'Indian mother[s] have yet to be taught what ambitions to hold in their hearts for their children' and that these ambitions ought to be those which best serve the interests of their British government's 'ideals of progress'.

I would argue that the conflict at work in Sorabji's writing is, if anything, between two western discursive traditions — that of 'expert male authority', and the more anecdotal, particular idiom she shared with her female English friends, whose letters and novels she refers to with admiration. Sorabji repeatedly makes asides to the English reader, and complains that she had, in the time in the zenana 'no English friend . . . with whom to share a wink'. However, the identity of this English friend seems to shift with the styles and identities which Sorabji herself adopts. A very interesting study could have been made which traced the literary influences that shaped Sorabji's work, sources which Burton alludes to as 'memoirs, devotional literature, personal narratives and a variety of prescriptive texts'; the places in the text in which these intersect and collide might reveal much about Sorabji's sense of self.

The strength of Burton's *Dwelling in the Archive* is that it provides the political and historical context with which to understand *India Calling,* while demonstrating the potential for further excavation of this context from within Sorabji's text. Burtons' central argument – that the domestic space and unofficial narratives of women are equally valid historical archives as more traditional sources – is a sound, but by now somewhat well-worn line of reasoning. However, in her attempt to weave three very disparate authors together in this work, which frequently focuses on their similarities rather than their differences, Burton at times neglects particularities which are potentially of great interest such as Sorabji's own identity and narrative voice.

Books Received

Cheeky Fictions: Laughter and the Postcolonial
Susanne Reichl and Mark Stein, eds
Rodopi, Amsterdam, 2005, pb
313pp ISBN 9 0420 1995 6 €65

Meet Me in Mozambique
E A Markham
Tindal Street Press, Birmingham, 2005, pb
246pp ISBN 0 9547 9137 1 £7.99

Gender and Slave Emancipation in the Atlantic World
Pamela Scully and Diana Paton, eds
Duke University Press, Hastings, 2005, pb
376pp ISBN 0 8223 3594 8 £15.95

The Barons
Ahmadu Kurfi
Spectrum Books, Ibadan, 2005, pb
442pp ISBN 9 7802 9543 7 £9.95

Kwani?1
Binyavanga Wainaina
Kwani Trust, Nairobi, 2003, pb
293pp ISBN 9 9669 8360 0 £11.95

Kwani?2
Binyavanga Wainaina
Kwani Trust, Nairobi, 2003, pb
416pp ISBN 9 9669 8364 3 £14.95

Tout Passe: Instantanés populaires et traces du passé à Lubumbashi (Cahiers Africans 71)
Danielle de Lame et Donatien Dibwe dia Mwembu, eds
L'Harmattan, Paris, 2005, pb
322pp ISBN 2 7475 9202 2 €29

A Life Elsewhere
Segun Afolabi
Jonathan Cape, London, 2006, pb
274pp ISBN 0 2240 7602 7 £10.99

Still Beating the Drum: Critical Perspectives on Lewis Nkosi (Cross/Cultures 81)
Lindy Steibel and Liz Gunner, eds
Rodopi, New York, 2005, hb
375pp ISBN 9 0420 1807 0 $103

Blood Child and Other Stories
Octavia Butler
Seven Stories Press, London, 2005, pb
213pp ISBN 1 5832 2698 2 £8.99

Dance the Guns to Silence: 100 Poems for Ken Saro-Wiwa
Nii Ayikwei Parkes and Kadija Sesay, eds
Flipped Eye Publishing and African Writers Abroad, London, 2005, pb
199pp ISBN 1 9052 3301 9 £5.99

African Theatre: Soyinka: Blackout, Blowout & Beyond: Satirical Review Sketches
Martin Banham, Judith Greenwood and Chuck Mike, eds
James Currey, Oxford, 2005, pb
216pp ISBN 0 8525 5595 4 £12.95

Brown Eyes
Nicole Moore, ed
Matador, Leicester, 2005, pb
268pp ISBN 1 9052 3714 6 £9.99

Gem Squash Tokoloshe
Rachel Zadok
Pan Books, London, 2005, pb
328pp ISBN 0 3304 4119 1 £6.99

Burning Whims and Other Poems
Liz Niven
Luath Press, Edinburgh, 2005, pb
110pp ISBN 1 8428 2074 5 £8.99

Wasafiri Vol. 21, No. 1 March 2006, pp. 92–93
ISSN 0269-0055 print/ISSN 1747-1508 online
http://www.tandf.co.uk/journals DOI: 10.1080/02690050500475971

Into the Blue Wavelengths: Love Poems and Elegies

Roderick Watson

Luath Press, Edinburgh, 2005, pb

84pp ISBN 1 8428 2075 3 £8.99

The Crisis of the Negro Intellectual

Harold Cruse

New York Review of Books, New York, 2005, pb

594pp ISBN 1 5901 7135 7 £9.99

Transnational America: Feminisms, Diasporas, Neoliberalisms

Inderpal Grewal

Duke University Press, London 2005, pb

280pp ISBN 0 8223 3544 1 $22.95

Among the Contributors

Diana Bridge is a New Zealand writer who began writing in India in the 1990s. Her fourth book of poems, *Red Leaves*, was published in 2005. She has a background in Chinese poetry and has taught in the Chinese department of Hong Kong University. She is currently working on the China poems of New Zealand writer, Robin Hyde.

Sarah Campbell studied English and Philosophy at York University and has an MA in Social Anthropology from Cambridge. Her dissertation combined ethnographic and literary methodologies in an analysis of oral narratives of migration.

Devon Campbell-Hall is a doctoral student at the University of Winchester. Her thesis focuses on the construction of multicultural British identity and how this is represented in contemporary Anglophone literature.

Sampurna Chattarji was born in Africa in 1970. Her poetry features in several journals and anthologies including *100 Poets Against the War, Chandrabhaga* and *Fifty-Six Indian Poets (1951–2005)*. Other publications include *Abol Tabol: The Nonsense World of Sukumar Ray* (Translation/Puffin) and *The Greatest Stories Ever Told* (Fiction/Puffin).

Shirley Chew is Emeritus Professor at the University of Leeds. She has published widely in the field of Postcolonial Literature, and is the founding editor of *Moving Worlds: A Journal of Transcultural Writings*. Her work in progress includes the *Blackwell History of Postcolonial Literature.*

Anthony Downey is Head of the MA in Contemporary Art at Sotheby's Institute, London. He is a regular contributor to *Third Text, Flash Art, Wasafiri, Contemporary*, and the *New York Arts Magazine.*

Victor Ehikhamenor was born in Udomi-Irrua in Edo State, Nigeria. He studied English at Bendel State University, Ekpoma, Nigeria, and was later awarded an MSc in Technology Management from the University of Maryland, University College, USA. He lives both in Nigeria and the USA.

Aminatta Forna is an author, broadcaster and journalist. Her book, *The Devil that Danced on the Water* (2002), was a runner-up for the Samuel Johnson Prize in 2003 and her documentary series 'Africa Unmasked' was shown on Channel 4 in 2002. She was a judge for the Caine Prize for African Writing in 2005 and her latest book, *The Ancestor Stones*, will be published in 2006.

Suman Gupta is Senior Lecturer in Literature at the Open University. His books include *Marxism, History and Intellectuals* (2000), *Corporate Capitalism and Political Philosophy* (2002), *The Replication of Violence* (2002), and the forthcoming *The Theory and Reality of Democracy: A Case Study in Iraq* (2006).

John Haynes spent most of his working life at Ahmadu Bello University, Zaria, Nigeria. He lives in Hampshire with his Nigerian wife and two children. His *Letter to Patience*, a book length poem, set in a

Wasafiri Vol. 21, No. 1 March 2006, pp. 94–96
ISSN 0269-0055 print/ISSN 1747-1508 online
http://www.tandf.co.uk/journals DOI: 10.1080/02690050500475989
Routledge Taylor & Francis Group

northern Nigerian township, is due next spring. He has two previous collections, *Sabon Gari*, and (under a Hausa name) *First the Desert Came and then the Torture*.

Shirley M Hughes was awarded an MA in Literature by the Open University in 2004. Her thesis was on Ben Okri's *Infinite Riches* (third of the *Songs of Enchantment* trilogy) and *In Arcadia*.

Anthony Ilona is mainly interested in writing from the Anglophone Caribbean as well as in black and Asian British writing. He has taught and written on a range of subjects in the field of postcolonial literatures. He currently works for *The Guardian* newspaper in London.

Erica Johnson Debeljak is the American-born author of two books of literary non-fiction. Her stories and essays have appeared in literary journals in the United States, Slovenia and other European countries. She is also a translator; her most recent book is a translation of the selected poems of Slovenian poet, Dane Zajc.

Tabish Khair is Associate Professor at Aarhus University, Denmark. His latest publication is the novel, *The Bus Stopped* (2004). He has edited *Other Routes: 1500 Years of African and Asian Travel Writing* (2005) and is working on a novel titled *Filming*.

Ursula Kluwick is a Lecturer in English Literature and Cultural Studies at the University of Vienna. She has written a doctoral thesis on Salman Rushdie's magic realism.

Hena Maes-Jelinek is an honorary professor of the University of Liège and a member of the Belgian Royal Academy. She has published extensively on British and post-colonial fiction, especially on Wilson Harris. Her book on Harris, *The Labyrinth of Universality* will be out early in 2006. She is general co-editor of the series *Cross/Cultures* published by Rodopi.

Christine Matzke teaches in the Department of African Studies, Humboldt-University in Berlin. Her research interests include theatre and cultural production in Eritrea, African women's writing and popular literature. She is co-editor (with Susanne Mühleisen) of *Postcolonial Postmortems: Crime Fiction in a Transcultural Perspective* (forthcoming).

Stefano Mercanti completed his doctorate on Raja Rao's short stories at the University of Udine, Italy and is currently working on a funded research project on partnership and multiculturalism in postcolonial literatures. As an Indian Council for Cultural Relations scholarship recipient, he has obtained a further doctorate on Indianness in Raja Rao's novels at the University of Bangalore.

Michael Niblett studied English and Cultural Criticism at Cardiff University. He is currently a doctoral student at the University of Warwick working on Caribbean Literature; his thesis focuses on issues of memory and identity in the works of Patrick Chamoiseau, Wilson Harris, and Earl Lovelace.

Amardeep Singh is Assistant Professor of English at Lehigh University in Bethlehem, Pennsylvania. He has written articles and reviews for journals such as *Polygraph*, *SAMAR*, and *The Journal of Commonwealth and Postcolonial Studies*. He has also completed a book-length manuscript called 'Literary Secularism: Religion and Modernity in England, Ireland, and India'.

Lou Smith is a poet, online magazine designer and radio programmer based in Melbourne, Australia. Her poetry has appeared in *Kunapipi* (forthcoming), *Muse*, *Strange: Shapes*, *Undergrowth*, *Neopoetry* and *Mod_Piece*. In 2004 she co-edited the anthology *Scrapbook to Somewhere*, a collection of writing and visual art responding to concepts of 'place'.

Florian Stadtler is a member of the Centre for Colonial and Postcolonial Research at the University of Kent. He is currently researching Indian popular cinema and its deployment in South Asian and South Asian diasporic writing.

Sara Upstone is Lecturer in English at Kingston University, where she specialises in postcolonial, American, and contemporary British fiction. Her research interests include cultural and critical theory, popular culture, and theories of spatiality. She has published articles on subjects including Toni Morrison, Ben Okri and J R R Tolkien.

Notes for Contributors

Wasafiri welcomes original contributions from poets, fiction writers and critics from all cultural backgrounds. We are particularly interested in publishing informed and lively essays on the work of established and emerging writers or interviews with them. Submitted work is peer-reviewed by established writers, critics and academics, ensuring *Wasafiri*'s long reputation for forging new perspectives and publishing the best in contemporary writing today. A modest fee is paid by *Wasafiri* to reviewers and those whose creative work is accepted. All material should be sent direct to: **Susheila Nasta, Editor, *Wasafiri*, The Open University, 1–11 Hawley Crescent, Camden Town, London NW1 8NP**. Books being sent for review should be marked for the attention of the **Reviews Editor**.

Manuscripts should be submitted according to the following:

General

- Two hard (paper) copies and an electronic copy of your work are required. Please ensure hard copies are firmly stapled together and marked MS in the top right hand corner. If you wish to have your MS returned enclose a self-addressed envelope.
- Length: Articles/Fiction (5000–6000 words); Review Essay (up to 2500 words).
- Include Author(s) names(s) and affiliation, full correspondence address, fax, landline, mobile, and email for author (top right hand corner of first page). Include short biography in submission letter, 50 words (and as electronic file). Please make sure that the hard copy is an exact printout of the electronic version.

Format

- Type/print on A4 plain white paper, one side only, double spaced.
- Font: Times New Roman, 12 pt, align left, unjustified.
- Title: align left 20 pt, Sub title 16 pt followed by author(s) name(s) 14 pt.
- No centring throughout text, no headers or footers, no page numbers.
- Single space after full stops.
- Tab for paragraph indent — 0.5 cm, no space between paragraphs. Do not indent first paragraph, or first paragraph of a new section. Leave one line space before a new section.
- Use parenthetical referencing for bibliographical material. Other notes (which should be kept to a minimum) should appear as endnotes, numbered consecutively in Arabic numerals. Any notes should be part of the main body text and be typed normally at the end of the text. These should be kept to a minimum. Do not use the footnote or endnote facility of your WP program. Do not use auto numbering facility.
- Picture captions: All slides, transparencies or photographs should be numbered and where known, the photographer's name should be given. If the picture is of a work of art then artist, title, date, dimensions, medium photo credit should be given, in that order. Electronic picture files should be provided as 300dpi tif files. These files should be burnt onto a CD and sent with the manuscript. Please mark in the text of the manuscript the approximate position of all images, highlight in red.

References

The magazine uses a slightly modified version of the format advocated by Joseph Gibaldi and Walter Achtert, *MLA Handbook for Writers of Research Papers*. The Modern Languages Association of America, 1999 (www.mla.org). References conform to the MLA style with the following exceptions:

- Use single quotes (not double) throughout.
- The quotation mark should always be inside punctuation. (Except when the quotation is a complete sentence, when the fullstop is within the closing quotation mark.)

Reference citation in the text should be as brief as possible while directing the reader to the correct reference in the list of Works Cited. Footnotes should be kept to an absolute minimum. NEVER cite bibliographical information from memory; verify each entry carefully in your bibliography against the original source; and NEVER insert quotations from memory, always check against the text. We must rely on our contributors to be accurate in their citations. Here are some examples of how to list Works Cited:

BOOK BY SINGLE AUTHOR
Kipling, Rudyard. *Kim*. 1901. New York: Penguin Classics, 1987.

ANTHOLOGY or COMPILIATION
Lopate, Phillip, ed. *The Art of the Personal Essay: An Anthology from the Classical Era to the Present*. New York: Anchor-Doubleday, 1994.

AN ARTICLE IN A JOURNAL WITH CONTINUOUS PAGINATION
Hanks, Patrick. 'Do Word Meanings Exist?' *Computers and the Humanities* 34 (2000): 205–15.

BASIC ENTRY DOCUMENT FROM INTERNET SITE
Zeki, Semir. 'Artistic Creativity and the Brain'. *Science* 6 July 2001: 51–52. *Science Magazine*. 2002. Amer. Assn. For the Advancement of Science. 24 Sept. 2002 <http://www.sciencemag.org/cgi/content/full/293/5527/51>.

A full style sheet, including how to reference within the text, can be found on our website at www.wasafiri.org or will be sent out when a piece has been accepted.

Early Electronic Offprints. Corresponding authors can receive their article by email as a complete PDF file. This allows the author to print up to 50 copies, free of charge, and disseminate them to colleagues. Alternatively, corresponding authors can choose to receive the traditional 50 offprints. A copy of the journal will be sent by post to all corresponding authors after publication.

Copyright. It is a condition of publication that authors assign copyright or licence the publication rights in their articles to *Wasafiri*. This enables us to ensure full copyright protection and to disseminate the article, and of course the journal, to the widest possible readership in print and electronic formats as appropriate. Authors may, of course, use the article elsewhere *after* publication without prior permission provided that full acknowledgement is given to *Wasafiri* as the original source of publication, and that *Wasafiri*/Taylor & Francis are notified so that the records show that its use is properly authorised. Authors retain a number of other rights under the copyright and licensing policy documents. These policies are referred to at http://www.tandf.co.uk/journals/authorrights.pdf for full details. Authors are themselves responsible for obtaining permission to reproduce copyright material from other sources.

Wasafiri

Subscription Information
Wasafiri is a peer-reviewed journal published three times a year (March, July and November), by Routledge, an imprint of Taylor & Francis, 4 Park Square, Milton Park, Abingdon, Oxfordshire OX14 4RN, UK.

Annual Subscription, Volume 21, 2006 (Print ISSN 0269-0055)

Institutional	US$210	£120
Individual	US$47	£27
Online only	US$200	£114 (plus tax where applicable)

An institutional subscription to the print edition includes free access for any number of concurrent users across a local area network to the online edition, ISSN 1747-1508.
For more information, visit our website: http://www.tandf.co.uk/journals
For a complete and up-to-date guide to Taylor & Francis journals and books publishing programmes, and details of advertising in our journals, visit our website: http://www.tandf.co.uk/journals

Dollar rates apply to subscribers in all countries except the UK and the Republic of Ireland where the pound sterling price applies. All subscriptions are payable in advance and all rates include postage. Journals are sent by air to the USA, Canada, Mexico, India, Japan and Australasia. Subscriptions are entered on an annual basis. Payment may be made by sterling cheque, dollar cheque, international money order, National Giro, or credit card (Amex, Visa, Mastercard).

Ordering Information
USA/Canada: Taylor & Francis Inc., Journals Department, 325 Chestnut Street, 8th Floor, Philadelphia, PA 19106, USA. Tel: +1 (800) 354 1420; Fax: +1 (215) 625 8914. **Europe/Rest of World:** T&F Customer Services, T&F Informa UK Ltd, Sheepen Place, Colchester, Essex CO3 3LP, UK. Tel: +44 (0)207 017 5544; Fax: +44 (0)207 017 5198; Email: tf.enquiries@tfinforma.com

Advertising Enquiries
USA/Canada: The Advertising Manager, Taylor & Francis Inc., 325 Chestnut Street, 8th Floor, Philadelphia, PA 19106, USA. Tel: +1 (215) 625 8900; Fax: +1 (215) 625 2240. **EU/RoW:** The Advertising Manager, Taylor & Francis, 4 Park Square, Milton Park, Abingdon, Oxfordshire OX14 4RN, UK. Tel: +44 (0) 207 017 6000. Fax: +44 (0) 207 017 6336.

Back Issues
Taylor & Francis retains a three year back issue stock of journals. Older volumes are held by our official stockists: Periodicals Service Company, 11 Main Street, Germantown, NY 12526, USA to whom all orders and enquiries should be addressed. Telephone: +1 518 537 4700; Fax: +1 518 537 5899; E-mail: psc@periodicals.com

The print edition of this journal is typeset by Datapage, Dublin, Ireland and printed on ANSI conforming acid free paper by Hobbs The Printers, Hampshire, UK. The online edition of this journal is hosted by MetaPress at http://www.journalsonline.tandf.co.uk